THE
WEALTH CHOICE

SUCCESS SECRETS OF BLACK MILLIONAIRES

Featuring the Seven Laws of Wealth

DENNIS KIMBRO

with The Napoleon Hill Foundation

palgrave
macmillan

First published in 2013 by PALGRAVE MACMILLAN® in the United
States—a division of St. Martin's Press LLC, 175 Fifth Avenue, New
York, NY 10010.

Where this book is distributed in the UK, Europe and the rest of the
world, this is by Palgrave Macmillan, a division of Macmillan Publishers
Limited, registered in England, company number 785998, of Houndmills,
Basingstoke, Hampshire RG21 6XS.

Palgrave Macmillan is the global academic imprint of the above
companies and has companies and representatives throughout the world.

Palgrave® and Macmillan® are registered trademarks in the United
States, the United Kingdom, Europe and other countries.

ISBN 978-0-230-34207-1

Library of Congress Cataloging-in-Publication Data
    The wealth choice : success secrets of Black millionaires / Dennis
Kimbro.
        pages   cm
    1. Success in business. 2. African Americans—Life skills guides. 3. Self-
confidence. I. Title.
HF5386.K496   2013
332.024'0108996073—dc23

                                                                    2012030390

A catalogue record of the book is available from the British Library.

Design by Letra Libre, Inc.

First edition: February 2013

10 9 8 7 6 5 4 3 2 1

Printed in the United States of America.

CONTENTS

ACKNOWLEDGMENTS

THIS SEVEN-YEAR EFFORT IS NOT ABOUT THE POWER OF one, but the support of many. I've learned so much in the process of writing *The Wealth Choice*. First, and foremost, I could not have done it alone. In my case, friends, family, and well-wishers stood patiently behind the scenes helping me put forth my best effort. As a result, I had the pleasure of working with some real pros. They include:

My agent, Wendy Keller, who believed in this project when a number of her colleagues passed. I don't know what I would do without her sound and sage advice. My editor, Emily Carleton, improved the manuscript beyond measure. Donna Cherry, my fact-checker extraordinaire; trust me, she is one of the best in the business. Don Green, the executive director of the Napoleon Hill Foundation, critiqued an early draft of the manuscript before pulling out all stops. I also owe special thanks to Teri Dean, Cheri Henderson, Andy Ingraham, Sophia White, Tony Martin, Randal Pinkett, Pennae Lewis, Wendy Welch, and Rudy Vincent who made several key interviews possible. Thomas Jenkins, Terry Ramdayal, and Gail Seegars pitched in when I needed help. As usual, David Smith kept my energy level up and refused to accept excuses.

In short, this book is about dreams and the power to make those dreams come true. No one knows more about this concept than my wife, Pat. The wind beneath my wings and an expert on achieving the impossible, her wisdom and insight can be felt on every page of this book. To my three daughters, Kelli, Kimberli, and MacKenzie, who personally crunched and collated so many numbers that she probably knows the data by heart. Kennedy and Logan, my two granddaughters, were there to cheer me on. The future belongs to them.

And finally, a special round of thanks goes to the countless Black millionaires—hundreds upon hundreds of determined and ambitious men and women who unselfishly embraced my survey and granted me entrance in to their world of wealth, power, and achievement. A partial list includes:

John Barfield	Daymond John
Shirley Bailey	Harry Johnson
Ken Brown	John H. Johnson
Leah Brown	Robert Johnson
Les Brown	Lillian Lincoln Lambert
John Hope Bryant	Spike Lee
Tom Burrell	Victor MacFarlane
Herman Cain	Rueben McDaniel
Pasha and Steve Carter	Colleen Payne-Nabors
Valerie Daniels-Carter	Clarence Otis
Lisa Nicole Cloud	Henry Parks
Johnnie Cochran	R. Donahue Peebles
Trish Millines-Dziko	Roosevelt Peebles
Joe Dudley	Tyler Perry
Kirk Franklin	Lisa Price
Tyrese Gibson	Antonio Reid
Nathaniel Goldston	Michael Roberts
Earl G. Graves	John Rogers
Farrah Gray	Barbara Smith
Carla Harris	David Steward
Steve Harvey	Ephren Taylor
Michele Hoskins	Willie Watkins
Janice Bryant Howroyd	Mark Wilson
Cathy Hughes	Amos Winbush
T. D. Jakes	

Their quotes are the result of these interviews. I hope and pray I have made them proud.

INTRODUCTION

A WEALTH OF KNOWLEDGE

THE MOST POWERFUL ECONOMIC WEAPON

The First Law of Wealth

If you don't know better, you can't do better.

—John Hope Bryant

"WHY AREN'T YOU RICH?" JOHN H. JOHNSON, THE founder and chief executive of *Ebony* magazine, the nation's leading Black publication, fired at me as I sat across from his desk in his plush Chicago headquarters. Caught off guard, I had never considered his question. "I suggest that you consider the gifts that you've been given," Johnson continued. "You and your generation live in an era of unprecedented wealth and growth. More men and women have become wealthy in the last 20 years than any other time in human history. You've been given a sound mind and sound body, not to mention an energetic spirit as well as opportunity at every turn. And to top it off, you've earned a degree from one of the finest schools in the country."

Again, the publishing tycoon repeated his question, this time demanding an answer. *"Why aren't you wealthy?"* I sat motionless and ashamed. Ashamed that I could not answer his question, ashamed that

I had failed to grasp past opportunities. Ashamed that I had failed to realize that wasted time means wasted energy, wasted talents, and wasted potential. I now know that time is money. No one should waste an hour any more than we should waste a dollar bill. But most important, I was ashamed because I had failed to cultivate, nurture, and emulate Johnson's passion and purpose for life. The millionaires among us are men and women of laser-like focus and concentration: wealth creators who have hammered away at one place long enough to accomplish their purpose. In a world of mostly have nots, the wealthy and influential tend to be individuals with one overriding objective, one unwavering aim. Ironically, the man or woman who is forever looking about to see what he or she can find never finds a thing. In short, we find what we seek with all our heart and, if we look for nothing in particular, *guess what?* We find just that.

I was ashamed because I was finally forced to answer to a man who served as my judge and jury. Johnson, a onetime have not, had spent the better part of three decades crafting articles at night and peddling them during the day before he was given the chance to demonstrate his powers of persuasion to the world of commerce. After starting *Ebony,* he became a multimillionaire by age 40. A weaker spirit would have quit years ago. And this remarkably committed individual unselfishly carved out a piece of his day to school me on the demands of wealth.

"If you want to know how people feel about themselves," Johnson reasoned, "look at their bank account. Money is the greatest measurement of your mind-set. There are thousands of men and women who have lost every material possession and yet, because they possess a stout heart, an unconquerable will, and the determination to push ahead, they are just as far from poverty as before their loss. Here lies the good news. Wealth is less a matter of circumstance than it is a matter of knowledge and choice. With such wealth no one should ever be poor. You must take control of your life—you must make the decision to be wealthy."

WHEN THE STUDENT IS READY . . .

During an economics class at Atlanta University, an inquisitive student asked the scholar and educator W. E. B. Du Bois for the quickest and surest way to prosperity. "What I am about to share," Dr. Du Bois replied, "you would do well to write on your heart and place in your purse. Many a ruined man dates his downfall from the day he began buying what he did not need. If you are in debt, part of you belongs to your creditors. To whom you give your money, you give your power."[1] More than a century later, Du Bois's words still resonate. Money is, arguably, one of humanity's greatest tools. Regardless of the heat it generates, money is like any other resource or commodity—neither good nor bad, neither sinful nor sacred. Unlike other resources, however, money evolves from the thought processes of those who possess it. It is an instrument, a standard that can be used for both good and evil, by the rich and the not-so-rich, by the haves as well as the have nots. Too many of us, like the inquisitive student just described, fail to understand the importance of financial management.

Only one path connects poverty and great wealth: the long and rugged road of faith, family, and hard work. What the marketplace wants are men and women with the ambition and nerve to work and wait, whether the world applauds, criticizes, or condemns them. Wealth requires a Janice Bryant Howroyd, who spent more than 25 years staring down hard times and toiling as a little fish in a big pond, building her one-woman temporary employment agency into a major corporate player. Long dismissed by the competition, Howroyd built her business brick by brick from a tiny southern California office. She was raised as one of 11 children in the segregated South, and it wasn't until Howroyd took an economics course in college that she realized the depth of her childhood poverty. But in spite of this, her family surrounded her—as they did each of their children—with love, self-confidence, and an insatiable thirst for academic excellence. With less than $1,500 in savings and personal loans, this devoutly spiritual woman founded the ACT-1 Group, one of the largest female- and minority-owned companies in the country, boasting annual revenues of more than $600 million. What is the source of her wealth? Not genius, deep pockets, or well-placed contacts but an unshakable faith matched by tireless passion and energy. Here's the secret that she personally shared with me nearly a decade ago: "To some people half a billion dollars seems like a vast sum of money. However, I've invested darn near every dime I earned back into my company. I refuse to fall prey to the bling-bling life. I've learned early on the power of the words 'I can't afford it.'"

Each day men and women go to their graves in obscurity because timidity prevented them from making a start or at least an initial effort. If they had just begun, in all likelihood, they would have found their calling and achieved financial success.

Reginald F. Lewis never knew when he was beaten. The words that were written on his heart throughout his life are now etched on his headstone: "*Keep going, no matter what.*" This was Lewis's mantra as he struck the single deal that not only transformed his investment firm, the TLC Group, but Black-owned business as well. In 1984, with only $1 million in cash and $24 million in borrowed funds, Lewis snapped up the Manhattan McCall Pattern Company, intent on revitalizing the 117-year-old sewing pattern maker. Just a year later, he shocked the financial community by selling McCall's to the John Crowther Group, a British textile maker, for $63 million.[2] Moreover, Crowther agreed to take on $32 million in debt owed by the pattern company. For TLC, the deal meant a remarkable 80-to-1 return on its initial $1 million investment. That coup ensured Lewis a top spot in Wall Street's financial community as he engineered TLC's next major transaction: the takeover of Beatrice International, a global food manufacturer valued at $985 million.

The odds may be a million to one against reaching your financial goals, but ever-present opportunities can shift the prospects in your favor if you just use your God-given talents and act! Why stand there with folded arms begging the Creator for blessings that He has already bestowed? Hasn't He given you the necessary faculties and strengths? Hasn't He blessed you with a sound mind and sturdy body? Is there no way in which you can utilize each passing moment to improve your condition and be of benefit to others? Are all the seats taken? Are all the positions filled? Are the resources of our great nation fully developed? Is the competition so fierce that you won't even try? With a world stacked with work that needs to be done and countless examples to encourage you to dare and find your highest good and true calling, why wait? Remember, when the Israelites found themselves caught between Pharaoh's army and the crashing waves of the Red Sea, Moses asked for divine help. And the response? The Lord of heavenly host questioned: "Why does thou criest unto me? Tell the children of Israel to go forward." In other words, pay heed to your passion and seize the hour.

SO YOU WANT TO BE A MILLIONAIRE?

Lack of opportunity is the excuse of the timid and the fearful. *Opportunities?* They are everywhere. A new era is dawning. Thousands of men and women have made their fortune from ideas that others pass by or dismiss. Just as the bee creates honey from the same flower that the spider saps its poison, some men and women will produce their riches from the most common, trivial ideas that others discard. Countless positions that were closed only decades ago are now inviting you and me to enter. There is latent power everywhere waiting for the observant eye to discover. If it is wealth that you seek, study yourself, your own needs and wants.

Opportunities? Every life is full of opportunity. Every breath, every moment, and every encounter is an opportunity! An opportunity to look past the traditional, to step over outdated methods, and to ignore the words "That's the way it has always been done." Every classroom, every book, and every lesson is an opportunity; an opportunity to *prove and improve* yourself, an opportunity to say "Yes" though the world says "No," an opportunity to put it all on the line, and an opportunity to immerse yourself in the dream buried in your heart. Every business transaction is an opportunity—an opportunity to serve, an opportunity to make a difference, an opportunity to test market conditions, an opportunity to stamp your brand, and an opportunity to "let your light so shine and glorify your Father in heaven."

"Spot and seize opportunities as if they were gold" are the words written above the door leading to prosperity, and who should know better than Don Barden? Growing up in the shipyards of Cleveland, Ohio, Barden valued ambition and determination over money and connections before finding his place in the field of enterprise. Extremely driven, Barden told those in his inner circle, "I had to control the events of my life. It was my call. Either sulk and languish in poverty or carry out my plans regardless of the opinion of others. In the end, if you take care of business, your business will take care of you."[3] Barden realized that the only way you can truly get ahead is by venturing into areas where others fear to tread. At last count, this casino operator and real estate developer was worth more than $500 million.

Wealth requires a Maggie Lena Walker to hold her ground and push without fear or trepidation. At the turn of the twentieth century,

Walker was not a promising candidate for financial success by any measure. She was penniless in a world that valued wealth, a female in a society that favored males, and a woman of color who sought riches in an arena where skin color mattered most. In 1903, through sound fiscal policies and boundless energy, Walker became the first woman—Black *or* White—to charter a U.S. bank, the St. Luke Penny Savings. Refusing to be intimidated by poverty or racial injustice, she would counsel all those who would listen: "No one can prosper when they expect to remain poor. Let's invest our money and reap the benefit ourselves."[4] As her financial empire grew, Walker knew that besides providing the power to transform ideas, wealth equals freedom. The giants of the race have been men and women of exquisite concentration—individuals who just kept hammering away at one place until they reached their objective. If you're wondering what makes people wealthy, look no further than perseverance in spite of every difficulty, courage that enables you to overcome all trials and disappointment, and a single unwavering aim matched by intense purpose. There is no open door to the temple of wealth; whoever dares to enter must forge his or her own way.

"There is no secret to amassing wealth," Lisa Nicole Cloud declared as she stood before a room packed with teary-eyed women from every economic strata and walk of life. "Ladies," this powerhouse of a motivator barked during a standing-room-only sales rally, "the key to wealth is within your reach. But you must design your life or someone else will.

"I've walked in your shoes," she continued. "I've been rejected, ridiculed, and kicked to the curb. Believe me, I know what you're going through. My journey from bootstraps to big time did not occur overnight. Plenty of nights I sank to my knees asking God to reveal His purpose—His divine plan. My turning point occurred when a dear friend—a mentor, someone who I respect and admire, said to me during one of the lowest points in my life, 'Lisa, you will either live your dreams or live your fears. The only barrier that stands between you and what you want out of life is the will to try and the faith to believe in your dreams.'"

Those words of wisdom changed her life. Five years ago, Nicole Cloud navigated the same road of uncertainty and instability as most employees who struggle within the corporate framework. As a pharmaceutical sales rep, each day she wondered if and when she would fall victim to corporate downsizing. She realized that the security she had once felt in her career was gone, and she had to do something different. She began exploring a variety of businesses opportunities and soon discovered a new venture in the Voice over Internet Protocol (VoIP)/direct sales arena. With a modest start-up investment, Nicole Cloud decided to launch her own VoIP telecom business in the direct sales industry. Devoting every spare moment to realizing her dream, her strong work ethic has paid off handsomely. Not only has she created unbelievable success for herself, she is internationally known as the Millionaire Maker, training and developing tens of thousands of direct sales associates around the world, many of whom boast seven-figure incomes.

Nicole Cloud's message is on point and simple: "Turn potential into performance and adhere to the traits and qualities of the financial elite who live life on their terms. *Opportunities,* you ask? Opportunities are endless!" And she should know. Still in her mid-30s, she has already been dubbed the "queen of direct sales."

At a time when opportunity and wealth call out and demand the best in each of us, Tyrese Gibson stands as the ultimate icon of nerve, imagination, and fortitude. Gibson wasn't destined for stardom. Raised by a single mother in the rough and unforgiving neighborhood of South Central Los Angeles, he was statistically more likely to be a victim of a drive-by shooting than a financial success. Gibson was six years old when his father left the family of four children. Instead of succumbing to the crime-infested streets, Gibson decided to battle his way out. "It was far from easy," he shared with me after speaking to my freshman business seminar class. "But I always believed in myself and that I could overcome any odds. Poverty and confusion are not deterrents to success." As a child, his household was filled with the sounds of the soulful balladeers, including Stevie Wonder, Donny Hathaway, and Marvin Gaye. Between those rhythm and blues giants and his mother, Gibson was inspired to never be caught without a song in his heart or a melody on his lips. In other words, he pursued his hobby of singing.

In 1995, that hobby turned into a career. Gibson answered a casting call posted on the wall in his high school. A local public relations firm was combing the area searching for an African American male to serve in the lead role in a soft drink promotional campaign. Gibson didn't hesitate. Unable to find a ride to the audition, he rode a city bus instead and was two hours late for his appointment. Ironically, the producer and ad agency director were caught in the same traffic. Despite the delay, and never one to be weakened by excuses, the budding entertainer convinced the director that he, Gibson, was born for the part. When the curtain fell on his first take in a makeshift back-alley studio, his reputation was made. Thanks to his achievements, Gibson is now known to millions as a multi-platinum singer, songwriter, actor, fashion model, and author. When I asked for the keys to financial empowerment, he stood to make his point: "Attack your dreams with a solitary purpose and vision, and learn to get out of your own way."

Opportunities? They are all around us. The surest and quickest way to a fortune is through humanity's prime necessities. Each of us is forced to toil for our own food, shelter, and clothing. Although initially people may struggle, anyone who is wise enough to supply society's wants; prudent enough to improve the methods that humanity can use; and clever enough to offer comfort, leisure, and peace of mind to the well-being of others will eventually rise to distinction. Riches are lying everywhere for the observant eye. Many of us who believe we are poor are rich in possibilities.

WHY *THE WEALTH CHOICE,* AND WHY NOW?

In spite of Black America's advances—only 40 years removed from the civil rights movement—with more successful, educated, and accomplished entrepreneurs and corporate professionals than at any other time in history, the journey is far from over. To be honest, it is only beginning. These pockets of prosperity, a gulf as vast and deep as the Nile, separates the majority of the Black community from its financial elites as well as from virtually every other ethnic group in our society. The abyss between wealthy Blacks and poverty-stricken Blacks is more than disturbing. The unemployment rate for young Black males in some urban areas is fast approaching Great Depression levels. More Black males than ever are incarcerated, attend miserably failing segregated inner-city schools, and live in gang-infested, crime-ridden neighborhoods. These impoverished enclaves have become the equivalent of a domestic third-world country. But these are not problems without solutions. Though the challenges that confront this market segment may be deep and vast and may desperately need addressing, the purpose of this book is to highlight the infinite possibilities that are available to all who inhabit the world—possibilities that have been brought to my attention and clarified by Black America's wealthiest.

Unfortunately, you would be hard pressed to find a course in our educational system titled Wealth 101. Few of us are even taught the basics rudiments of money—how to make it, keep it, share it, and open our hands to it. Over the years, I have learned that much of the accepted wisdom about race and economics is based on conjecture rather than fact. It would take a lifetime to untangle the myths, inaccuracies, and stereotypes that cloud the "Black experience." And the most mindless idea of our time is that wealth, in general, or millionaireship specifically, is attainable only by those of a certain class, race, or economic stratum. As this book will prove, nothing can be further from the truth. You, the reader, will come to understand that building a seven-figure income requires more than a successful enterprise or career—in fact, much more. The wealth creators interviewed for this study were quite clear regarding the path to wealth, not to mention the bigger picture: financial empowerment. The millionaires profiled here are convinced that Black America's top priority for the twenty-first century should be closing the wealth gap. With regard to wealth, prosperity, and fiscal fitness and awareness, what do Black millionaires know that so few people fail to comprehend? These wealth creators know that our prosperity as a nation depends on the personal financial prosperity of each individual. They know that proper preparation is the key to financial success. They know that if you invest in yourself, you will never be poor, and that if you ask for little, you will receive little. They know that debt is like any other trap—easy to tumble into but difficult to escape. They know that nothing makes a man or woman independent as ready cash and that an investment in knowledge will always return the highest dividend. They know that prosperity flows only through channels that are open to receive it and that anyone can overcome poverty, but that the individual who has nothing but money confronts another form of poverty, one that can never be conquered. They know that thrift not only safeguards the future but allows one to work with confidence. And, most important, Black millionaires know that true wealth can be found in these words: Make all you can, save all you can, and give all you can. These principles and laws lie at the heart of *The Wealth Choice.*

OPERATION NEW LIFE

I have read countless books on finance and economics, and I have worked for years with the financial elite. As a result, I've found one common chord that resonates among those who control vast resources: They don't implement wealth-generating habits only when they feel the need to do so; rather, they habitually live in a state of wealth. In other words, there is more to wealth than just learning about money. Black millionaires repeatedly take certain actions, consistently adhering to routines that allow them to create and maintain considerable wealth. They save, dream, plan, invest, and give in a never-ending cycle. Behind their routines and habits lies a basic core of beliefs—the first of which is that money is plentiful for those who understand the simple laws that govern its acquisition.

On November 4, 1986, my life forever changed. Though I never met Napoleon Hill—famed author of the seminal classic *Think and Grow Rich*—I did meet and develop a relationship with his manager and business partner, W. Clement Stone. Stone's slicked-back hair, bow tie, pencil mustache, and omnipresent cigar marked him as a creature from the Roaring Twenties. But when I met him in his Chicago office when he was 84 years old, his handshake was viselike. Stone, a visionary and an icon, was once named the world's wealthiest. Seldom can a single individual affect the lives of an entire generation for the better, not to mention the lives of future generations, but Stone did so. As the founder and president of Combined Insurance Company of America, no one spoke on the subject of wealth and achievement with more authority or experience. Stone was the foremost spiritual descendant of Benjamin Franklin, Samuel Smiles, Orison Swett Marden, and the other giants in the self-help field. During our meeting, he shared a few pearls of wisdom:

- *Desire is the beginning of all human achievement.*
- *When you go for something, don't return until you get it.*
- *Success is achieved by those who try. When there's nothing to lose by trying and everything to gain if successful, by all means try.*

- *If you cannot save 10 percent of all that you earn, the seeds of greatness are not in you.*
- *Prayer is mankind's greatest power.*[5]

Above Stone's desk hung a portrait of George Washington kneeling in prayer before battle, a testament to Stone's lasting belief in the oldest self-help philosophy in the world. "I never engage in any action," Stone confessed, "without praying for guidance."

But the Great Depression hit Stone hard. By 1937, his company's 1,000-employee sales force had shrunk to 135, and he was $28,000 in debt. As fate would have it, he was given a copy of Napoleon Hill's *Think and Grow Rich*. Stone devoured the book. He distributed copies to his reps and watched company revenues explode. By 1952, Stone had personally earned more than $100 million from his Combined Insurance Company of America.

What was in that book? The answer to that question goes back to 1908, when author Napoleon Hill was a 25-year-old magazine reporter. During an interview, steel giant Andrew Carnegie tossed the young journalist a massive challenge. Carnegie promised Hill he would introduce him to the greatest wealth creators of his day, provided the aspiring writer would devote the next 20 years compiling their success secrets into a book. Hill would receive no pay. Moreover, in Carnegie's vest pocket was a stopwatch. He told Hill that an individual who makes fast decisions can be trusted to carry them out. If Hill hesitated more than 60 seconds, the deal was off. For the next two decades, while supporting himself through a variety of positions in sales, advertising, education, and public relations, Hill interviewed more than 500 successful men, among them Henry Ford, Charles Goodyear, John D. Rockefeller, George Eastman, Marshall Field, and Thomas Edison. His *Law of Success*, published in 1928, won worldwide acclaim. However, it was Hill's blockbuster, *Think and Grow Rich*, published nearly a decade later, that truly hit a nerve in Depression-era America. At last count, this single volume has sold more than 60 million copies.[6]

When I met Stone, I was 36 years old, married with three small children, and, financially, at the lowest point of my life. Prior to this encounter, I was one of those men leading a life of quiet desperation. Although I had finished college and graduate school, I was dead broke. I had spent most of our income and every dime of our savings researching and interviewing Black achievers and peak performers for a book that would eventually become *What Makes the Great Great*. Outside of my writing, life was a living hell for me and my family. It seemed that no matter how hard my wife, Pat, and I worked, we were always in debt up to our eyeballs. But I knew life held so much more. Back in the mid-1980s, in the outskirts of Atlanta, Georgia, I lived in a nice house on a cul-de-sac overlooking a pristine wooded area surrounded by neighbors who were and are like family. As idyllic as the view was then, and still is today, I often found myself dreaming of a different view and a different life—not necessarily a better life but a richer, fuller one. I wanted to see all that this world has to offer; to know some of the most interesting people; and to experience, learn, and truly grow as an individual. Quite simply, I wanted to succeed—especially spiritually and financially—though I was unsure exactly what success meant.

I didn't realize it at the time, but I was about to take a long step into the future. Slowly but surely, word got out about my research. Because there was such an obvious void in the literature, I was asked to write a series of articles about the wealth creators at the center of this study. As fate would have it, one such article found its way onto the pages of *Success Magazine*. Finally, in spite of all the tough years, I was earning a living as a writer. One year later, another break came my way. The Napoleon Hill Foundation caught wind of my writings, and, out of the blue, I received Stone's phone call requesting a meeting in his palatial Chicago office. As Carnegie did with Napoleon Hill, Stone not only sought out me, an unknown writer, but he guided my development through his personal philosophy and principles while providing me with the offer of a lifetime: to update and complete Hill's final work, a spin-off of his greatest effort, dedicated solely to the economic advancement of Black America. On November 4, 1986, the day I walked into Stone's office, I hoped that he would see my ambition and strong desire to learn and know—qualities I knew he admired and valued. My curiosity is perhaps the character trait of which I am most proud. I am and always have been intrigued by those men and women who, by dint of their own talent, creativity, promise, and perseverance, reached impressive goals and objectives and amassed high levels of wealth as a well-deserved by-product of their accomplishments. Interestingly enough, the most successful people I have met along my journey share this one critical element: boundless, near-insatiable curiosity. When it comes to growth, success, human development, and receiving all that life has to offer, they simply *need to know.*

When *Think and Grow Rich: A Black Choice* was released in 1991, I set a simple yet achievable goal: to turn one-time victims into victors and to transform the least, the last, and the lost into peak-performing, high-achieving men and women. "Operation New Life" was what Wally Amos, the chocolate chip cookie tycoon, called the moment. "You are going to create a new and improved you. Turn the page," Amos urged, "and get started on the greatest journey of your life."[7]

"True success," I added, "is guaranteed when each of us discovers our inherent purpose, lives courageously, utilizes our creative gifts, and incorporates integrity into everything we do." To increase the prospects of both prosperity and personal empowerment, I identified 12 sure-fire principles that would set anyone on to the fast track of success.[8] Along the way—with my follow-up effort, *What Makes the Great Great,* again through countless interviews with Black America's best and brightest—I've constantly refined and expanded my inquisition to include practical advice as well as pearls of wisdom. "We all possess the seeds of greatness," I pointed out. "*What Makes the Great Great* provides the tools to discover and nourish those seeds." As of this writing, I am happy to report that both works have been enthusiastically embraced by people from all walks of life, from private and professional associations to churches, colleges, and the nonprofit sector. And with this book, the message has widened.

THE WEALTH CHOICE

Each year, approximately 50,000 manuscripts find their way to editors' desks and are eventually published. Bookstores generally contain about 15,000 different titles. And yet, of all the books you could be reading, you are holding *The Wealth Choice*. Is it fate, luck, chance, or coincidence? I don't believe it is any of these things. Nothing is coincidental. I am convinced that many times during the course of our lives, the Creator challenges us to be more and do more than what we thought possible.

I know nothing of your particular circumstances, whether you are young or old, male or female, rich or poor. I do know, however, that you are in search of a better life and increased abundance. What I am about to reveal to you has until now been known by only a fortunate few. Ironically, this key has evaded both the educated and the illiterate. Some who have been blessed with this wisdom have rejected it. They resisted and refused to listen, just as you may wish to do. This is your chance. Forget the past and welcome this day. You would be wise to understand that at any moment, the decisions you make can alter the course of your life forever. If you follow the instructions outlined in this book, the results will be automatic. You'll suddenly realize that you are capable of achieving, earning, and possessing far more than you ever thought possible. And you will realize your potential simply by applying the seven laws of wealth—"million-dollar habits" of men and women who have gone from rags to riches in one generation. I beg you to adhere to the words written by business philosopher Jim Rohn: "Let others lead small lives, but not you. Let others argue over small things, but not you. Let others cry over small hurts, but not you. Let others leave their future in someone else's hands, but not you." And remember the four things that never return: the spoken word, the speeding arrow, the wasted life, and the neglected opportunity.

Now the choice is yours.

THE START OF A NEW REVOLUTION

Since its publication, more than 500,000 readers have purchased a copy of *Think and Grow Rich: A Black Choice*. If history is any guide, perhaps half of them ever bothered to open the book. Two hundred thousand may have read as much as a chapter or two or heard me speak. One hundred thousand were diligent enough to absorb it from cover to cover. Ten thousand dog-eared a page, highlighted a few passages, or wrote notes in the margin. Believe me, I know. After my many speaking events, I am regularly asked to sign books. Through my unscientific poll, the number of copies featuring bent pages and highlighted is shockingly low. But regardless of how many readers actually absorbed and heeded my writings—or failed to do so—a new revolution is about to take place. The zeal to do something, to implement a new approach, to take the first step along a new path is clear. Let me explain.

Nearly three years ago, as I prepared to catch a flight from Atlanta's Hartsfield-Jackson airport, I received a phone call. One of the top investment houses in the nation wanted to partner with me in an effort to reach a little-known and untapped market segment: Black America's wealthiest—at a minimum, men and women whose annual household income exceeded $250,000 and, in particular, those who have reached millionaire status.

The game plan was simple enough. Leaning on my name recognition as a draw, I would serve as the opening act to roughly 300 invited guests in seven different cities. Once I concluded my remarks, a company representative, usually a high-ranking senior vice president, would share his or her insights on the economy and present the firm's wide array of financial services. Each 90-minute session closed with cocktails, hors d'oeuvres, and small talk. It was during the small talk with these financial high fliers that the subject of my next book revealed itself, and I accepted the proposal. It would be a study that would shatter many cherished, misguided beliefs, including a widely held notion that wealth and financial independence are the result of some mysterious, jealously guarded secret. Or, even more insidiously, that wealth is the result of being blessed with superior intelligence, talents or skills, influence or good luck. Wealth, as stated clearly by the millionaires I met during my initial presentations, is the result of a mind-set that embraces tried-and-true habits backed by consistent and persistent action.

In this book, I argue that a revolution is imminent, wherein the average American, particularly African Americans, are rethinking the tried and, as it turns out, not-so-true keys to wealth creation. Historically, at the heart of all revolutions stand no more than a handful of committed souls. Perhaps among them today are those 10,000 who have underlined key points in *Think and Grow Rich: A Black Choice*. However, now is the time to begin a new phase. The urge to do something—*anything*—is clear. A quick glance at the data I describe spells out what needs to be done. Before you read any further, allow me to offer a word of advice. You may want to release, or at least reconsider, any preconceived notions you've held regarding Blacks, Whites, and money. For starters, consider these statistics:

- According to a 2009 Pew Research Center study, the median wealth of White households was 20 times that of Black households and 18 times that of Hispanic households.

These lopsided wealth ratios are the largest since the federal
government began publishing such data in the 1980s. Whites'
20-to-1 wealth advantage over African Americans has been
known to buffer and soften any economic downturns in
the economy. Moreover, the net worth of Black households
fell from $12,124 in 2005 to $5,677 in 2009, a decline of
53 percent. Surprisingly, more than one-third of Black (35
percent) households had zero net worth during the same
period.[9]

- Approximately 35 percent of African Americans had no wealth
  or were in debt in 2009. To magnify this point, the Consumer
  Federation of America calculated that 25 percent of U.S.
  households were "wealth poor," holding net assets less than
  $10,000. This statistic is a far cry from the 45 percent of Black
  households that fall into this category. Home ownership rates
  are highest for Whites—74 percent—and lowest for Blacks—46
  percent. Strikingly, Black unemployment rates are twice those
  of Whites, and the median Black family's net worth stands at
  $8,300, a fraction of that of White households, at $56,000.[10]

- Twenty-four percent of African Americans spend more than
  their income compared with only 14 percent of all Americans;
  32 percent of Blacks don't save at all. Less than one-fourth
  of all Americans fail to do so. To underscore these statistics,
  according to Earl Graves, Jr., CEO of *Black Enterprise*
  magazine, Blacks are six times more likely than Whites to
  purchase a Mercedes-Benz automobile. Furthermore, Graves
  continues, the average income of an African American who
  buys a Jaguar is nearly one-third less than that of a White
  purchaser of the same luxury vehicle.[11]

- Nearly one-third of White households own 401(k) or thrift
  savings accounts, compared with less than one-fifth of African
  American households. Moreover, White households are more
  likely to own stocks and mutual funds (31.9 percent) as IRA or
  Keogh accounts (27.5 percent). Ten percent or less of African
  Americans own these assets, and their median value, $8,000, is
  far below that of Whites ($20,000).[12]

- When using the term "millionaire," few tracking institutes
  or organizations refer to those with investments in excess

of $1 million. "Investments" include such income-bearing
tools as stocks, bonds, mutual funds, equity shares in private
businesses, annuities, net cash value of life insurance policies,
mortgages, certificates of deposit, Treasury bills, savings
bonds, money markets, checking accounts, cash, as well
as gold and other precious metals—basically, anything of
value that is reasonably liquid. Capgemini, a French-based
information technology firm, defines a millionaire as "anyone
with investable assets of $1 million or more, excluding primary
residence." By their conservative measure, nearly 10 million
millionaires exist worldwide. Credit Suisse, the international
financial services conglomerate, asserts that a millionaire is
an individual whose net assets exceed $1 million. The "Credit
Suisse Global Wealth Report" estimates that 24 million
such people exist across the globe, which equates to more
millionaires than the number of people living in Australia.[13]
Some 41 percent of these wealth creators reside in the United
States, 10 percent live in Japan, and 3 percent live in China.
Closer to home, according to the Federal Reserve, this is
not the traditional way of expressing a household's level of
wealth.[14] In the context of wealth creation, home ownership
and equity (the appraised value of the home minus the
mortgage owed) proves to be the most valuable and widely
held asset. Against this backdrop, in 2000, nearly three-
quarters (74 percent) of White households held home equity.

In contrast, fewer than one-half of African Americans are home
owners. To compound matters, Whites are three times more likely to
own rental property than Black Americans as well as to own and operate a business—12 percent compared to 3.4 percent. Black Americans
spend more than $700 billion annually, yet Black-owned businesses
receive less than one-half of 1 percent of all sales receipts generated in
the United States.

- According to the 2007 Federal Survey of Business Owners, of
  the 1.9 million Black-owned firms, 1.8 million are classified
  as sole proprietorships. The average receipts for these
  nonemployee firms were a paltry $21,270.[15]

- And, if the future weren't bleak enough, according to a 2009 Child Trends Research Brief report, 34.5 percent of African American children—compared with only 11 percent of Whites—are raised in poverty.[16]

Once upon a time, immigrants who traveled to this country thought that the streets in America were paved with gold. These newcomers believed that fame and fortune were possible to anyone who was armed with an idea, who backed his or her dreams with hard work and determination, and who stayed true to the guiding principles on which this country was built. Eventually, experience demonstrated that this wouldn't be true for everyone. But what *is* true is that wealth and prosperity come to those who know where to look for it. The high-net-worth men and women outlined in this study, more than 1,000 Black millionaires, know where to look.

STUDY POPULATION AND METHODOLOGY

As I repeated throughout my presentations, I was thrilled and honored to be selected as a spokesperson for such a series of events. And my reasoning was simple: From the earliest days of humanity, humankind has been comprised of two camps: the haves and have nots. Since childhood, I've been obsessed with learning what invisible barrier, if any, separates the two camps. Why are some people rich and others poor? Why are some individuals well off financially while others continually struggle to make ends meet? When I asked the adults who lived in my neighborhood, to my amazement, they knew little about wealth creation and money management. They simply repeated what they had been told or what they thought to be true: "Either you have it or you don't."

As a have not, I wanted to know why so few African Americans managed to climb to the ranks of the wealthy, specifically the 1 percent, in a land where financial freedom, regardless of race, creed, or color, is allegedly available to all. Case in point: More than 25 years ago, my father died absolutely broke, despite attending college and working nonstop for nearly 30 years. I remembered wondering how, in a country brimming with opportunities and endless possibilities, anyone could work so hard during his or her life and end up with little or nothing before falling into the lap of social security. That was the moment I promised myself that it would never happen to me. Regardless of how long or how hard I had to search, how many books I was forced to read, or how many people I had to ask, I was determined to uncover the key to financial freedom and wealth creation. And now the answer that I and so many others seek is closer than we think.

During these talks, I questioned each invited guest. In the process, I compiled enough life-altering information to fill several notebooks as I attempted to draw a composite picture of Black America's wealthy and financially independent population. I spoke with the old and the young; male and female; educated and uneducated; the professional and the working class; doctors, lawyers, accountants, business owners, college graduates as well as high school dropouts, corporate executives—high-achieving men and women of all types. Each proved what is possible when you possess clarity of purpose, backed by persistence, determination, and an indefatigable commitment to a program of wealth creation and financial investing. In short, Black millionaires adhere to nine key disciplines while creating their fortunes.

THE NINE DISCIPLINES OF
BLACK MILLIONAIRES

I am often asked what common traits I observed as I interviewed many of today's Black wealthy.

Amazingly, the answer is simple because nearly all successful men and women share two common factors: (1) a relentless commitment to lifelong learning, and (2) a tenacity of purpose—in other words, tightly crafted goals matched with the discipline to achieve them. The difference between the haves and have nots does not rest with possessions or lack thereof. *No!* The disparity can be found in their individual life's purpose and what each group is willing to do to attain its goals. How can you apply these fundamental truths? By deciding what your long-term financial goals are and working toward them one step at a time.

When I first took on this project, my goal was to provide a road map for financial growth and development—a textbook that would be packed with the best and the latest insight into the behaviors and mind-set of Black America's financial elite. I want to arm you, the reader, with the skills and strategies that lead to abundance and prosperity. I want you to refer to this volume again and again, knowing that you will find exactly what you need at just the right moment. But, most important, I want you to become aware of the nine disciplines—internalized character traits and attributes that all Black millionaires share and practice—with the hope that you will incorporate these principles into your life.

Discipline 1. Be Passionate and Focus on Unique Strengths; Develop Clear, Delineated Goals

Each of us is driven, to some degree, by the mantra "Get a life." But millionaires have done that and more. The wealthy have discovered a cause, a consuming, almost obsessive purpose, that drives them to try, to do, to grow, and to expand. They got a life—and not just any life, but a blessed life, a good and productive life, a life that is fearless, that isn't burdened by risk or the possibility of failure; a life wherein they are willing not only to take a leap of faith but to keep that faith through daily prayer; a life that can be still while listening for God's voice. A life that asks not for material possessions but for guidance, knowledge, and wisdom. A life that is overflowing with self-control, confidence, and discipline. A life that focuses on its unique strengths and refuses to undertake tasks where it cannot perform at its best. In other words, a life that is motivated by the question: "Where can I apply my talents and gifts to render the best advantage?" A life built with warmth and laughter. A life not based on money but built on adding value and service. Or, as one respondent shared, "Never do anything for the sake of money. If you find a vocation that you really love and adds value, take my word for it, money will find you." A life filled with compassion and generosity. A life that is glorious and cannot be taken for granted.

At their core, today's Black financial elite view themselves less as wealthy or successful and more as individuals who have worked hard to pursue their passion. In my focus groups, they spoke at length about the importance of loving their work, establishing meaningful goals, and enjoying what they do. It shouldn't be necessary to ask people if they enjoy their work. Their faces should answer the question without words.

It was passion that set the actions of the Atlanta, Georgia–based Paschal brothers apart from so many entrepreneurial start-ups. In 1947, James and Robert Paschal opened a 30-seat luncheonette in the heart of downtown Atlanta where they sold sandwiches and sodas. As their business grew, they expanded the menu to include both lunch and dinner. Owning neither a stove nor a car, or even the basic necessities, they prepared the food at their home and had it delivered to the luncheonette by cab. Both Dr. Martin Luther King Jr. and future president Bill Clinton strategized their next political moves over Paschal's fried chicken and peach cobbler.

Passion caused Byron E. Lewis to dive headfirst into an uncertain global marketplace. When Lewis launched the Uni-World Group in 1969, the agency's existence was a radical notion. Marketing to African Americans and Latinos? At the time, these two ethnic groups comprised less than 20 percent of the U.S. population. Today, ethnic and segmented markets *are* the market, and Uni-World, the oldest multicultural marketing agency in the country, continues to be the trendsetter. Nearly 30 years after its launch, Lewis's agency boasts annual billings of more than $133 million and provides a wide array of in-house advertising, public relations, event marketing, broadcast production, and entertainment-oriented services. And what is Lewis's secret? He clearly is intoxicated with his work—completely absorbed. "Passion never has to beg for advancement," he explained during a conference keynote that I attended. "The individual who masters his trade and is engaged in his work will be escorted to the front."

Discipline 2. Autonomous and Independent:
Deep Need for Internal Control;
Highly Motivated Self-Starters

Whenever I'm asked what I believe is the purpose of life, my response is the same. Of all the great earthly pursuits, one resides head and shoulders above the rest. Every virtue, treasure, and reward in life is obtained only through this quest. Simply stated, it is fulfilling your potential. Robert Louis Stevenson, the nineteenth-century Scottish writer, said it best: "To become what we are capable of becoming is the only end in life." Unfortunately, most people deny life's endless possibilities and fail to exploit their God-given gifts. There's an anonymous quote that the greatest waste in the world is the difference between who we are and what we could've become. And what is our response to this underutilized and discarded time and effort? Abraham Maslow, the father of Third Force psychology, wrote, "If you plan on being anything less than you are capable of being, you'll probably be unhappy all the days of your life."[17]

The emerging picture from this study does more than suggest that the Black financial elite are intensely goal oriented. They are also ambitious self-starters who possess a deep need for internal control of their lives. They know what they want, and they are focused single-mindedly on achieving their objectives. For the most part, the wealthy adhere to the unwritten rule of financial success: It doesn't matter where you come from; all that matters is where you're going. And where you are going is determined solely by your thoughts and actions. When asked for his prescription to success, a Dallas, Texas–based millionaire replied, "I get up early, stay up late, and do a whole bunch in between." Another member of his peer group chimed in: "I discovered that the best way for me to predict my future is to create it. It serves no purpose to either play it safe or small. If that means that I must continually grow and stretch myself, so be it." By definition, these men and women are self-made. In short, they take complete responsibility for the outcome of their lives, regardless of their struggles and failures. The two words you will never hear the wealthy utter are *"If only."* This habit alone allows them to rise from obscurity to positions of power and influence.

Discipline 3. Industrious: Strong Work Ethic; Bias for Action

What is the one attribute that all millionaires exhibit? What quality is the bedrock of their financial success? What is the one feature that translates into prosperity and abundance? *Hard work!* The affluent have adapted this positive compulsive behavior in the belief that sacrifice, grit, and toil produce character, integrity, and value. As one respondent emphatically stated, "You can always work your way out of poverty and failure." Another participant who scoffed at the current market downturn continues to set the pace on Wall Street as an investment banker. In between my classes, he visited me in my office long enough to share his keys to success: "It seems so cliché," he said, "but it's true. You'd be surprised how much money you could earn if you'd only show up. You can have anything in life that you desire as long as you are willing to earn it."

Millionaires love their work, and they love *to work*. Nearly each member of the seven-figure club knows both victory and defeat, but their ambition, persistence and drive, and ceaseless appreciation for hard work have earned them millions in spite of the occasional bump in the road. And they lead by example. When asked what term describes them best, nearly three out of four respondents cited hard work. And to further underscore the point, regardless of their vocation, the majority in this study said they identified with the label "hardworking."

As a boy growing up in Dayton, Ohio, Henry Parks, the marketing genius who would blaze the trail for future Black entrepreneurs, saw a sign hanging outside a neighborhood store: "Boy wanted." Young Parks immediately removed the sign and walked boldly inside. The store owner indignantly asked what he meant by removing the sign. "You won't need it anymore," Parks asserted. "I'm going to take the job." And he took it. Tyler Perry has made no secret of the pains he expended as he created his most memorable scenes in his films.[18] It is said that Alex Haley rewrote *Roots* dozens of times, and even then he was unsatisfied. He would cut, splice, and edit whatever he wrote until he was completely satisfied. Maya Angelou would spend weeks over a single sentence; Lisa Nichols, hours over a word; Toni Morrison, a month over a short composition. And E. Lynn Harris thought four lines were a good day's work. During a crown forum symposium lecture at Morehouse College, his alma mater, Spike Lee gave the secret to his success, both professionally and financially. "Hard work and perseverance made me what I am today," he shared as he stood before a room packed with ambitious students. "I am most fulfilled when pursuing my labor of love." Hard work is the parent of all worthwhile endeavors, whether in business or the arts. If the wealthy could offer a fresh beatitude to the eight blessings provided in the Book of Matthew, it would be: "Blessed are those who have found their work." Wealth will never open its doors to those who are unwilling to pay the price in terms of sweat, sacrifice, and hard work.

Discipline 4. Creativity and Innovation: Recognize the Powers of Ideas

> Innovate or die? I know that sounds dramatic. And while you might not physically die, your greater hopes and dreams and your chances to accomplish your big goals will. Innovation has always separated leaders from followers, those who succeed and those who just get by. Innovation is what creates progress, and progress is what advances companies and people beyond the competitive herd of the masses, average and the status quo. . . . Innovation is not a task, project or something you only do at an off-site meeting. Innovation is a constant mindset and perspective. It's a way of looking at the world. Instead of seeing what is, it is looking for what could be. Being an innovator is seeking the greater potential in every person, in every situation, process, experience and outcome. The fundamental desire of an innovator is to help, serve and solve.[19]

Daymond John can neither sing nor dance. So, in his early twenties, using his inexhaustible creative power, he hooked into the burgeoning 1980s rap scene in New York as his path to success. John worked as a roadie for renowned rappers Run-DMC and LL Cool J and in the process discovered his enthusiasm for fashion. As the founder of the urban clothing line FUBU (For Us, By Us), John built his empire with determination, creative marketing, and groundbreaking branding strategies. Known as the "godfather of urban fashion," John runs a number of multimillion-dollar clothing enterprises while offering branding expertise to some of the top companies and celebrities in the world.

However, as recently as 1992, John wasn't successful or wealthy—far from it. He had little direction and almost no understanding of the apparel industry. What he did possess, however, was a strong desire to utilize his creative skills and revolutionize the sportswear industry by branding a distinctive line of jerseys, jeans, and outerwear with a decidedly urban appeal. After pricing competitive brands, he decided to design and manufacture his own line instead. At breakneck speed, he began sewing his logo onto every piece of clothing he could produce—hats, hockey jerseys, sweatshirts, and T-shirts—before even considering a marketing strategy.

In 1998, FUBU raked in more than $350 million in revenue. John's business ventures have brought in more than $4 billion in sales since the line was released. He is amused by the nickname "godfather of urban fashion," but knows that it is a result of his relentless effort, determination, and knowledge of what it takes to build a successful business.[20] "I've learned, especially in this industry, that all aspects of this business revolve around preparation, sales, and marketing. I was rejected by 27 banks. I was turned down because I was poorly prepared. I didn't know what potential investors needed to see. I didn't know how to write a business plan; I had no concept of business forecasting and strategic planning. To be blunt, I didn't know a thing. But it was a learning curve, and the only skill set that is more expensive than education is ignorance. I now know what the wealthy and affluent have known all along: The marketplace pays for results, not effort. In other words, focus on the future and keep the ideas flowing.

"Anything and everything can be branded," he shared during our interview. And what lies at the heart of an effective brand? "*Creativity and innovation*—your ability to develop ideas, connect with others, and impact the bottom line."

Discipline 5. Never Consider the Possibility of Failure

If you are afraid to fail, I suggest that you read no further. Close this book and retreat back to the huddled masses, to the humbled crowd, to the status quo. Each day countless obscure men and women march to their graves simply because timidity and lack of courage prevented them from trying or taking a chance. Even worse, the fear of failure stopped them. Perhaps the greatest common trait among the wealthy is their willingness to face failure and rejection and their resilience in picking themselves up and moving on. Self-made millionaires are realistic enough to expect challenges and setbacks. Further, they do not become discouraged or depressed by difficulties or temporary defeat. Mention the word *risk* to a millionaire, and he or she will only hear the term *money*. As a result, they find promise where others find pessimism. As one respondent shared, "In the process of chasing your dream, optimism is not a luxury but a necessity." They know that success builds character, but failure reveals it. Failure is never fatal; it's the down payment you pay for success.

Growing up in the housing projects of Omaha, Nebraska, neighbors told Nathaniel Goldston that he would never rise above anything more than a head waiter. Thirty years later, Goldston, the chief executive officer (CEO) of Gourmet Food Services, was in charge of a company that surpassed the $170 million mark. It mattered not who or what stood in his path—not ridicule, poverty, or the possibility of humiliating defeat would deter him.

"Over the course of my career I've failed more times than I can count," Goldston admitted during our interview. "And each time failure has always rendered a special gift—it's called wisdom. So if at first you don't succeed, welcome to the club."

There's little point in dismissing an idea by saying it might fail. *Any* idea might fail. If you're committed to achieving your financial goals, you'll suffer your fair share of failure. Bank on it.

Discipline 6. Inquisitive; Strong Desire to Know; Quick to Absorb and Apply New Information

During a time when society's reading habits wane, both at home and in school, and as television viewing steadily increases, the wealthy shun this wasteful habit and continue their never-ending quest to grow, study, and absorb new information. So many people fail to increase their earnings because they don't make financial literacy a priority. According to the Nielsen Wire, the global leader in consumer insights, the average African American household spends more than seven hours each day—40 percent more than the overall population, and nearly nine times that of the average Black millionaire—*watching television.* The wealthy, however, read—nearly two books per month. *And the genre?* Mostly history, biographies, or money management—basically any subject or topic that might provide advice, useful information, or cautionary tales.

As you've learned by now, a formal education is not required to join the seven-figure club. Truth be told, a handful of the multimillionaires in this study never ventured past the tenth grade. Although I found these men and women to be no more gifted than others, each had developed an insatiable desire for knowledge and information. They stand out because they had taken the time to prepare, to read and study, and to develop their full potential without the benefit of formal schooling. Affirming a commitment to wealth means becoming a *student* of wealth; you must learn the language of money. It means living by this maxim: *If you wish to be wealthy, you must study the acquisition of wealth.* The millionaires among us are inquisitive; their curiosity propels them forward. They take classes to augment their financial literacy and ask for advice from those who are where they want to be. The wealthy possess a voracious hunger for knowledge and absolutely no appetite for ignorance.

Discipline 7. Strong Sales Skills: "Sell" Is Not a Four-Letter Word

Millionaires not only openly engage in the sales process, they embrace the activity. Although some may detest being labeled a "salesperson," those profiled in this study are proud of the term. *Why?* Because the selling process is the most effective and efficient way to increase your earnings and reach your financial goals. In short: *Sales equals income.* The Black financial elite are thoroughly prepared, completely engaged sales professionals tough enough to deal with any rejection, resilient enough to overcome any objection, and caring enough to help customers and clients achieve their goals.

For this special group, selling takes on a positive, proactive, and even creative aura. It provides continual opportunities to understand real customer needs, to be responsive to changes in the market, and to create value, a subject I touch upon in chapter 5. The wealthy know that selling is not just a business skill but an essential life skill. They live by this mantra: Nothing occurs until somebody sells something. *Nothing!* Hear me loud and clear: There's no way to avoid it—wealth creation requires effective sales skills.

Barbara Smith has always had big dreams—but, more important, thanks in part to her convincing sales skills, she has made those dreams a reality. When she was barely 20 years old, driven by her deep love for fashion, Smith auditioned numerous times for the Ebony Fashion Fair line before convincing Eunice Johnson, the wife of publisher John H. Johnson and director of the annual traveling tour, that her looks and grace could entice top European designers. Her persuasiveness paid off. As she strode down the runway, her artistry and authenticity convinced French and Italian fashion icons that not only should Black women be in their shows but women of color should be in their clothes. After landing a position with the Chicago-based couture trendsetter, Ebony Fashion Fair, Smith moved to New York, the heart of the fashion world, where she had a rewarding career as an international runway, print, and commercial model. In 1976 Smith, the first Black woman to do so, landed the cover of *Mademoiselle* magazine.

Most models retire by age 30. But Smith continued working and kept her sights on loftier goals, pursuing another childhood love—*food*. Smith learned the restaurant business at night and modeled during the day, and although she hadn't intended to create a lifestyle brand, the end result was clear: a multimedia empire that includes two books and two television shows—*B. Smith with Style* and *B. Smart Tips for a Better Life*—that air in a variety of markets. "It's taken me longer," she proudly asserts, "but I've done it my way, and the business is 100 percent African American owned." At last count, Smith's products and licensing produce $75 million in annual sales. This one-time high-priced fashion model clearly knows how to sell her ideas, and that's the millionaire's brilliance.[21]

Every millionaire brings his or her own unique talents, knowledge, and experience to a business venture. But all, in one way or another, sell. They sell themselves, their concepts, their business plans, their products or services, even their hopes and dreams. Clearly, if you hope to join this most influential body, this overlooked skill must become your most practiced and prized asset. As a participant in an Atlanta, Georgia, focus group told me, "Marketing, promotion, and advertising no longer provide the path to growth. If you hope to generate a million-dollar income, you must win the war in the marketplace by mastering the art of one-on-one selling. You must be able to sell *your* story as well as your experience, mission, and expertise."

Discipline 8. Savings: Thrifty and Frugal in Nature

Raised by his mother in Chattanooga, Tennessee, Usher Raymond is a prime example of a young man of modest means making good. His parents split when he was an infant, and he has not had much contact with his father since then. His mother remarried and gave birth to another son, James. While working as a medical claims examiner, her oldest son began performing with a local group. The first to gauge his innate talent, she decided to expose him to more opportunities and moved the family to Atlanta, Georgia, then the center of a humming new urban music scene.

One year later, after singing in a *Star Search* contest, Usher signed with BMG's LaFace Records, which was headed by Antonio "L.A." Reid. Usher's debut album, released in 1994, sold more than 500,000 copies. Three years later, worldwide sales of his second album reached 5 million and allowed the performer to cash his first major check—for $1 million—through a deal with EMI Music Publishing. The young man had just turned 17. Today, Usher sits atop the hip-hop and R&B music scene. His music is downloaded worldwide. He tours internationally, performing in sold-out venues. He stars in films and rubs shoulders with Hollywood legends, and dates supermodels. Still in his 30s, he has everything he could ever want. He lives in a $2.8 million hideaway mansion and owns a stake in the NBA's Cleveland Cavaliers, occupying a courtside seat and high-fiving other stars and celebrities. To date, his record company, Sony BMG, has paid him more than $20 million. In 2005, he grossed more than $20 million on a 64-city tour and made deals to star in movies, commanding a salary of $8 million each. On top of that he renegotiated his music contract, securing a (pretty much nonrefundable) advance of more than $50 million.

But this story is not about a young superstar or the next King of Pop. Nor should you, the reader, be concerned with one man's life of wealth, excess, and comfort that few have ever experienced. No, this eighth discipline centers on a simple question addressed to those who wish to enter the hallowed gates of affluence and prosperity. Yes, Usher has grown quite wealthy very fast—*but will he stay wealthy?* Falling prey to the trappings of notoriety and success—fast cars, expensive homes, and large entourages—young entertainers lose their fortunes as fast as they make them. Over-the-top spending, shoddy financial advice, or dealings with shady handlers can leave them broke even before their brief fame ends. But let me be clear, I am not to judge. Usher is entitled to spend his money as he pleases. He has settled on a chosen profession and is a firm believer in his talents and abilities. Though he makes succeeding look easy, he has fought hard for every inch of ground he has covered. He deserves to reap his rewards and the fruits of his effort. And now, thanks in part to his team of advisors who constantly drill the basic tenets of thrift and frugality, this A-list performer vows to keep his spending under control.

"During our initial meeting," says Reuben McDaniel, Usher's investment advisor and head of Jackson Securities in Atlanta, "he was running through his money so fast it frightened him. But then Usher confided: 'I don't want to be some old, washed-up performer singing in lounges for the rest of my life. I know I have the talent to entertain. I just want to be a great businessman.' He solemnly pledged that he will never be broke. From there we developed a strategy that will place him on solid ground—fixed-income investments, blue-chip stocks and real estate—and consuming less than 10 percent of his total earnings. This plan as well as other investment opportunities will create and maintain his earnings long after anyone cares to hear him sing or watch him dance. We got him to buy into the philosophy: *If it doesn't make money, it doesn't make sense.* And now he applies the same outlook to all of his business ventures. When, like any smart money manager, Usher was ready to diversify, he turned to a cadre of mentors—Dick Parsons of Citigroup, former basketball great Magic Johnson, and hip-hop moguls Russell Simmons and Sean 'Puffy' Combs—individuals who are skilled in all phases of creating wealth."[22]

There's no magic formula. These steps call for no extra effort; they call for no personal sacrifice. But few individuals know how to utilize their earnings properly. For example, today, U.S. credit card debt is at an all-time high—$60 billion—and the average family owes more than $7,000. Eighty-nine percent of the U.S. population operates less than four paychecks away from disaster, and nearly one-half of all African Americans will retire on less than $900 per month. McDaniel is a member of the seven-figure club because, among other things, he knows the devastation of living beyond your means. Like his fellow millionaires, he thinks deeply before he spends and loathes debt. When it comes to our money, we can earn it, hoard it, spend it, save it, waste it, or worship it. But to *deal with it wisely,* as a means to an end, is an education worth its weight in gold. As the Book of Matthew instructs, "*What is a man profited, if he shall gain the whole world and lose his own soul?*"

Thrift and savings are the first steps to prosperity and abundance. More than talent, intellect, education, or skill, the habit of saving is the key to amassing a fortune. The philosophy of the wealthy versus the poor proves that *the rich invest their money and spend what's left; the poor spend their money and invest what's left.* "Pay yourself first," Black millionaires admonish. The habit of thrift not only opens the door to opportunity but is a safeguard against our own weaknesses and the tendency to scatter our earnings. It is by the mysterious power of savings that your resources grow; that the loaf is multiplied, that little becomes much, that scattered fragments grow to unity, and that out of nothing comes the miracle of something. Such disciplined habits allow anyone to surprise the world with gifts, even if he or she is poor. Unless you make it a cast-iron rule to lay aside a certain percentage of your earnings each week, each month, your dream of financial independence will be just that: *a dream.*

In closing, the lesson is clear: You must learn to save and budget if you hope to join the ranks of those who boast seven-figure incomes. You must understand the concept of compound interest—how it works in your favor when you add money each month into your 401(k) and hurts you when you pay the minimum on your credit card debt. You must learn that low monthly payments don't equal *affordability.* You must read the fine print. You must learn how to pay cash because *cash hurts.* You must be aware of the seductive power of marketing and separate your wants from your needs. And finally, if you do nothing but change the way you manage your current income, your life will change for the better. It's not what you earn that makes you wealthy, *it's what you keep!*

Discipline 9. Spirituality: The Gospel of Wealth

Where do Black millionaires draw their inspiration and, in turn, inspire us? From a close personal relationship with their Creator and a belief that the Almighty has a plan for their life. This relationship is the elixir the soul craves, the glue that holds spirit and dreams together. An active faith, a faith that provides inner strength on a consistent basis, is the first and last order of business of Black millionaires. This faith is the language of their heart, the center of a truly—regardless of their millions—humble life. Their deeply personal crusade is not so much the fervor of a come-lately Christian but the steady quest of a peaceful soul bent on doing good and one day hoping to meet their Maker. Believe me, the Black financial elite have found God—not the God we meet every Sunday in church or the power we frequently pray to but the Heavenly Father who keeps them standing in good times and in bad. The God who sits high and looks low; the all-knowing, all-seeing spirit they embrace for meaning in their lives. The God who can mold a mere lump of breathing clay; who can chip away and pound us remorselessly to bring out our possibilities; who can strip us of our ego and vanity; who can humble our pride, humiliate our ambition, knock us off the ladder of success only to eventually lift us to heights and sights unseen.

Many of the people we call financially secure have overcome incredible struggles. More than a few have seen everything go up in smoke. Some have endured loss of family and friends, homelessness, bankruptcy, and bouts with depression so horrific it seems a miracle they survived. At one time, nearly all those surveyed within this study have danced with disaster. Yet it's not tragedy that forms the essence of great comebacks. It's tenacity, perseverance, and an ever-present abiding faith. Case in point: Gospel artist and mega-producer Kirk Franklin's road to wealth has been anything but easy. Adopted at age four, Franklin was reared by an aunt, a deeply spiritual woman who scraped up enough money from her monthly social security check to pay for her nephew's piano lessons. It was money well spent. As a child, Franklin was a quick study. The natural musician could sight read and play by ear. By age 11, he was leading the adult choir at Mt. Rose Baptist church near Dallas, Texas.

But in spite of his religious upbringing, Franklin's rebellious ways got the better of him. Not until a close friend was accidentally shot and killed in his teens did the young musician realize the error of his ways. Hoping to bring an end to his grieving, Franklin channeled his efforts into composing and producing his own music. The result? His debut album, *Kirk Franklin and the Family,* spent nearly two years on the Billboard Gospel charts. Amazingly, a few of his tracks crossed over into R&B, the first of its type to do so. Follow-up projects, such as *Stomp* and *Nu Nation*—highly charged hip-hop efforts—aired on urban radio across the country. As his music leaked to the pop charts, Franklin became known as the king of gospel with a lifestyle to match. But fame and adulation wouldn't last long.

Although more traditional gospel artists paved the way for the blending of gospel with more contemporary sounds, Franklin was dismissed by many in music circles because of his up-front appropriation of hip-hop, R&B, and pop culture. Often, critics argued, it was difficult to determine whether Franklin was truly singing gospel—at least the old-school gospel our forebears rocked to on Sunday mornings. Though he expanded his artistic reach by producing music with performers such as Mary J. Blige and Bono, by 1998, Franklin's own album sales weren't impressive. With his influence in decline and faced with fickle fans, it wasn't long before he lost his home, cars, and nearly his marriage. The king of gospel was literally forced to change his tune.

Trapped by material success in a spiritual world, once again Franklin faced his demons outside of the bright lights. "What does it value the man who inherits the world but loses his soul?" he asked as he leaned on his favorite biblical verse. "Few of us stop to realize and appreciate the undeserved blessings that have been heaped our way. I've been given more than I could ask, but what truly matters? The love of my wife, my children and friends, plus a talent to share. I mean, let's face it," he continued. "I still wear the finest suits, but that chapter of my life is no longer important. You can only drive one car at a time no matter how many you own. What kept me going during those down years? Look no further than Romans 8:28: 'All things work together for good to those who love God, to those who are called according to His purpose.' In other words, it's all good!"

The true character of a man or woman will emerge in the toughest of times, and this may be the greatest lesson for you. Instead of giving in to despair, use the difficulties of the day to strengthen your deepest layer of mettle. As the aforementioned profiles underscore, you are urged to "work hard, be honest in all business dealings, and *trust in the Lord.*" As one interviewee told me, "If you have the faith, God certainly has the power."

WHY ARE SO MANY POOR IN SPIRIT?

Most of these principles are not startling. In fact, most are common sense. I should also note that not all principles were present or obvious to the same degree in every interview or focus group. But in every case, many if not most were clearly visible. Furthermore, the application of these principles calls for no formal education. What is required is simply the willingness to listen, learn, and understand that the accumulation of money cannot be left to chance, good fortune, or luck. Sadly, too many of the traits that lead to financial success are absent or lacking throughout our society. It's true that the poor will always be among us, and noted lecturer and business writer Brian Tracy explains why:

> With regard to money and earnings there are five reasons why so many people remain poor. One, it never occurs to them that they, too, can be wealthy. Two, if it does occur to them, they never decide to become wealthy. Three, if people do decide to improve their financial lives, they procrastinate which, in turn, hastens the obvious. Four, so many individuals lack the ability to delay gratification; spending all that they earn in the process. And five, the majority of men and women operate within a short-term perspective [more on this later]. They think and act day to day.[23]

Yes, similar to wealth, poverty begins in the mind. The have nots have not because so many are born poor and expect to remain poor. This is their unvarying trend of thought, their fixed conviction. *You doubt me?* Walk or travel among have nots and, invariably, you will find them discussing poverty, explaining poverty, and bewailing their fate, their hard luck, the cruelty and injustice of it all. They walk, it is said, "in the shadow of death." They will share how they are ground down and kept down by the upper class, by unsympathetic employers, or by the unjust order of society despite the fact that limitless abundance, an inexhaustible supply to meet their needs, is just waiting to come to light. It is in the unseen world that humankind, animated and inspired by the consciousness of their partnership with divinity, will find the secrets of wealth and prosperity. No matter how poor you may be, if you hold to the right mental attitude and keep your mind fixed on the laws of abundance and prosperity—if you truly believe that you are a child of the Creator, the possessor of all things, "in Him in whom all fullness lies," and that you were not intended for poverty—*you* will not be poor long. Every discovery, invention, improvement, and achievement—everything that humanity has created for our use and benefit—has been preceded by divine intelligence and cosmic thought. Just as the first step in an architect's building is a plan, we, too, must envision a plan or mental image of the prosperity we desire. The seven laws of wealth that I discuss later are as definite as the law of gravity, and they work just as unerringly. The stream of plenty flows toward the open mind, the expectant mind, toward faith and confidence, and away from doubt. It is because the millionaires profiled and researched within this study understand the importance of adhering to these seven laws that there is such a difference between them and the have nots. If embraced, these laws can spell the difference between poverty and hope, poverty and courage, poverty and the expectation of better days, and poverty and the faithful effort to improve your condition.

Surprisingly, so many people point their finger at God when they should be praising Him. If the have nots are to be saved spiritually, it is hope that will save them. If they are to be rescued, it is faith that will lift them above the rising tide. If they are to be transformed from rags to riches, it is their thinking that will extend a helping hand. Have we not been instructed "be ye transformed by the renewing of our mind"? The Almighty can do *for* you only what He can do *through* you.

Now hear me out. I beg of you, don't get me wrong. It's so easy to parade the likes of Oprah Winfrey, Bob Johnson, Cathy Hughes, or any of the other Black billionaires or 35,000 Black millionaires who currently operate within the confines of our economic system and exclaim, "Follow their lead. Do what they did. They overcame the odds." Indeed, they did, and I, like so many within my community, am ecstatic and brimming with pride as I soak in their accomplishments. However, their achievement doesn't ease the plight of the child born to a single mother living in the inner city. Their success doesn't remove the heartache or anxiety of the millions who are trapped in impoverished neighborhoods. The question society should address—and the focal point of this study—is this: Can *anyone* overcome similar odds if they were born to that poor woman or living in similar circumstances? In other words, instead of asking why these wealth creators made it, I suggest that each of us turn within and ask *how* they made it. I suggest that you, the reader, turn to biography. Every great and good life is rich in experience and hopeful promise. These members of the financial elite chose fields that suited their temperaments and talents. When opportunity arose, every power in their nature came into play.

For a group of people who have been in this country for more than 400 years, we, Black Americans, have yet to claim our divine inheritance. Rather than combating any and all economic barriers to wealth and prosperity, we are unconsciously bred to think of ourselves as victims, quick to point fingers and heap blame on any outside cause that has kept us stuck in poverty. When we relish the habit of living on marginal incomes, spending beyond our means, spurning the need to save, embracing the need to impress others, forsaking a basic education, and justifying an existence within an endless cycle of debt and liabilities, we don't even realize that we reinforce and strengthen the preconceptions surrounding lack and limit and our inability to foster and preserve wealth.

YOUR FIRST STEP ON YOUR ROAD TO WEALTH

Perhaps you are what the world calls poor. So what? *Who cares?* Most of the men and women found on these pages were and are the offspring of poverty. Each knew the pressure of limited resources and the fragile nature of their monetary means. Each began their trek to riches right from the ground floor. However, these obstacles and others do not prove that poverty is indeed a barrier to financial success. Each of us must aggressively pursue our individual right to wealth. Falling down does not constitute failure; refusing to rise and fight again surely does. It is poverty that makes the financial elite rich. The wealthiest men and women will always be those who have risen from the ranks.

On a personal note, as I look back over the course of my life, I must admit I've been blessed. Today—thanks, in part, to all that I am about to share—I do not want for much. In terms of creature comforts, I possess all that I need. However, I must constantly remind myself that it was not always this way. Indeed, in my youth, I knew poverty all too well. Moreover, I was constantly surrounded by adults with little hope of rising above a state of economic hopelessness. At one time, I, too, wallowed in that hopelessness until the fateful day when I met the one individual—as well as a cadre of like-minded men and women—who helped uncover the laws that govern the accumulation of wealth. What they taught me changed my life forever, as it would the life of anyone who applies these few basic rules that govern prosperity.

These are the laws and lessons that I now share with you. These are the foundational principles that will guide you down the path to abundance—that is, if you choose to embrace and apply them in your life. Nearly all of the affluent enjoy sharing what they've learned along the way as they built their personal financial empire. I've enjoyed writing this book and pointing out, as clearly as I can, not the secrets but the techniques, practices, truths, and laws that are instrumental to financial success. Just as physical laws govern the universe, laws of prosperity and abundance are equally sure and true. It doesn't matter whether you know them or use them; they exist nonetheless, and they will govern your life. Those who learn these laws and apply them will achieve a level of purpose, success, and prosperity of which others can only dream. But before you begin, I must warn you. Simply reading this book, even contemplating the principles contained herein, will do little good if you do not act and apply the principles. It is through recognizing the successful truths and concepts within these pages, relating them to your own personal life, and developing daily habits of action that you will find yourself among the financial elite.

In addition, I have learned a host of valuable lessons during the course of this research, including the first law of wealth:

Wealth begins in the mind but ends in the purse.

All the world cries, "Where is the man or woman who will save us?" Don't waste your time searching for this individual, for he or she is at hand. This man, this woman, is *you* and *me*. This individual is *each of us*. You are the architect of your own fortune. Your fortune is not something to find but to unfold. We do not *go* through life, we *grow* through life. Your greatest strength is developed and your best work is done when you struggle for that which you have yet to possess. "How did you find your place?" I asked Harry Johnson, the Houston, Texas–based attorney who single-handedly raised more than $120 million to build the Martin Luther King, Jr. memorial. "I didn't find it," Johnson admitted. "My *place* found *me*." True, but after it found the well-known lawyer, his *place* would not have taken him far had it not found him prepared.

Stick to your dreams and carry them through. Believe that you were made for the place you're about to fill and that no one can fill it as well as you. "Do what you want to do," R. Donahue Peebles, arguably Black America's top real estate developer, shared with me during a conversation. "Don't wait for or seek the approval of others. Don't sit around wondering what will happen next. Push the envelope. Push the pedal to the metal and make the most of your life!" And, if Johnson's and Peebles's words aren't enough to compel you to act, listen to one focus group participant who experienced years of toil, opposition, and repeated failure but now operates one of the largest automotive supply companies in Detroit. "When it comes to earning a seven-figure income," he stated, "there are no elevators in life. Each of us must use the stairs." Whether we are haves or have nots, we will be better served once we understand that a constant struggle, a ceaseless battle to win success in spite of every barrier, is the price of financial achievement.

To be truthful, it is not knowledge that provides prosperity and fulfillment but the judicious use of wisdom. Wealth without wisdom corrupts and destroys; wealth with wisdom ennobles and expands. In short, *the pocketbook can't grow until the mind grows. Knowledge can be taught, but wisdom must be acquired.* Wealth and abundance are not measured in terms of possessions and money but in relationships, values, knowledge, and action; in what we *do*, not what we know. If you are to walk among the financial elite, the first step on your journey is to develop a wealth consciousness, for it is in the depths of your mind that your vast treasure resides. So I encourage you to read this book and the lessons it contains. Identify ideas of action and place them into practice. Continue to follow these fundamental codes, and you will forge, in the crucible of your life experiences, the faith, knowledge, and wisdom that will surely plant the seeds of abundance and prosperity. As a result, you will uncover your personal road map to financial success.

MILLIONAIRE LESSON NO. 1

"If you want to know how people feel about themselves, look at their bank account. Money is the greatest measurement of your mind-set. Wealth is less a matter of circumstance than it is a matter of knowledge and choice."

—*John H. Johnson*

ONE

DECISION

RESOLVE NOW THAT YOU
WILL NOT BE POOR

The Second Law of Wealth

The greatest of evils and the worst of crimes is poverty. Our first duty, a duty to which every other consideration should be sacrificed, is not to be poor.

—George Bernard Shaw

THE WEALTH CHOICE BEGAN YEARS AGO, AS SCRIBBLES ON scraps of paper, before morphing into a PowerPoint lecture that I used in an MBA class. From there, with the help of U.S. Census Bureau, Federal Reserve, and U.S. Trust Survey data, I developed a one-page questionnaire for my survey participants. I tried to make the pool of respondents as authoritative, comprehensive, and objective as humanly possible, given the constantly shifting ground beneath the data. I do recognize, however, that no matter how rigorous the research, any respondent list is but a snapshot in time. My goal was to move beyond anecdotes of crucial career events and wise money moves and highlight the underlying factors that spell financial success. What emerged was a surprising set of habits and disciplines from a diverse body of people. At this point, I had the material collated by industry, gender, and net worth. This project eventually grew into bound pages of notes that begged for empirical qualitative analyses. Based on an 18-page,

118-question survey as well as crates of data, endless coding, personal interviews, and focus groups, I was able to piece together a composite picture of Black America's wealthiest—the top 1 percent of wage earners—that flies in the face of conventional wisdom. To keep the search moving, I cast a broad net, combing the country for Black men and women who had attained millionaire status.

Since the goal of this research was to secure at least 1,000 responses—a significant statistical representation—I collected names and data from many sources and utilized a network of professional associations and organizations. Individual surveys were confidential, held in complete anonymity, and reported in aggregate form only. Respondents did not sign the survey. In short, there was little need for me to know any proprietary information. Although the eventual choice of respondents was a decidedly statistical objective call, in order to remain true to the core data, I decided early on to omit athletes, celebrities, and entertainers, a subject that I will address in full detail later. I felt that if I were to crack the code on Black millionaireship, it would be best to focus on those participants whose wealth wasn't fleeting or temporary. This book is not about conspicuous consumption or high-tech bling. Instead, I chose to focus on the types of personal choices and decisions that are informed and driven by specific values.

When all was said and done, the project required not only seven years of random face-to-face interviewing, crunching numbers, and countless computer runs but ongoing field research and the subsequent write-up as well. Clearly I had touched a nerve. It turns out that respondents—even high-net-worth candidates, those with in excess of $5 million—wanted to think about, learn about, and talk about what this group of men and women know that others do not. I spoke directly with three of Black America's five billionaires and darn near 500 millionaires, not to mention their handlers. My ultimate objective is to highlight how you, the reader, can create your own fortune. It would be of little to no use to discover that your relationship with your parents or your childhood experiences failed to match some standard millionaire's profile. More important are the segments of the equation you can control—namely, the habits and strategies that you can emulate. To this end, the final chapter offers a chance for a bit of self-assessment. Armed with the knowledge that self-made millionaires display a tendency toward certain character traits and adhere to the laws of wealth, you can strive to correct any shortcomings and strengthen those traits within your own personality.

What distinguishes the haves from the have nots are not key connections, superior intelligence, or wealthy parents—although those advantages seldom hurt—but rather the nine disciplines discussed in this book. The affluent African American is not the son or daughter of the boss. Nor is he or she likely to feature an IQ in the ninety-ninth percentile.

The vast majority of Black millionaires profiled in this study began their careers like most others—with a solid education, tons of ambition, and precious little relevant experience. Like accumulating compound interest, these men and women achieved financial success slowly and consistently. The story of how Black men and women became millionaires, and how that event influenced their lives, takes nothing away from the mystery that surrounds the rich. But it does offer a lesson. These individuals did not necessarily set out to achieve material success; they just worked hard in a field in which they could apply their talents and gifts. Before they knew it, they were standing in a pool of liquid gold. Or, as one respondent shared, "I've heard that money changes you. That's why, though I am grateful for the blessings of wealth, it hasn't changed who I am. My feet are still on the ground. I'm just wearing better shoes."

PROFILE OF THE AFFLUENT AFRICAN AMERICAN

As *The Wealth Choice* reflects, I discovered the inner workings of Black America's most affluent as well as the habits and attitudes of those who join the millionaires' club. For example, did you know:

- The average Black millionaire is a 52-year-old male nearly 12 percent, and growing, female; born in the Northeast and Midwest; the majority raised in a home where both parents were present; more often than not their mother was a housewife
- Average net worth: $4 million
- Average income of parents: $10,000 to $20,000 per year
- Married 15 to 20 years
- Children: two plus

- College degree: approximately 69 percent
  - SAT score: greater than 1,000 (earlier version)
  - College GPA: male: 2.9; female: 3.4
  - Major: 52 percent business majors; 20 percent MBA
- Daily routine
  - Rise 5:30 A.M.; retire by 11:00 P.M.
  - Exercise: 3.5 hours per week; golf and tennis most popular with men and golf, tennis, aerobics, yoga, and gardening most popular with women
- Cars: four plus (Mercedes or Lexus; General Motors or Ford)
- Church habits
  - Attendance: twice per week at churches with fewer than 2,500 members
  - Donations: women tithe; men give 10 to 15 percent of their earnings to charity
- How they made their money? 90 percent entrepreneurship; 30 percent real estate
- Smartest money move? "Diversifying my portfolio": 31 percent. "Buying a home": 26 percent
- Investment strategy: stocks, mutual funds; "Earn it, grow it, give it away!"
- Best way to get rich? "Start a business": 30 percent
- Savings plan: 10–20 percent of income
- Average credit card debt: $2,500
- Appraised value of home: $200,000 to $299,000
- Average debt not including mortgage: Less than $10,000
- Definition of success: "Ability to effect change and the capacity to enjoy their work"
- What money means to them: "Freedom and security"
- Most important public policy issue facing Black America: economic development and education
- Golden rule to Black millionaireship: earn six figures ($100,000) or more by age 30

To say the least, this was a far cry from what I expected to hear concerning the creation of wealth and success. And now, in city after city, in hotel suites and meeting halls across the country, over soft drinks, cocktails, and coffee, I was finally given full access—the opportunity to discover the keys to financial success—in short, the million-dollar secret that unfortunately has eluded mine and previous generations. I had been given the chance to hear the answers to a host of questions that I had asked over the course of my adult life, answers that I am more than willing to share with a waiting audience.

To quote the American novelist and journalist Ernest Hemingway, when friend and fellow writer F. Scott Fitzgerald observed that the rich are different from you and me: "Yes, they have more money." And here lies the heart of the issue: What is the difference between you, the reader, and Victor MacFarlane, the California-based real estate developer who currently boasts a net worth in excess of $300 million? Between you and Oprah Winfrey? Between you and Lisa Price, the famed female entrepreneur who launched Carol's Daughter? Or between you and Daymond John of FUBU; Dave Steward of World Wide Technology; Sheila Johnson Lee, the team president and managing partner of the WNBA Washington Mystics and the first woman to manage three different sports franchises; or the hundreds of Black millionaires surveyed for this book? Why do some people generate wealth while others face a life of financial struggle? Is the difference found in their education, intelligence, skills, work habits, contacts, luck, or vocation?

So who are these wealth creators and what do they stand for? They believe in hard work, and they invest in themselves and constantly work toward self-improvement. They are more likely to place emphasis on receiving financial gain from their work and do not allow failure to deter them. And they don't waste their hard-earned money on the indulgences of the very rich; rather, they live and spend according to middle-class values. These are individuals who are driven by an unwavering aim; who cut their way through the opposition and forge to the front; who, in this information age, where everything is push or be pushed, dare to hold their ground and push hard. What are stumbling blocks to the poor and defeated are but stepping-stones to the strong and determined; poverty and humble birth do not bar the progress of men and women with the grit to seize their chance.

For those who believe that millionaire status isn't what it used to be, I suggest that you speak to the 35,000 Black millionaires—an all-time high—who boasted a net worth of $1 million or more in 2009, excluding the value of their primary residence.[1] Well, that's what I've done. I asked—not all 35,000 but a representative sample. Enough to realize that both Hemingway and Fitzgerald were correct in their assessment in more ways than one. If I learned anything over the course of my seven-year study, I've discovered that despite our enduring fascination with those we classify as rich or high net worth, most of us misunderstand wealth. We mistake the *trappings* of money for genuine affluence. In a culture that encourages living above your means, Black millionaires work extremely hard, save their money, hold dear to their values, and plow their profits back into their business and/or vocation. In a nutshell, that's why they're millionaires. Needless to say, this image runs counter to how the masses view the well-to-do. More than intellect, education, or luck, *discipline* is the key to joining the ranks of this elite class.

LET'S TALK ABOUT MONEY . . . AGAIN

Without considering temporary setbacks and extraordinary fortunes of inheritance or luck, if you wish to know how average individuals feel about themselves, look at their bank accounts. Money, or the lack thereof, is the greatest measurement of your mind-set. The age-old maxim that water seeks its own level also applies to income. Money will meet you where you are. Or, stated another way, your net worth will equal your *self-worth*. More than just a clever quip, the statement is a wise truth—and a stark reality for some. Money is neither good nor bad; it is only a resource. Money is the instrument of exchange for valued production and is earned only by the producer. The accumulation of wealth is accomplished only by consistent applied effort and discipline. Money possesses an energy of its own, and it is largely attracted to those who understand its value and respect its power. Although there are exceptions to every rule, money tends to flow to those individuals who can use it in the most effective and productive manner and who can invest it to create opportunities that will benefit others. It takes money to acquire food, shelter, and clothing. It takes money to build schools, churches, and institutions. It takes money to purchase cars, homes, and education as well as all of life's magical moments.

Money is not acquired, as many believe, by fortunate speculation or foolhardy enterprises but by the daily practice of faith, family, and hard work. Those who rely on these values will rarely be destitute, and those who succumb to thoughts of lack and limit will generally be broke. At some point in time, as this study points out, the wealthy break away from the crowd and ignore conventional wisdom to journey into the unknown armed only with their creative imagination and courage of conviction. Optimism, curiosity, creativity, and drive are universal qualities found in the profile of the "average" millionaire. Most in this study did not begin in pursuit of fame and fortune; they focused on solving a problem or by pouring themselves into the task at hand. Whether churchgoers or not, Black millionaires emerge from a culture shaped by spiritual values. The optimism and trust, the commitment and faith, the discipline and altruism that their lives reveal and their works require can flourish only in the midst of a moral order with spiritual foundations.

Over the course of seven years, I have found the Black wealthy to be constant learners and calculated risk takers unafraid to attempt new ideas, even at the risk of appearing foolish to their peers. Their financial windfall is the by-product of these qualities. When money flows freely and circulates, it blesses humanity. But when hoarding, squandering, or abuse interrupts the circulation, money becomes a curse. In itself, money does not increase the personal merit of its possessor. It is not a sign so much as a test of real worth. It constitutes opportunity and means for either virtue or vice. Its faithful use or foolish abuse determines the owner's character.

THE MASTER KEY TO WEALTH

If you asked the average person what it takes to become a millionaire, he or she would probably cite a number of predictable factors. Topping the list would be intelligence, inheritance, contacts, hard work, ambition, persistence, and luck, to name a few. It may be difficult to dislodge this misguided belief, but my study of Black millionaires reveals a critical skill that so many were forced to master prior to earning their millions. The listed qualities can and eventually may play a role, but none is the sole source of wealth accumulation. Consider the following profiles. Compare each and observe how these men and women are united by a single common chord: *the golden rule.*

Consider the words and deeds of Madame C. J. Walker, America's first Black female millionaire. Walker's accomplishments as an inventor, entrepreneur, and philanthropist are nothing short of amazing, considering the time in which she lived and the short stack she was dealt. Born four years after the abolition of slavery, she was orphaned, married, and widowed by age 20. She also suffered from a scalp condition that caused hair loss. In the early 1900s, she began testing various homemade cures, and by 1905, she had developed a revolutionary hair care system aimed specifically at Black women. And with that, this visionary blazed a new trail for Black women. Not only did she offer products designed for women of color during a time when the rest of the market ignored this segment, she opened the door for a small army of women, known as Walker Agents, to earn additional income pitching her products door to door. As the business grew, she embraced vertical integration, manufacturing the treatments in her own plants and selling them in company-owned beauty shops. Soon she and her sales force were nationwide.

A *Black Enterprise* feature article on this skilled entrepreneur also highlighted her shrewd real estate investments:

> Walker owned properties in Chicago, Pittsburgh, Indianapolis, St. Louis, and New York, including an apartment building overlooking Central Park. Her crown jewel, however, was "Villa Lewaro," a $250,000, 20-room Georgian mansion on New York's Hudson River. True to her principles of Black empowerment, she hired a Black architect to design her elegant estate, which was located in the same community as those of the Rockefellers, Tiffanys, and Vanderbilts.[2]

With her million-dollar fortune—a rarity for her race and gender—Walker gave as lavishly as she lived. "There is no royal flower-strewn path to success," this entrepreneurial wizard admonished. "And, if there is, I have yet to find it. For if I have accomplished anything it is because I have been willing to work hard. I was raised at a time when everybody had something to do, and they did it. Don't sit down and wait for opportunities to come—*get up and make them!*"

When traveling across this vast continent, people are often impressed by the immense unutilized wealth contained in its unmined mountains; in its millions of acres of rich, uncultivated soil; in its dense forests of heroic proportions replete with every variety of timber and wood; and in its mighty waterfalls—resources as far as the eye can see and beyond the ability of human thought to estimate. But what of the incalculable amount of human faculty, of unused ability, of undeveloped mental power within the countless souls who are using only a fraction of their limitless possibilities? There are no wastelands except to the blind, no useless resources to those who know how to utilize them. The future never takes care of itself; it is taken care of, shaped, molded, and colored by the present. Our todays are what our yesterdays made them; our tomorrows must inevitably be the product of our todays. Those who neglect opportunity and shirk responsibility do so at the peril of any possible financial attainment or advancement. So, throw away your money, if you will; waste, if you must, your possessions, your homes, or your resources, but never discard opportunity. No power, no force in the universe can restore to you its value or the possibilities for growth and accomplishment contained within.

"There are no longer any chances for my generation," complained an inner-city youth to Jon E. Barfield. The grandson of Alabama sharecroppers, Barfield graduated from Princeton University before entering Harvard Law School and built his high-tech personnel firm with a string of blue-chip clients. But it was by his father's side that he would master his greatest lesson. It was Barfield's father who launched the family business. In 1954, John Barfield went north to Detroit from Alabama and created a cleaning venture with his wife. At a time and place when African Americans were given no quarter and fewer breaks, the hardworking Barfields saw their little enterprise grow. In 1969, the elder Barfield sold his cleaning business to the ITT Corporation for an undisclosed amount and assumed his place in the motor city as a respected entrepreneur with strong ties in both the Black and White communities. Twelve years later, with the company's revenue surpassing more than $4 million, the younger Barfield took the post of president while his father served as chairman.

"*No chance, no opportunities?*" questioned Barfield's father. Here is a man who made his mark, although the world seemingly turned a cold shoulder. "How quick we forget. In a land where a fatherless Black boy has become president of the most powerful country on the face of the earth, too many of us have forgotten that the key to success has been given to the weakest as well as the strongest. There's no need to search for opportunity—it's everywhere."[3] And each day more opportunities are being created. There's always work to be done, value to be created. The most common mistake we make is looking outside of ourselves for what we can only find within. Wealth is no exception. It is a sorry day for our youth who cannot see opportunities where they stand. Like Paul during his darkest hour, they need only to "unlock the door."

HOW ONE MAN FOUND AND USED THE KEY

With neither capital nor influence, it is not an easy task to accrue great wealth in any undertaking that those around you believe to be both foolish and fleeting. But fortunately for the cause of human progress, there are brave spirits with determination and mettle enough to stand their ground and push even when the world opposes. There are no more interesting pages in biography than those that record how Berry Gordy Jr. took his first steps toward prosperity. Without his insight, there would be no "Baby Love," no "My Guy," no "Let's Get It On," and no "Billie Jean." Moreover, there would be no Temptations, no Diana Ross, no Marvin Gaye, no Stevie Wonder, no Gladys Knight, no Lionel Richie, and no Michael Jackson. Gordy opened a path into the White mainstream for Black musicians and demolished the notion that Black popular music was a passing fad. His ability to reach across the racial divide with a unique sound that would touch all people made him a historically significant figure. Never before had an independent record label like Motown produced so many hits with artists who walked in unknown and walked out stars.

Armed with a dream and a $700 loan, Gordy proceeded to build the most successful independent label of the 1960s. Born during the Depression and reared in Detroit, he has been described as brilliant, charismatic, a genius, and highly driven. At the age of five, Gordy, the seventh of eight children, took classical piano lessons from his uncle. As a teenager and young adult, he worked in his father's small construction company, sold cookware, and applied and trimmed chrome on the assembly line at the Ford Motor Company. After a stint in the army, Gordy returned to Detroit and launched his first venture—a record store—his initial foray into the world of music. Though the business failed, it made him want to be part of the industry even more. Gordy's big break came in the 1950s, when he began writing songs for local rhythm and blues acts, acquiring a reputation as a songwriter and producer. It was against this backdrop that Gordy met an aspiring artist named William "Smokey" Robinson, who created a group aptly named the Miracles. Gordy soon became their manager, and together he and Robinson forged a creative partnership and produced a number of hits.

With the success of the Miracles, a stream of young, talented aspiring artists found their way to Gordy's doorstep. Soon Marvin Gaye, the Temptations, the Supremes, Martha Reeves, Stevie Wonder, and the Four Tops created the foundation of what would become the Motown sound. An effective and efficient manager, Gordy created a competitive environment where every artist and group contended and vied with each other. The result of this strategy propelled the Motown label up the charts. The Motown sound had its roots in rhythm and blues, but it was Gordy's plan to appeal to listeners of all races and backgrounds. The label's tagline—"The Sound of America"—reflected the founder's desire to achieve widespread popularity. Gordy's move of his base of operations to Los Angeles in 1972 marked the end of an amazing era, though the Motown label continued to flourish. Nonetheless, the music created during those golden years sounds as fresh and energetic as it did the day it was produced.

Gordy and his fellow wealth creators are the real achievers of our society. Their courage, determination, and belief in themselves to pursue their dream and overcome obstacles cannot be overestimated. The greatest among us are those who revolutionize business, open opportunities for others, and change and challenge the way we think and live. Their impact is felt for generations. The lessons we deduce from their ingenuity, spirit, and courage are invaluable. If people are to achieve their financial goals, they must stand erect in spite of difficulties while others bow and tremble in fear. "There's nothing magical regarding my success," Gordy stated during an award ceremony. "I refused to give up or give in. In short, don't judge yourself by others' standards—develop your own. Don't get caught up in the trap of changing yourself to fit the world. The world has to change to fit you. We stuck to who we were at Motown, and the world eventually came around."[4]

THE POWER OF A SINGLE PURPOSE

There is no grander sight than the man or woman who is committed to a single purpose, one aim. It is a divine purpose that gives meaning to life. It unifies all powers, binds them together; makes strong and united what was weak, separated and scattered. To be financially successful is to identify your mission and pursue it, to find your place and fill it. Individuals driven by an unwavering aim are bound to win; the world stands aside and allows them to pass. Defeat only gives them new power; opposition only redoubles their efforts; danger only increases their daring. Regardless of what may come—sickness, poverty, or disaster—they never turn their eyes from their objectives. Even Christ knew that a single idea rules life best when He taught, "No man can serve two masters."

It was this one critical skill that brought Tyler Perry—the director, playwright, and actor—back from the brink. Scoffed and ridiculed, and with little industry experience, Perry felt the dream that beat in his chest and stood his ground. The words "Hollywood producer" were engraved on his heart, and he would sacrifice his reputation, possessions, resources, past friendships, or even life itself if need be. This entertainment mogul has built a maverick media company by transforming urban theater into mainstream movies and television shows.

Nearly five years ago, Perry started Tyler Perry Studios in Atlanta, one of the first movie studios in the United States owned by an African American. His first two films, *Diary of a Mad Black Woman* (2005) and *Madea's Family Reunion* (2006), were produced with Lions Gate Entertainment for a total of only $11 million. Surprisingly, each movie opened at number 1, and they earned more than $110 million combined, stunning an industry known for narrow profit margins. His third feature, *Daddy's Little Girls,* opened to similar appeal and receipts. Since 1998, his touring stage plays have made more than $150 million.[5] Perry even captured first place on the *New York Times* nonfiction best-seller list with the publication of *Don't Make a Black Woman Take Off Her Earrings: Madea's Uninhibited Commentaries on Love and Life,* written in the voice of Madea, the boisterous grandmother he has portrayed in his films and many of his plays.

Amazingly, Perry has maintained ownership of all his work. In a business where it is commonplace to use OPM (other people's money), he has used his own to build a library of substantial and growing value. But perhaps his most surprising feat happened on the small screen. In 2007, in a deal ultimately valued in excess of $200 million and based on the success of a ten-episode test run, the Turner Broadcasting

Station (TBS) bought 100 episodes of Perry's half-hour sitcom *House of Payne*. Perry was able to avoid the entire standard sitcom route—selling a show to a network, airing a new episode every week, and hoping to stay on television long enough to go into syndication. He put up $5 million to produce the test episodes, maintained creative control, and, when TBS and others showed interest, landed an incredibly lucrative deal that would allow him to air his show five nights a week, something unheard of in the world of sitcoms.

The son of a carpenter, Perry grew up poor. As he told me and an invitation-only audience at Atlanta, Georgia's Fox Theater, his father "worked his entire life, paying $116 a month for 30 years for a tiny house in a tough section of New Orleans." Witnessing his father pay a mortgage on the cramped space he shared with his wife and four children—while others sold the houses he built for far more than the elder Perry had earned—at a young age Perry vowed that entrepreneurship held the key to his future and that he would be the owner. "The key to longevity and building generational wealth," a principle he hopes other African Americans will embrace, "is ownership of the finished product."

But there were challenges. His father's hammer and saw soon gave way to alcohol and guilt before he took his frustrations out on his son. This abusive environment left Perry confused, angry, and without anyone to lean on. "Where I come from," he continued, "you can have your dream, but you've got to keep it private because others will try their best to suppress it and snuff it out. That was the mentality of my surroundings."[6] Not knowing which way to turn, a friend suggested that he accompany him on a trip to Atlanta. This engaging southern city offered Perry the one quality he needed most—hope; the city's prominent Black middle and upper class raised Perry's level of vision. This was the environment that he sought. "After my first visit I just knew I was in the Promised Land. I had never seen so many Black people doing so well. I felt as if I were home." Finally in his element, Perry returned to New Orleans, packed his bags, and moved to Georgia in 1990. He was 21 years old.

Seeking a fresh start, Perry began chronicling the events in his life. Two years later and again with the encouragement of friends and $12,000—every dime to his name—those writings became his first stage play, *I Know I've Been Changed*. Full of hope that he had finally turned the corner, Perry was devastated—and broke—when only 30 people attended the show. This setback marked a six-year period in which he moved from one job to the next—from bill collector to used-car salesman, among others—barely keeping his head above water and saving enough to stage one play each year, all of which failed. Finally, having been evicted from his apartment, he hocked his furniture to eat and was living in his car. By 1998, Perry was prepared to throw in the towel. But first he decided to stage one final show at Atlanta's House of Blues, the centerpiece of the city's theater district. However, this time his approach was different. He selected choir members and pastors from the city's most well-known Black churches as his cast members. On a freezing opening night, with little to no heat in the theater and fearing that he had wasted his life, Perry looked out the window and saw a line stretching around the corner. He sold out eight nights at the House of Blues and another two at the 4,500-seat Fox Theatre. He realized that he had found his audience.

Perry's media empire features 6 million Facebook followers and more than $1 billion in sales, through his movies, sitcoms, plays, publications, and DVDs. Wealthy men and women have found no easy road to prosperity. It takes courage to look beyond obstacles, to see the way over difficulties, to brave opposition, and to allow nothing to swerve you from your course. Millionaires know that you cannot keep determined souls from reaching their objectives. Place stumbling blocks on their paths, and they will transform those obstacles into stepping-stones that they will use to reach their financial goals. Limit their financial resources, and they will turn a dime into a dollar. Ridicule or abuse them, and they will remain firm, as Tyler Perry did before becoming the highest-paid African American film producer. It was in this manner that he moved his economic prospects from homeless to hopeful.

There is something about devotion to an inward vision, the intense desire and concentrated effort to fulfill what you believe to be your mission on earth. If it is riches that you seek, you will find critics and pessimists at every turn who will forecast your failure. These "experts" will point out that you can never build a business without sufficient capital in these times of intense competition. Moreover, you will encounter obstacles at every turn. Wealth attainment demands a stiff backbone as well as plenty of grit to keep you pushing toward your goal. Nothing else will win the day.

Look at Toni Morrison. From birth, the odds were stacked against her. The child of a scorned and branded race, without resources, privilege, or connections, she triumphed over all by winning honors with her literary skill and scholarship. With what delight we read Morrison's *Beloved,* perhaps the most powerful depiction of the slave experience that ever came from an American pen. A fellow writer has said that, if there were any doubts about Morrison's stature as a preeminent American novelist, of her own or any other generation, *Beloved* will put them to rest.[7]

But the notebooks of this demure and reserved mere mortal reveal the secret to her wealth and genius. For nearly 20 years she pressed on, unrecognized and unknown. Every page captures that persistence, patience, toil, and faith. Nothing was too trivial to be condensed in her notes. Everything she felt, heard, or saw was duly preserved in her journal and compelled to pay tribute in her fiction. Morrison's Pulitzer Prize in 1988 for her fifth novel and the Nobel Prize for Literature five years later brought her the national recognition many critics and readers believed were long overdue. She had earned the slot of first Black woman ever to win the field's highest honor, and she attracted millions—in readers and earnings—in the process.

It can be debated whether Clarence Otis would be the chief executive officer of Darden Restaurants and one of the few African Americans who occupy the c-suite in corporate America had it not been for the vision and foresight of his father. A janitor as well as a high school drop-out with only a tenth-grade education, Otis's father may have been short on academics, but he was long on wisdom. His routine Sunday drives through the affluent neighborhoods surrounding Beverly Hills were a far cry from his family's impoverished South Central Los Angeles home. As he had hoped, his son took his father's lessons to heart, soaking in the palatial mansions with the exquisite manicured lawns. This was his father's way of pointing out to his son that another world existed, a world where wealth and power ruled the day, and a world that was not beyond his reach.

During a Darden sales retreat in Puerto Rico, Otis shared that on paper his family would probably be labeled poor. "But in the context in which we lived," he continued, "my parents were really high achievers. They had the ambition and drive to dream boldly even in the shadow of doubt."

As a child, Otis found an escape from the racial strife and isolation of the 1960s in his local library. Like clockwork, each week he would check out and absorb dozens of books on a variety of subjects. By ninth grade, he had read nearly every novel and biography his neighborhood branch had to offer. Encouraged by a high school guidance counselor, Otis earned a scholarship to Williams College that placed him physically, if not financially, in the land of wealth, power, and prestige. After graduating Phi Beta Kappa, Stanford Law School waited in the wings before he landed on Wall Street with First Boston, serving as vice president in the public finance department. In 1995, a headhunter recommended him to Darden, which had just branched out from General Mills. Otis signed on as vice president and treasurer, attracted to a company positioned for growth. Leaning on his strong leadership skills as well as a tireless work ethic, in less than a decade, he became the seventh African American to lead a Fortune 500 firm.[8]

After decades of painfully slow progress, Black executives have begun to wield power within the halls of corporate America. Today, the upper echelons of Fortune 500 America include men and women such as American Express CEO Ken Chenault, Ursula Burns of Xerox, A. Barry Rand, CEO of AARP, and Donald Thompson, president and chief executive officer of McDonald's. These men and women stand in unanimous agreement: The marketplace does not demand that you master the world of enterprise—that you become a successful business-man, entrepreneur, or merchant. It does not dictate what you *shall* do. But it does require that you master whatever field you enter. Hold true to this counsel, and not only will the world applaud your efforts, all doors will open to you. Be greater than your calling; go to the bottom of your business if you would climb to the top. Nothing is too small; master every detail. Performing world-class work is a central part of life. Do you hope to become wealthy in a single generation? If so, like those before, you will be required to nurture the faith, fortitude, and creativity when your hour arrives. Before you can become a millionaire, you must learn to think like one.

THE GREATEST SKILL . . . HAVE YOU FOUND IT?

What is the greatest skill a millionaire can possess? Is it intelligence, knowledge, or what the world calls "smarts"? What about IQ? Surely you've heard the phrase "knowledge is power." Have you considered hard work, persistence, talent, faith, courage, tenacity, attitude, or personal contacts? And what about that ever-so-fickle, evasive occurrence we call luck? Where does a life of abundance, wealth, and prosperity begin? In the mind, the body, the heart, or the soul? Perhaps I can offer a clue.

I find it amazing how the world makes way for those ambitious men and women who possess and utilize their God-given gifts. Nothing or no one can defeat them. Poverty cannot dishearten them, misfortune can't deter them, and hardship won't stifle them. Come what may, those armed with this power to create wealth simply fix their eye on their goal—to live a life of true abundance—and press ahead.

> For all we know about balance sheets, income statements and cash flow accounting; for all of our understanding about marketing strategies, tactics and techniques; and for everything we have learned about management principles and practices, there remains something essential, yet mysterious, at the core of entrepreneurship. It is so mysterious that we cannot see it or touch it, yet feel it and know it exists. It cannot be mined, manufactured or bought, yet it can be discovered. Its source is invisible, yet its results are tangible and measurable. This mysterious core is so powerful that it can make the remarkable appear ordinary, so contagious that it can spread like wildfire from one to another in an organization, and so persuasive that it can transform doubt and uncertainty into conviction.[9]

This quality burns all bridges behind it, clears all obstacles before it, and arrives at its destination no matter how long it may take, regardless of the sacrifice or cost.

At this moment, there are literally thousands—*no, millions*—of wealthy men and women in all lines of work who are where they are today because they've tapped into this life-changing force. When I first glimpsed this power, it was an enormous help to me. It led me to decide, once and for all, how to reach and exceed my financial goals. It unified my thinking and provided me with a straight, clear path to my objectives and aspirations. I've sat in richly paneled, thickly carpeted executive offices before highly celebrated business leaders—some of whom were old enough to be my parents—and listened as each shared how this power altered the course of their lives. After they fully digested this miraculous force, these men and women possessed a unique knowledge that enabled them to turn thoughts into things, dreams into reality. So-called fate or exterior circumstances were no longer in command. Those who had been passengers on a ship to nowhere—tossed between the rocks and reefs on which so many flounder—were suddenly, as the nineteenth-century English poet William Ernest Henley suggested, masters of their fate and captains of their soul.

When those who are profiled in this study took hold of this persistent power, they were born anew. Doubts, fears, apathy, and indifference that had dogged their steps in the past vanished in the blink of an eye. As aptly pointed out by the nineteenth-century writer Orison Swett Marden, all of their slumbering faculties had awakened to activity. Truth be told, if you examine your own circle of friends or acquaintances, you can point to one or more who have had no greater opportunity than you and who appear to possess no more—perhaps less—ability yet who are achieving far greater success. Search diligently and you will discover that these wealth creators have acquired the habit of implementing this God-given force. Far from working harder, they work *smarter* and with greater ease by virtue of this secret. Each of us should look on our true self—the potential to generate abundance—as artists envision their masterpiece, as a vision of their personal best, on which they focus with infinite pride and the satisfaction that nothing else can provide. Yet many fail to do so.

When used constructively, this powerful weapon will plant you firmly in the world of prosperity. Conversely, when mishandled or, worse, not unleashed at all, your negligence may undermine all chances of wealth. Poverty and failure are self-invited more times than we care to admit. The hardship that far too many dread arrives right on schedule. Trust me. If you interview the great legions of "failures"—those who've neglected to set specific goals or take full advantage of their potential as well as the opportunities this prosperous country presents—you will find the same sad story.

YES, IQ, INTELLIGENCE, AND KNOWLEDGE MATTER, BUT . . .

It has been said that the world is a great university. From the cradle to the grave, we live and learn in God's eternal kindergarten, where everything and everyone is our instructor. Who can estimate the value of books that spur our ambition and awaken slumbering possibilities? Some of us are constantly in school, continually storing up and retaining precious bits of information. Every experience offers a lesson for the eye that can see and the mind that can appropriate. Haven't we been instructed "In all thy getting, gain understanding"? Hasn't it been written that the Creator sends experience to paint humanity's portraits? You and I were created for growth and development, and to reach our full potential. It is the object, the essence of our being. To possess an ambition to expand larger and more broadly each day, to push the horizon of ignorance a little further away, to become a bit richer in knowledge, a tad wiser, and more of what we were created to be—that is our worthwhile objective. The daily habit of absorbing information to be used later in life, the reading of books that will inspire and stimulate to greater endeavor, the constant effort of engaging self-improvement is the best type of capital—worth far more than any bank account. This act alone can lead to great mental wealth, wisdom beyond all material riches. It is neither necessary nor desirable that a formal education be crowded into only a few years of life. Education is not an end but a process. The best educated are those who are always learning, forever absorbing information from every possible source and at every opportunity.

It's true, millionaires are exceptional learners. They learn from everything and everybody. They learn from experience. They learn by doing. They learn from past mistakes as well as the mistakes of others. They learn from associates. They learn from what works and, more important, from what doesn't. The millionaires in this study focus on personal growth. To underscore, approximately 34 percent of respondents either attended graduate school or hold a graduate degree. Conversely, only 4 in a pool of nearly 1,000 respondents failed to receive their high school diploma. Millionaires believe that in order to *earn* more, they must *learn* more. They view personal growth as the main objective of a life worth living. In their eyes, knowledge is a seed, and it takes time for seeds to develop into plants that bear fruit. They continually search for ways of thinking and acting that can be more fulfilling, not only in their lives but the lives of others as well. As one respondent admitted, "We learn to fail quickly and cheaply."

However, even education has its limits. If achieving wealth was only a matter of intelligence, there would be far more millionaires who possess superior IQs and academic honors.[10] But the world is overcrowded with men and women, young and old, who, while in college, stood high in their classes, shoulder to shoulder with the best and brightest. These students were scholars, people to emulate and admire, graduating with honors and distinction. "Most likely to succeed" was stamped across their files. Yet when it came to the course of life, they failed to make the grade; they couldn't catch on. Relegated to the rear, they've become round pegs in square holes. They've been pushed aside by those who've grasped the big picture and have found life much more understandable. Life is comprised of such contrasts. Surely, here is enough material for a hundred sermons.

Knowledge alone will not attract wealth. This misunderstanding has been the source of much confusion to those who repeat "Knowledge is power." According to the acclaimed author and philosopher Napoleon Hill, "Knowledge is only potential power. It becomes power if and when it is organized into definite plans of action and directed at a definite end."[11] The most telling question that confronts you in the practical world is: *What can you do with what you know?* Can you transfer your knowledge into power? Your ability to read your Latin diploma is not a true test of your education; a stuffed memory does not make an educated man or woman. Knowledge that can be utilized, that can be transferred into power, constitutes the only education worthy of the name. Ironically, the most prized possession that you can carry from your alma mater is not your degree. No, it is something infinitely more sacred, of greater value. It is your aroused ambition, your discovery of your unique gifts and limitless possibilities. There's a huge difference between absorbing knowledge and transmuting that information into working capital and power. In short, knowledge only becomes powerful *if and when* it is applied. So, if it is an education that you desire, when you find it, apply it as Alice Walker applied hers. The words *acclaimed novelist* may not be attached to her name today if she had not convinced friends and neighbors in her rural Georgia community to purchase her bus ticket to Spelman College. Apply your schooling as Sean "Puffy" Combs applied his. Hip, hopeful, and refusing to be tied to any outdated modes of operating, while a student at Howard University, Combs allegedly wrote and hawked term papers across the campus to make ends meet. This act alone ensured that he would one day fill his place as a Grammy award-winning producer and millionaire businessman.[12]

Pursue your education as the billionaire media mogul, Oprah Win-frey, pursued hers. As a precocious five-year-old, she insisted on being placed in the first grade. "There's no need for me to attend kinder-garten," she pointed out to the Nashville, Tennessee, school board. "I could read at two." After she aced a battery of tests, Nashville ad-ministrators were convinced of her academic acumen and reluctantly placed her in the first grade before moving her to the third grade the following year.

When asked to list the keys to their success, millionaires rank hard work first, followed by education. Some have confessed that what they absorbed in the classroom was less important than learn-ing how to *study and stay disciplined*. Granted, though more than 60 percent of Black millionaires hold advanced degrees, many others squeaked through school. Moreover, my research reveals that most Black millionaires did not graduate—from either high school or col-lege—with top honors. Nearly one-fourth in my study failed to finish college at all. And the well-educated can act as foolish as anyone else when it comes to their personal finances. And finally, with regard to the limits of education, over drinks and idle chatter in a downtown Atlanta hotel, one respondent set the record straight. "I've learned long ago," he shared, "that sooner or later A students will one day work for B students. And C students will eventually hire B students. And D students—those supposedly slow learners who were continu-ally reprimanded for daydreaming in class—well, buildings have been erected in their honor."

IS HARD WORK THE KEY?

Are tenacity and hard work the keys to building your fortune? Orison Swett Marden wrote, "The world admires the man or woman who never flinches from unexpected difficulties, who calmly, patiently, and courageously grapples with his or her fate; who dies, if need be, at his or her post." Hard work always commands respect. The challenge that all Black millionaires face—whether entrepreneurs, managers, or pro-fessionals with large responsibilities—is that their work is never done. Hard work is the quality that sustained A. G. Gaston, the dean of Black entrepreneurs, when he was half starved and thinly clad walking the dusty roads of Alabama filled with the hopes of selling insurance to a long-neglected Black market. When faced with the choice of either buying boots or chasing his dream, he mended his shoes with folded paper and kept pushing. This is what drove Joe Dudley to concoct hair care and beauty products on his kitchen stove during the night and sell his small line door to door the following day. At last count, his net worth exceeded $30 million. On his seventieth birthday, where most individuals would have retired to enjoy their hard-earned leisure, Dudley shared the secret to his success: "God and work have made me what I am. You would do best to realize that wealth is the offspring of industry. Pay the price and it is yours."[13]

This is what enabled Chris Gardner to make the long slow trek from homeless to prosperous. Perhaps no one ever battled harder and longer to overcome obstacles that would have stifled the weak. While working in an unpaid internship program at Dean Witter Reynolds, Gardner and his two-year-old son spent night after night in a church shelter or the bathroom of an area subway station in Oakland, California. Nobody at work had any idea this was going on. Eventually Gardner earned a position as a stockbroker at the firm, and two years later he headed to Bear Sterns, where he became a top earner. In 1987, he launched his own brokerage shop—Gardner Rich—in Chicago. Today, this multi-millionaire is a best-selling author, philanthropist, and international businessman who is about to establish his own private equity fund that will invest solely in South Africa. *His partner in the fund?* Nelson Mandela. Not bad for someone who, six years prior to building his company, was "fighting, scratching, and crawling my way out of the gutter with a baby on my back."[14]

There are a few unlikely ways to attain your millions. You could win the lottery, inherit a windfall, or, as in the case of Stormy Wellington, sell hope. Prior to her thirtieth birthday, this down-on-her-luck single mother of two small children owed thousands more than she possessed. Undeterred, Wellington put grit in place of her foreclosed home. Within six months, the former corporate account representative increased her earnings from $7,500 a month to more than $1 million per year promoting a slew of products manufactured by Ardyss International, a Mexican-based direct sales company. And Wellington is happy to spread the wealth. With Body Magic, the firm's flagship undergarment that promises to corral excess body fat, her team of

distributors set monthly sales records that few in the company or industry have yet to reach.

Simply put, work is more enjoyable when you are pursuing your
own financial self-interest. Ideally, work should represent opportunity,
not obligation. Here lies the reason that so many Black millionaires
in this study say they feel different about Sunday evening than far too
many have nots. Salaried workers are likely to mourn the start of the
new business week while the wealthy embrace it. Many even feel an
itch as early as Sunday morning, feeling a mild anxiety to get the week
under way.

T. D. Jakes completely broke down the first time he was asked to
speak before a congregation. Lacking any resources, he continued to
push his way up through the masses until he stood poised on the top
rung of spiritual and social power. Jakes, who at one time was scoffed,
ridiculed, mocked, and told he would never make it in the ministry
because he had such a heavy lisp, tells us that no one wins by accident.
"I know what it is like to be broke," he recounts. "I know what it is
like to be laughed at and scorned. I know what it's like to clean toilets
while envisioning Sunday sermons."[15] Jakes's own journey began in
Charleston, West Virginia, where his mother taught school and his
father ran a janitorial business. But times were tough. To help make
ends meet, Jakes sold vegetables, managed a paper route, and even
dropped off beauty products door to door for his mother's Avon business. He left high school early but later returned to earn a GED. Jakes
knew early on that he was called to the ministry. While growing up,
acquaintances remember the young boy preaching alone in his family's living room, loudly enough that he could be heard throughout the
neighborhood. In 1979, he founded the Greater Emanuel Temple of
Faith with a congregation of ten. Nearly 20 years later, he raised the
bar by moving to Dallas, Texas, where he built the Potter's House—a
27,000-member, $45 million, 191,000-square-foot mega-church. "My
critics weren't altogether wrong," he shared with me after a Sunday
service. "There is a lisp, but whether I had to stutter, stammer, spit, or
choke, I had something to say and I was going to say it!"[16] Victories
that are easy are cheap. Millionaires have found no royal road to their
triumph and fortune. It is always the same old route, by way of tenacity, industry, and hard work.

LIKE IQ AND KNOWLEDGE,
HARD WORK HAS ITS LIMITS

The millionaires in this survey share an almost unanimous belief in the virtue of hard work. Nearly seven out of ten respondents agreed with this statement: "Anyone can become a millionaire if he or she works hard enough." The millionaires in my sample work on average 60 to 65 hours per week, a far cry from the 35- to 40-hour workweek—according to the Census Bureau—of the average U.S. employee. Furthermore, the average workday for millionaires is far more likely to spill over into nights and weekends. Their days begin at 5:00 A.M. and end at 11:30 P.M. Millionaires are five times more likely to say they are always available for business by e-mail or phone and three times more likely to admit that they regularly work evenings and weekends. Moreover, the majority have taken less than three weeks' vacation in the past year. When long hours and hard work are the price of realizing opportunities, truly successful people seem more finely attuned than others to the value and finite nature of time itself. Maximizing its value is the true challenge.

Some of us have been led to believe blindly that if we keep at it, eventually we will succeed. Unfortunately, this is not always true. Working without a plan is as foolish as going to sea without a compass. Hasn't it been written that the race does not always go to the swift nor the battle to the strong? You and I can count among our acquaintances those who have worked hard their entire lives with little or nothing to show for it. Mere energy is not enough; all effort must be focused on a steady, over-arching vision. What's more common than an unsuccessful genius or impoverished failures with commanding talents?

What about contacts, connections, or being in the right place, at the right time? You may leave your millions to your son or daughter, but have you really given your children anything worth possessing? You cannot transfer the discipline, the experience, the grit; you cannot transfer the delight of achieving, the joy felt only in growth, the pride of acquisition. The majority of millionaires in this study confess that their greatest satisfaction and most memorable occasion occurred when they emerged from poverty into days of joy; when they felt that their meager savings were growing into multiple streams of income; when they first felt assured that poverty would no longer dog their steps; when they first felt that those whom they loved were being re-leased from the clutch of limit and want; that creature comforts were taking the place of bare necessities; that their children might not be forced to struggle quite as hard.

You can pass on your fortune, but you cannot transfer the skill, the prudence, the vision, the passion, and the attention to detail on which your wealth is founded. These qualities may mean a great deal to you, but they may mean nothing to your heirs. As you climbed to your fortune, you developed the muscle, stamina, and strength to succeed in spite of the difficulties, to keep your millions intact. You had the power that only comes from experience. You thought it a kindness to deprive yourself in order that your children might begin where you left off. You thought to spare them the tedium and bone-jarring obstacles, the hardships as well as the lack of opportunities. But you have placed a crutch in their hands instead of a staff. You have removed any form of incentive to self-development or self-help without which no real form of wealth creation is possible. As a result, heirs' enthusiasm will evaporate, energy will dissipate, and ambition gradually will fade away. If you do everything for your children and fight their battles, you've done nothing but produce a financial weakling. It has been written that the Lord loves poor people, but He demonstrated a way *how not to be poor.* Each of us is the architect of our own fate, but we must lay the bricks ourselves.

What makes these rags-to-riches stories so compelling? Is it the daring that seems to lie behind each millionaire's decision to chase his or her dream? The apparent willingness of the wealth creator to leap before he or she looks? Is it the amazing determination that the wealthy demonstrate in the face of adversity, setbacks, and catastrophes? The never-say-die attitude that can turn seemingly certain defeat into victory? Is it the quality and value each respondent brings to the marketplace? Is it his or her ability to delay gratification; to forsake to-day for tomorrow? Or is it the power to start with little or nothing and somehow magically generate products and profits? Something deeper is also at work in the have versus have not transformative process. Wealth creators truly believe in their ability to influence events, in their capacity to direct destiny, and in their power to shape the future.

The largest fortunes ever accumulated or possessed were and are the fruit of endeavors that began with little capital save energy, intellect, or faith. In Revelation we read: "He that overcometh, I will give him to sit down with me on my throne." In other words, opposing circumstances create strength. Opposition provides a greater power of resistance. Overcoming one barrier arms us with a greater ability to overcome the next. Wealthy men and women, it has been documented, owe more to their persistence and tenacity than to their natural powers, favorable circumstances, or friends and associates. Take my word for it: Intelligence will falter by the side of effort; great powers will yield to greater industry; though talent and connections are desirable, *nothing* will take the place of aim and perseverance.

"When did you become wealthy?" I asked a respondent in this study. "I was wealthy when I was dead broke," he replied. "I knew what I wanted to do, and I knew I'd do it. It was only a matter of time."

I asked Tom Burrell, founder and CEO of the advertising agency that bears his name, how he and his wife celebrated the moment they broke the seven-figure barrier. "The day we realized we were millionaires was a lot like any other day," he replied matter-of-factly. "There was no popping of champagne, no trips abroad, and no excessive or extravagant purchases. We simply spent a quiet night at home and roasted hot dogs."

"*Roasted hot dogs?*" I asked in disbelief. *Why hot dogs?*

"Because we remembered all too well the many days and nights we had little or nothing to eat."

WHAT ABOUT LUCK?

And what about that intangible quality we call luck? There is hardly a word in the English language that has been more cruelly abused than the word *luck*. Perhaps George S. Clason, the nineteenth-century writer and author of the *Richest Man in Babylon*, expressed it best: "Fickle fate is a vicious goddess who brings no permanent good to anyone. On the contrary, she brings ruin to almost every man upon whom she showers unearned gold. She makes wanton spenders, who soon dissipate all they receive and are left beset by overwhelming appetites and desires they have not the ability to gratify."[17]

Although I agree our youth should be taught that, sooner or later, circumstances eventually may decide outcomes, that money alone may

place unworthy candidates in high positions, and that *who* you know
sometimes outweighs *what* you know, as this study bears out, fortune
smiles on those who roll up their sleeves and place their shoulder to the
wheel. Our children should also be taught that diligence is the mother
of good luck; that he alone is great, who, by a life heroic, conquers
fate; that as a rule, the best individual *does* win the highest place. This
generation should be taught that nine times out of ten, what others call
luck or fate is but a limited belief of the indolent, the indifferent, and
those who are less than ambitious. If I were called on to express in a
word why so many capable men and women fail in business and in life,
"lack of luck" would never be the prime culprit. Yes, I have observed
what appears to be good fortune or luck in people's lives, but actually
it is the result of strong habits that are deeply a part of their self-belief
and character.

Wealth requires more than just luck. Fewer than 2 percent of the
respondents in this study inherited any or all of their fortune. Moreover, research has revealed that those who receive luck-induced wealth
far too often fail to retain their windfalls. One study points out that
of those who came into their fortune through lotteries, gaming, or
chance, more than 80 percent were bankrupt within five years. The
fate of those receiving other gifts or gains, such as insurance claims or
an inheritance, isn't much better.

"Bad luck" is made to stand as cause and sponsor of all the faults
and failures of men and women. Show me a man who according to
popular prejudice is a victim of bad luck in the world of enterprise, and
I will show you someone whose outlook or temperament probably invites disaster. Go speak with the shady businessman who has destroyed
his fortune through wild speculation. Go visit with the incarcerated;
they will try their best to convince you that they were victims of circumstances. Sit down with the shiftless and lazy and ask why they
failed to pull themselves out of poverty. In six words or less, they'll say,
"I could never catch a break." *What is luck?* Has any scholar defined
it? Has any chemist shown its composition? Has any philosopher explained its nature? Luck is not God's price for success—that would be
far too cheap. Luck occurs when preparedness meets opportunity, and
opportunity is ever present.

Lord, if only the next generation would begin life with the ideal
that every statement they utter be the exact truth; that every promise

made be redeemable to the letter; that every appointment be kept with the utmost faithfulness and with full regard and respect for the time of others; that they hold their own reputation as a priceless treasure and feel as if the eyes of the world were on them; that they criticize and condemn no one; that they learn the true estimate of value and self-esteem; that they are not deceived by appearances but place the emphasis of life where it belongs; and that they must not deviate one iota from what is upright and true. As the Almighty has made plain: "You are rich or poor according to what you've become, not according to what you own." It is not talent or opportunity that our children lack but the belief that fortune smiles on the pure and determined. Hold true to these ideals, and luck will be a forgone conclusion.

Unfortunately, far too many have nots who have read the compelling story of Bob Johnson, Black Entertainment Television's founder and owner of the National Basketball Association's Charlotte Bobcat team, have gained little inspiration or direction in terms of advancing their lot. For they view Johnson's success as luck, chance, or fate. "How lucky can one guy be?" they wonder. But luck, as it has been so often noted, played only a minimal role in his story. A full examination of Johnson's life reinforces the same lessons taught by the study of the lives of most of the wealthy: A loving mother, an innate drive that knows no defeat, a definite purpose that never wavers, a concentration that rarely loses its focus, indomitable energy, the identification of a calling, courage that never falters, a love of detail, an upbeat disposition matched only by unbounded enthusiasm, as well as the habit of hard work will always ensure the largest measure of financial success.

HOW THE WEALTHY BECAME WEALTHY

Who were the greatest moneymakers of our day? Look no further than a 36-square-block area in Tulsa, Oklahoma, known by many as the Black Wall Street. No finer example was ever recorded in the pages of economic history than that of the bold Black business owners who dared to utilize meager resources and face backbreaking discrimination to serve a waiting clientele. Despite strife, struggle, ridicule, and an environment that forced them to the rear, these men and women of commerce patiently toiled and created several financial empires. Ironically, so many of my race who constantly dream of some far-off success, who falsely believe they cannot make their mark where they stand, can learn a striking lesson from the Black capitalists who endured and, in their enduring, triumphed during the early 1920s. *How did they overcome the odds and create wealth? What force rested in their hands?* You tell me. Circumstances that others call unfavorable cannot impede the unfolding of your God-given powers. Like their White counterparts, most of Tulsa's Black residents arrived in Oklahoma during the late 1890s in the great boom years just before and after statehood. Some came from Mississippi, Missouri, and Georgia. For many, Oklahoma represented not only a chance to escape the oppression of the Deep South and the segregation mandates but the harsher racial realities of life under Jim Crow. The Sooner state represented a land of hope—a place to sacrifice and build; somewhere to start fresh. They arrived in wagons, on horseback, by train, or on foot. While some of the new settlers flocked to Tulsa, many first settled in smaller communities—many of which were all Black, or had large Black populations—throughout the state.

If "impossibility" ever existed, it could've been found somewhere between the birth and death of O. W. Gurley, the son of former slaves. A would-be real estate developer, Gurley never knew when he was defeated. He took his last cent and purchased property in the Greenwood–Archer–Pine area in 1906, where he immediately sought to build his financial empire. That same year, he built a hotel and grocery store attracting fresh migrants. Four years later, J. B. Stradford, a lawyer, son of a runaway slave, and Oberlin College graduate, built the 65-room Stradford Hotel—a $2 million facility and one of more than 600 Black businesses in the area. In the process, Stradford became the wealthiest business owner on Greenwood Avenue. This 36-block stretch of handsome one-, two-, and three-story redbrick buildings housed dozens of Black-owned businesses, including grocery stores and meat markets, clothing and dry good concerns, billiard halls, beauty parlors and barbershops, as well as the Economy Drug Company.[18] The segregated business district known as Black Wall Street featured these enterprises: 30 grocery stores; 21 restaurants; 21 churches; 2 movie theaters; 2 newspapers; 1 bank; 1 hospital; 1 post office; 1 library; 1 bus line; more than 1,200 homes, some of which were so palatial their pictures were often captured on postcards; countless private schools, where more than 30 college-educated Black teachers in segregated schools taught their young charges; and, lest we forget, 10 millionaires and far too many families with substantial savings to count.

Through guts and glory, full of riveting tales of isolation and perseverance, nearly a century ago, a small Black community managed to do what no other group of African Americans had ever done. Forbidden equal citizenship as well as the basic rights provided to their White neighbors, they were compelled to restrict their exertions to bartering, buying, and selling and to the accumulation of wealth in every possible way. Collectively, they spared no pains and considered no task too great in pursuit of their goals. These hearty souls were not easily discouraged. As a result, they became the inventors of letters of credit, bills of exchange, and basic financial and accounting methods. Having been shut out of other careers and forced to devote their entire energies to organizing their capital, they acquired a genius for the acquisition of wealth. They amassed millions when others settled for thousands; they grew rich when others lived day to day. In short, they became the wealthiest Blacks of their era.

WHAT IS THE GREATEST SKILL A MILLIONAIRE CAN POSSESS?

If it is not luck, intelligence, contacts or connections, talent, persistence, or hard work, what is the magic ingredient—the extraordinary principle—that is required prior to joining the ranks of those 35,000 African Americans who've attained millionaire status? As I shared during my presentations, I decided to write this book for two main reasons. The first reason is that I sincerely believe that each of us has an innate responsibility to share those ideals and values that produce positive results, not only in our own life but the lives of others. Years ago I started seeking highly successful men and women who were generous with their time and who openly shared the belief system and philosophy that empowered them to reach their full potential. As I adopted these attitudes and disciplines and made them a consistent part of my life, I began to experience extraordinary results too. Each of us has a song to sing, and *The Wealth Choice* is a part of my song. Whether teaching these principles or interacting with my readers, I experience a strong sense of purpose whenever the topic revolves around wealth creation and prosperity. So, in short, *to whom much has been given, much is required.*

Second, countless books have been written on every facet of financial success. Why did I feel compelled to add to this seemingly endless stream? Frankly, each book I've read revealed a different aspect regarding the art of financial fulfillment. Remarkably, all too often it is the smallest detail or distinction that spells the difference between success and failure—or, in this case, haves and have nots. Ironically, an unassuming writer can share thoughts on a difficult subject in a manner that literally flips a switch in a reader's mind and alters his or her life forever. It is my hope that I am that writer.

Who knows where this book will be decades from now? The ideas that I am about to discuss will never change. These ideals are built on natural law. Regardless of whose hands this book falls into or whose eyes glance over these words a century from now, this simple volume will still serve its purpose. So it is with a deep sense of faith and responsibility that I offer my thoughts.

We live in a strange and fast-moving world; each day a new and different voice is heard preaching his or her own brand of happiness and financial attainment. As you digest the next story, I suggest that you take good notes. This example will provide the key that will unlock the door to your hopes of financial empowerment.

"WE LIVED IN POVERTY, BUT POVERTY NEVER LIVED IN US"

Everyone has a story to tell. Few stories, however, prove to be as profound and inspirational as Ken Brown's. This restaurateur is a messenger of hope who inspires others to rely on their faith, integrity, and discipline as they search for the strength to withstand the most difficult times. As a child growing up in inner-city Chicago, Brown knows firsthand what it means to lose everything, including the house you call home. His family faced financial hardship during a harrowing period in which they were evicted ten times—twice in one year—and added to the city's welfare rolls.

In spite of it all, Brown's parents, who had five children under the age of eight while still in their teens, passed on a message of hope. His young father worked as a chef at Chicago's trendy Hyde Park Hilton hotel, and he stressed the importance of commitment and a solid work ethic. His personal lack of a formal education shaped a dream where— somehow, some way—his children would earn a college degree and forge their own way.

"I'm the product of two teenage parents," Brown told me as we dined in a Detroit hotel. "Together, they drilled that a sense of belief is the road map out of poverty. Though I've heard parents tell their children 'You were an accident' or 'You'll never amount to much,' there was no such negativity in our home. Sometimes we lacked the bare necessities: food, shelter, and clothing. One Christmas morning, our neighbor allowed us to run an extension cord through her kitchen window in order that my mother could prepare breakfast on a hot plate. Nonetheless, my parents never wavered in their faith. My child-hood was infused with positive confession. Clutching our coat collars against our necks to keep warm, my mother would state, 'This is not the end; there's a reason why you were born. God has something big-ger planned for your life.'"

Through their words and deeds, Brown's mother and father im-mersed their children in a living testimony that professed that anyone can achieve his dream in spite of humble beginnings if only he de-fines his purpose and places his faith in the Almighty. The importance of hope grew even as the Browns' financial condition continued to crumble.

"I'll never forget the day that I arrived home from school and I saw all of our belongings thrown in the street. I was beyond embar-rassed. I tried to come to terms with our poverty, but I couldn't. How my parents scrounged up enough money to find another place, I will never know. Though I wasn't fully aware of our dilemma, I knew we were losing ground financially. It seemed as if we were always behind on the rent and utilities, not to mention there was never enough to eat. One night, in the middle of dinner, our kitchen lights began to flicker. We didn't know what was going on. Moments later, the room went dark. The electric company cut off our power. I glanced out the window and peered at our neighbor's home; the lights from their liv-ing room could be seen through our curtains. It was at this point that my mother confessed that she hadn't made utility payments in three months. As we sat in the dark picking at our food, I was too worn out to cry. I shook my head and questioned what would be next. That was the lowest point in my life." It was at this fork in the road that Brown was taught a life-changing lesson. His mother, trying her best to free and shelter her children from the seductive nature and vice-like grip of poverty, instructed social workers in the Department of Family and Children Services to close her case and stop sending additional welfare checks. Brown remembers this bold move. "In spite of our instability, she said, 'I will not allow my children to develop a welfare mentality.' Without two nickels to rub together, my mother still held to her standards."

Brown's mother understood and internalized a key element of wealth that, even today, many fail to grasp. She knew that wealth is not now, nor has it ever been, tied to the physical assets we see, seek, or desire but to the vast untapped potential of creative thinking. She knew the strongest force known to humankind. This woman was more than aware of the power that can carry each of us from the deepest depths of poverty to the highest ranks of prosperity—from lack, ridicule, and humiliation to wealth, respect, and influence. Brown's mother was conscious of the power that turns stumbling blocks into stepping-stones. She knew of the source that has been known to propel humanity from the slums and ghettos of the world to the grandest level of grace, grandeur, and distinction. She knew that each of us is the architect of our own fortune. And now she was about to share this idea with her son.

HOW TO WIN THE WAR ON POVERTY

The greatest fallacy known to humanity is the necessity of poverty. Far too many have succumbed to the erroneous notion that some of us are destined to be rich while others, conversely, are preordained to be poor. Nothing could be further from the truth. Poverty, want, or lack has never commanded a place in the Creator's plan for humanity. The Almighty never placed the vast multitudes on earth in order that we, you and I, haggle over a limited supply. There need not be a poor person on the planet. The earth is replete with resources that we have yet to tap. As a result, we grow comfortable with our lack in the midst of prosperity and opportunity. Financial riches are lying everywhere, waiting for the observant to discover them. Wealth begins in the mind, and those who are hostile to it will never possess it.

Seated on the edge of his bed, Brown's mother shared her impressions and knowledge of wealth and poverty. Though life as a have not was all she had ever known, she told her son that wealth would forever elude his grasp until he came to grips with the root cause of poverty.[19] She admonished her son to incorporate the following thoughts into his spirit:

- *Be an optimist. Seize the moment. Live today to the fullest. Whatever good you desire is yours, but you must stretch forth your hand and take it. Success occurs by choice, not chance. Life has no limits except the boundaries that you set.*

- *We've been blessed by a mighty God who has a gentle heart. If this were not so, you and I would have been gone a long time ago. Blessings occur each and every day, in ways that we rarely notice. God exists within each of us; we all share a common humanity. Love yourself, whatever faults you possess, and love the world, no matter how bad it seems. Be grateful not for the hardship but for the character it built in you. Every challenge provides you with the opportunity to rise above your circumstances. Each of us is far richer than we realize; you and I are better than we've ever dreamed.*

- *Manhood can never be given, only earned. Your greatest strength is the power of your example.*

- *Prayer—the language of the heart—is the center of a humble life. Fear not. Never stop believing, never stop dreaming. Remember, He is our eyes when we cannot see, our voice when we are unable to speak, and our faith when we need it expressed.*

- *Haven't we worshiped the God of poverty and scarcity long enough? You must decide that you will not be poor. There is no philosophy that will help a man to succeed when he always doubts his ability to do so. There are multitudes of poor people in this country who have grown satisfied and comfortable to remain impoverished, and who have ceased to mount any assault to rise above their conditions. They may work hard, but mentally they have lost the hope, the edge, the expectation that will remove the bars that stand between them and their financial blessing. You will reach the direction in which you*

*face. If you look toward poverty, toward lack, you will rest
squarely in its grip.*

- *Abundance is your destiny. Rid yourself of the poverty
mentality. Money goes wherever it is welcomed. Decide that
you will be a good steward of the money you possess, and, as a
result, more money will be added unto you.*[20]

Considering his family's plight, Brown listened intently. His mother's words did more than ignite a spark; her preaching lit a fire. It then dawned on Brown that there was a way to end the continuous cycle of financial hardship for his family. Now on a mission, Brown set a goal to finish school and—of all things—go to college before returning home to launch a business and provide the type of stability his family sorely needed.

A recruiter from Southern Illinois University (SIU) saw something in Brown, who was long on commitment but short on grades, and slotted him for a special admissions program contingent that he earn at least a B average his freshman year. Although he arrived on campus with only $25 and a wicker chair, Brown couldn't care less. Eager to leave his past behind, he gazed at the broad Gothic buildings in a daze. "Under normal circumstances," he shared, "I wasn't supposed to be there. I was a child of teenage, out-of-wedlock parents. I was a welfare recipient, an inner-city nomad. But thanks to my mother's counsel, I was determined to prove my worth. By the time May rolled around, I finished my first year with 3.15 grade point average, and SIU accepted me into general admissions."

OPPORTUNITY COMES KNOCKING

Four years later, Brown graduated with a degree in food and nutrition, an ambition to own his own restaurant, and the first step to realizing that goal: a full-time position with a blue-chip food service company. But moonlighting as a waiter at a local Chicago bistro provided the keys to his future. A chance meeting in the late 1990s with a high-ranking executive eventually changed his life. Edie Waddell and her husband were regular customers at the upscale restaurant, and Brown had served them often. They were impressed with his professionalism as well as his attention to detail. After dining one evening, Brown presented her husband the check, and Waddell, in turn, offered her business card. "You're the type of individual we want at McDonald's," she explained. "All I ask is for your trust."

Waddell was swiftly climbing the corporate ladder with the fast-food giant; her timing couldn't have been better. Through previous conversations, she knew of Brown's desire to own a restaurant. After his initial training at McDonald's corporate headquarters, she suggested that he take over one of McDonald's corporate stores. Despite its location in the Chicago suburbs, the store underperformed. The current manager offered every excuse in the book for its soft bottom line, but Brown knew better. Intensely driven, within the first two weeks, Brown sat down with every employee and asked for his or her input. After implementing a few of their suggestions, he made other subtle changes. He purchased new uniforms for his crew and insisted that everything be in tiptop condition. Restrooms would be clean and tidy, windows would be spotless, counters would sparkle, and the surrounding lawn and flowers would bloom. In the dining room, two antiquated televisions hung from the ceiling. Not only were they inoperable, they were eyesores. Brown replaced them with state-of-the-art flat screens. Also, an old magazine rack sat empty in the lobby. Instead of hanging magazines and newspapers, he bought a throw rug and bean bag chairs from a local Wal-Mart and transformed the space into a children's reading area. As a result, sales soared, customer service improved, and his team took pride in their work. In short order, the franchise came to life. At a minimum, his staff knew they were led by a manager who preferred human service over customer service. Brown not only demanded performance, but he quickly became known as someone who rolled up his sleeves and worked side by side with his employees.

Opportunities flew Brown's way. Six months later, Waddell was promoted to director of the entire Michigan region, and it wasn't long before she contacted Brown with the offer of a lifetime. At age 35, Brown obtained a loan through Fleet Bank of Boston to consummate the deal that brought his dream to fruition, becoming the youngest owner operator in the history of the franchise. "[Waddell] invited me to fly to Detroit and select two stores," he recalls. "As I look back at every position that I held—whether it be Aramark, Wendy's, Marriott, Lorenzo's Bistro, or even McDonald's—I considered each opportunity as a paid internship. Each challenge created character, contacts, and relationships. Regardless of the roadblock, you can't focus on what you are going through, only what you are going to do." His inauspicious start in life might have discouraged most people, but not Ken Brown. His welfare-to-faring-well story rivals the best that Hollywood has to offer, ending with a man so passionate about his life's mission that he dives into storytelling and seldom comes up for air. He is excited, and understandably so. It is Brown's hope to use his portfolio, which now includes both restaurants and hotels, to make a difference. By sharing his guiding principles, Brown hopes to spread his formula for wealth creation to all those who will listen: "The starting point to all growth and development rests with a decision—the decision that you make can alter the course of your life forever."

NEW RULES OF MONEY: THE LAW THAT GUIDES THE THINKING OF THE RICH

In his own words, you have witnessed one man's legacy, a road map for the suffering as well as the successful to reach those places within the soul that give life meaning. Here is one individual's overarching testimony that would give anyone pause, and it all began by mastering the greatest skill. *Do you wish to become wealthy in one generation?* If so, you will be forced to nurture the courage to make a decision—a decision that, sooner or later, all millionaires have reached. The reason that so few of us are financially independent is due, in part, to the negative mental roadblocks that have been placed in our minds. I suggest that you hold fast to the second law of wealth:

Decide now that you will not be poor!

The conviction that we are poor and must remain so is fatal to humanity. As long as we envision despair, we shall never arrive at the gates of delight. As long as our state of mind anticipates hard luck, reconciles misfortune, broods over shortcomings, and dwells on lowly conditions while minimizing all that is divine, penny-pinching and tough times will follow as surely as an architect's blueprint precedes the foundation. The Winfreys, the MacFarlanes, the Browns, and the Robertses think wealth, and they get it.

When you make up your mind that you are done with poverty forever; that you will not entertain a single unproductive thought; that you are going to erase every trace of this debilitating disease from your dress, your appearance, your demeanor, your decorum, your speech, your actions, your home; that you are going to show the world your true mettle; that you will no longer conduct your affairs in an apologetic stooping, slipshod manner, as if you lacked confidence or ability; that you will adhere to the words of the Master who admonished us to turn the other cheek and squarely and persistently face a life of plenty, power, prayer, and untold riches—here lies the very heart of a wealth consciousness: the conversion process. This outlook converts spenders into savers, the nonbanked or unbanked into banking customers, renters into homeowners, entrepreneurial hopefuls into business owners, and the economically uneducated into the financially literate. This outlook helps people help themselves and creates wealth in the process. Before you can become a millionaire, you must learn to think like one. You must *decide!*

And it need not take ten years to make the leap. Those individuals who have left their mark on the world of wealth and commerce have been men and women who possess the ability to render prompt decisions. Nothing will provide greater confidence than the reputation of promptness. The individual who is trapped by indecision, ever juggling two opinions, forever debating which course to pursue, cannot control him or herself let alone his or her financial future. In contrast, the man or woman of prompt and calculated decision does not wait for favorable circumstances. To hesitate is to be lost. In fact, those who are forever shuffling and procrastinating, weighing and balancing will never rise above minimum wage.

No, it need not require a lifetime in order to make the leap. Throughout my focus groups, millionaires who transitioned from paycheck to paycheck to a life of affluence replied that the process took less than five years. Furthermore, shifting from affluence to a seven-figure income, on average, required an additional three to four years. However, clearing the big leap—jumping from a weekly paycheck to millionaireship—demanded nine to ten years of focus, effort, grit, and determination. And yes, you, the reader, must *choose* to make this change. In all likelihood, this task is similar to the diet you've scheduled to start, the marathon you hope to run, the poor habits you plan to break, and the money you wish to save. Here lies a choice that you must confront each day.

If you are driven to reach your financial potential, you must expand your wealth consciousness and belief system and assume the part it demands. You must decide that poverty has no place within your life. No one can achieve prosperity while, in the still moments, envisioning poverty. It's up to you, the reader, to decide whether you will conquer poverty once and for all. The road to abundance does not lie on private property; anyone who chooses can walk it. Prosperity begins in the mind but ends in the purse.

MILLIONAIRE LESSON NO. 2

Abundance is your destiny. Rid yourself of the poverty mentality. Money goes wherever it's welcomed. Decide that you will be a good steward of the money you possess. As a result, more money will be added unto you.

TWO

THE HAVES AND
THE HAVE NOTS

THE DIFFERENCE THAT
MAKES THE DIFFERENCE

Open the door, and I'll get it myself.

—James Brown

AMERICA'S BLACK MILLIONAIRES LIVE IN A WORLD WHERE 4 BIL-
lion people are categorized as poor. Oddly, these wealth creators command little political power or means of defense. Like all capitalists
innately face, government regulation or excessive taxation could
seize their earnings. So why, on a planet ripe with famine, poverty,
and disease, should this tiny minority—approximately 35,000 driven
Black men and women—be allowed to control riches thousands of
times greater than their needs? Why should a few thousand families of
color command wealth far exceeding the endowments of most third-
world countries? More specifically, why should Ephren Taylor, the
video game designer and youngest African American to take a company public on Wall Street, command a net worth of $20 million,
and Walter Taylor, a janitor at a local Atlanta, Georgia, high school
earn less than $20,000 per year? Why should the annual compen-
sation of American Express CEO Ken Chenault exceed $50 million
while nearly 40 percent of African Americans continue to navigate life
only a day's march ahead of financial ruin? Why should former Time

Warner CEO Richard Parsons live in the lap of luxury and manage a personal portfolio of nearly $100 million while the average household income of Black America falls below $32,000 per year? Why should Valerie Daniels-Carter command a fortune in excess of $90 million while untold thousands of homeless Black men roam from shelter to shelter in search of a warm meal and an empty cot? And why should the net worth of St. Louis–based hotel developer Michael Roberts inch closer to the $1 billion mark while so many of his race teeter on the verge of economic collapse? *Does this make sense? Does this comparison seem fair?*

When spread across demographics, the question is just as stark. Why should the top 1 percent of families own 20 percent of the nation's wealth while the bottom 20 percent, awash in debt, possess no measurable net worth at all? On a global level, the disparity is deadly. Why should even this bottom fifth of Americans be able to discard enough food to feed a continent while millions of Sudanese die of famine? And, to drive the point home, why should our pets eat far better than most of the men, women, and children who live outside our shores?

The reason for the huge wealth disparity between Ephren Taylor and Walter Taylor; between Valerie Daniels-Carter and so many young, unsettled Black males; between Ken Chenault, Richard Parsons, and Michael Roberts and the average African American; and, for the most part, between the haves and have nots is *knowledge* and *commitment. Who succeeds financially, and why?* We all know some people who seem to possess an innate ability to rise above any challenge or sidestep any roadblock. Even during their most difficult moments, these men and women soar above the fray, in social settings, at work, and with their finances. You've seen them and wondered, "What do they have that I don't?" It's not that they were born into wealth. It's not that they caught a lucky break. It's not that they are smarter than you or me or that most had an elite education. They simply knew what they wanted; they plotted a course and arrived. Every day they thought about what was to come, and they set clear goals with intention and purpose. And today, as a result, they are surrounded by people whom they care deeply about—and who return the favor. They wake up happy and go to sleep fulfilled. And they don't toss and turn over unpaid bills.

Millionaires set their own wages, goals, and lifestyles. Even without start-up capital or influence, they reach their objectives. They strike when the time is right, when the iron is hot. They do what is unpopular; they follow their gut when others are paralyzed by fear. They stand their ground and push hard even when the world opposes. And as far as rules are concerned, they rewrite them. Have nots, however, force their lifestyles to fit whatever wages they receive. They fail to call on innate talent, gifts, or prowess, robbing themselves of a say in their own economic welfare. But if they wish to blame their misfortune on external circumstances, they will find small comfort in statistics compiled by those who have investigated the subject. According to Census Bureau data:

- There has never been a better time to crack the seven-figure mark. At the beginning of the twentieth century, a mere 5,000 millionaires existed. Today, more than 10 million men and women have reached that coveted but not-so-elite status, and this number is expected to double within the next ten years.[1]
- Eighty percent of all millionaires can be classified as first generation. In other words, these wealth creators built their fortune with little to no capital, savings, or inheritance.
- When Martin Luther King Jr. led the Montgomery bus boycott, five Black millionaires had made their mark. As of this writing, 35,000 African Americans have leaned on their faith, learned from their mistakes, and empowered themselves as well as countless others. Although this number remains a fraction of their White counterparts, Black millionaires play to win, approaching every task with a level of confidence, commitment, and creativity that few dare to display.

The story of Black millionaireship is best embodied not in the theory of a writer but in the life of the wealth creator, a story that leads from the old frontier to the new.

PORTRAIT OF A WEALTH CREATOR

The wealthy share one quality, regardless of how else they may differ. Call it a sense of quiet assurance or inner resolve, but never mistake it for lack of backbone. We've heard it said of the best: "Everything he undertakes succeeds" or "Everything she touches turns to gold." It's that low-key attitude of command, based on self-knowledge that says, in effect, "I've faced difficult times, and I've passed the tests. I know who I am, so there's no need for me to impress others." By the force of character, such a man or woman wrings success from the most adverse circumstances. Their poise and ability increase in direct ratio to their number of accomplishments. As time goes on, they are reinforced not only by their own success but by their associates' faith in those abilities. Earl Graves possesses this quality. Over the past 40 years, he has built an empire that he runs with a personal touch. It's called Earl G. Graves, Ltd., and it specializes in publishing, media relations, and beverage sales.[2]

As I walked into Graves's Fifth Avenue Manhattan office, I began to size him up right off the bat. I immediately knew I had never met anyone so focused. When you're organized, you lay claim to a special power. You walk and conduct your affairs with a sense of purpose. Your priorities are clear and in full view. You orchestrate complex events with a masterful touch. In Graves's spacious office, adorned with awards and handsomely framed pictures, I sat attentively. For the next few hours, I was utterly captivated.

Graves came of age during the civil rights era and has dedicated most of his professional life fostering change to America's balance of wealth and power, so that any person of color can increase his or her net worth. His platform, *Black Enterprise* magazine, was the first publication devoted to African American entrepreneurs and corporate executives. Founded in 1970 with the help of a $175,000 Small Business Administration start-up loan, Graves has since created a media empire that at last count earned more than $50 million in revenues.[3] Like most African Americans who aspire to business, Graves had few resources and far fewer Black role models to inspire him when he decided to step into a field usually reserved for the well-to-do and the well prepared.

Graves's father, a West Indian shipping clerk who plied his trade in New York City's garment district, drilled that education was the ticket to prosperity and financial independence. "He constantly drove home the message 'Be the boss—buy it, own it, run it.' It was only natural that I would produce and market a magazine targeted to Black men and women who wanted to get ahead."[4]

If Martin Luther King Jr. was the spokesperson for civil rights and Bishop Tutu the voice for human rights, then Earl Graves, through *Black Enterprise* magazine, has been Black America's champion for economic rights. "As a young entrepreneur," Graves continued, "I was intrigued by the concept of tapping into the minds of the nation's most talented African Americans—business owners and professionals—providing a forum for their ideas and advice." But what Graves has really done is to influence others through his creativity and innovation, taking an idea in an industry where nine out of ten start-ups fail, molding it editorially, motivating and inspiring its audience, and launching the project in the worst business year—1970—of the past four decades. And, further, he marketed it to reluctant advertisers.

Marketing a business magazine has never been an easy task. Bruce Forbes started the biweekly *Forbes* in 1917. After a decade-long struggle, his eldest son, Henry Luce, launched *Business Week* and *Fortune* in 1930 while he was still an undergraduate at Yale. "But here is a new type of magazine," said an openly excited Graves in 1970. "It's Black, and it's about business! The time is absolutely right for *Black Enterprise*." Nearly four decades later, the magazine is considered the source book that records the economic, political, and social ups and downs of Black Americans.

Wealth creation has always been Graves's focus. He reached his current status by working at his craft, perfecting his skills, and playing to his strengths. Over the years, he and a loyal cadre of employees have increased the magazine's circulation to 230,000, with a readership in excess of 2 million. What's unusual is that this occurred as the monthly magazine made the transition from closed to open circulation.

"We had, arguably, the most successful switch-over in publishing history," Graves shared. "We converted our readership while increasing circulation." In 1981, *Black Enterprise* went newsstand and added to its already impressive growth. The idea of change, particularly the type of change that the world of enterprise can generate, turns Graves on. It permeates his being. It's what fuels the man, what drives him and his staff. Ironically, what he is trying to change is the only idea that slows him down: the notion of being Black in an economic world. Graves is masterfully using his voice to seek nothing less than a revolution throughout the marketplace, to prove that "blacks are just as capable of generating wealth as any other group."

WHEN PREPARATION MEETS OPPORTUNITY

After graduating from college, Graves entered the Army in 1958. "The only options open for Blacks were to teach, join the civil service or the Army." The military was just what he needed. There he developed a talent for organization. He learned to lead, delegate, and plan with authority. Although he made captain ahead of schedule, the military was clearly not the career he coveted. He dreamed of running his own ship. Gradually an idea took shape. When his tour was up, Graves returned to New York and dabbled in real estate. In his first three months, he sold nine houses—enough to pay for a wedding and furnish a modest apartment. In 1965, he went to work for the Justice Department, a job that eventually led to an assignment with Robert Kennedy, then a New York senator. Graves's official title was administrative assistant responsible for monitoring various economic programs and special events.

"Working for Kennedy," Graves admitted, "played an enormous part in my personal development. Robert Kennedy was a man totally unfamiliar with failure. I joined Kennedy's staff as an administrative assistant. I was now working for an icon from a family of icons. Kennedy's world was filled with a steady stream of power brokers, elite athletes, and other celebrities. As one of his aides, his world of power and privilege became accessible to me. In turn, I shared my world: Brooklyn and the voters that other politicians had often ignored. When he announced his presidential candidacy in 1968, we were all optimistic that his dedication to civil rights and social justice would change the country."[5]

For three years, Graves was on the Kennedy fast track as the senator seemed destined to become president. But his plans were shattered when Kennedy was cut down by an assassin's bullet. Graves lost a dear friend and mentor, and he was out of work with a wife and three small children to care for. Stunned by these circumstances, Graves lost his way. He tried his hand in real estate again, hoping for the same thrill that Kennedy provided, but it didn't measure up. Several Fortune 500 companies came calling, and some even offered a position or two. But he declined. Almost as a diversion, he started a consulting firm, mainly as an excuse to give himself more time to ponder his next step, but with his meager savings, time was a precious commodity.

"Fortunately, as a Kennedy staffer, I was marked as a candidate who was highly employable. I was offered both a job with IBM and a Ford Foundation fellowship. Those were IBM's halcyon days, and a job there would have been a steady meal ticket. But to me it sounded like fixed income. I didn't want any limitations on what I thought I could earn. I wanted to be my own boss. So I accepted the Ford fellowship, essentially a work-study grant. Contemplating a career as a consultant to Black businesspeople, I studied entrepreneurship and economic development in Barbados, home to my grandparents. When I returned, I set out to advise business on tapping an emerging Black market."

Graves dove headfirst into his research. He immediately began to draw comparisons between what he saw abroad and what existed at home within America's Black communities. Even though the results were disheartening, he knew he could make an impact. "There was no medium for Blacks," he recalls, "to learn the successes and failures of those who had gone before." Graves starting piecing together a business plan and assembled a team of advisors to help push his idea forward. The result? A board of advisors that read like a who's who in politics and business: Senator Edward W. Brooke of Massachusetts; Julian Bond, House Representative of Georgia; and William Huggins, former president of Freedom National Bank. Here was an august group of prestigious Blacks who saw a need to further Black economic development. By lending their names, they helped convince corporate America that *Black Enterprise* was worth a second look.

BUILDING AN EMPIRE

Graves, who saw his market as Blacks of "advanced means," began the tedious task of sifting through mountains of African American organizational directories. The result was a list of 100,000 businessmen and women, doctors, lawyers, teachers, clergy, elected officials, and college students—present and future leaders of Black America. He sent free subscriptions to these individuals. With a draft of the magazine in hand, Graves approached area banks, whose initial response was lukewarm at best. Many rejected the idea outright. But after discussing the concept with Chase Manhattan Bank's Capital Corporation, Graves hit pay dirt. Chase Manhattan's president believed in gutsy banking and unique ventures that showed promise. Besides, Manhattan Capital had made a number of loans to Black businesses and liked the idea of a tool that might help its clients succeed. The bank financed *Black Enterprise* with $150,000 loan and $25,000 in equity. Graves later bought the investment shares back for $500,000.

"By the late 1960s, roughly 100,000 Black-owned businesses existed in the U.S., and most were mom-and-pop operations. But I knew that the number would grow. The Civil Rights Act of 1964 cleared the way for policies designed to level the playing field for minority-owned businesses. In 1969, President Nixon signed Executive Order 11458, which directed the Secretary of Commerce to coordinate the federal government's efforts to promote minority enterprise, in effect creating the Minority Business Development Agency. That's the environment in which Black Enterprise magazine was created. With the support of my wife, I took out a $175,000 SBA-backed loan. We were determined to place the words 'Black and capitalism' in the same sentence."

Graves was in his element. The next step was to convince advertisers. However, he would alter his approach. Instead of making cold calls to ad agencies, as he had with banks, Graves personally initiated a letter-writing campaign to the heads of those corporations he believed would make profitable advertisers—IBM, Ford Motor Corp., and Coca-Cola, to name a few. "Time and again, I had to educate White advertisers about the Black consumer. I ran around trying to convince executives that Black people smoke, drive cars, stay in hotels, and use credit cards. That was anything but easy." As a result of his efforts, Graves received $500,000 in commitments long before the first issue would ever hit the mailbox. *Black Enterprise* magazine was profitable from day 1. The cover and lead story of the first issue—August 1970—featured Charles Evers, who "Started Small and Made It Big" in politics and business. "Lacking capital, managerial and technical knowledge and crippled by prejudice, the minority businessman has been effectively kept out of the marketplace. We want to help change this," Graves declared in the first issue.[6]

"It was nearly two years before we were taken seriously," Graves remembers. "But by 1972, advertisers and distributors began calling us, and three years later, my input was being sought in the highest of circles." *Black Enterprise*'s first-year revenues were $900,000. The magazine has transformed since its initial issue. Today, the graphics

regularly win design awards, circulation was converted to paid subscribers, and the editorial coverage has been broadened beyond the
realms of business to include other key issues. Revenues have reached
$50 million. From Graves's perspective, the market isn't so much a
principle as it is a collection of people, all of whose wants and needs
must be taken into account. His world is a sphere of customers, both
actual and potential, who ultimately will determine how well he satis-
fies those needs. As he redefines his market, he searches for virgin turf
to conquer. For example, in 1988, en route to a speaking engagement,
Graves exchanged business cards with a fellow passenger. The gentle-
man, as Graves discovered, was a senior-level executive with Pepsi-
Cola Corporation. During the course of their conversation, the soft
drink executive revealed his company's desire to broaden its base by
completing a deal with an equally stellar Black businessman or woman
for its Washington, DC, operations. Graves couldn't believe his ears.
He hid his emotions as, once again, the door to opportunity swung
open.

By his own admission, Graves knew nothing about the bottling
business, but he also knew that with a good organization behind him,
he could glide into the industry. For the next two years, he would
step up communications between his headquarters and the soft drink
distributor and place together the intricate pieces of a financial puzzle
that would establish him as Pepsi's largest minority vendor.

Some of the pieces began to fall in place the same year. Graves and
basketball great Earvin "Magic" Johnson met in New York, and the
two hit it off immediately. During their conversation, sports soon gave
way to business, and they shook hands on a deal. Johnson would lend
his name and persona to the Pepsi franchise; Graves would retain two-
thirds ownership. Both walked away elated as the meeting produced
the results each wanted. Meanwhile, Graves continued to iron out the
details until the $60 million deal was finalized in September 1990.

Black Enterprise magazine continues to thrive. In 2001, the company, headquartered on Fifth Avenue in Manhattan, enjoyed $5.7
million in sales, with 4 million readers. The company also includes
a book publishing arm, sponsored seminars for entrepreneurs, and
a private equity investment fund. The *Washington Post* called its
founder "one of the most influential Black businesspeople in the
country" and, said Graves, "has used *Black Enterprise* to tell the

community how to: work together, dress smart, pull strings, borrow money, live revengefully well."[7]

Two of Graves's three sons serve as executives with his company, while the third holds a post with PepsiCo. In addition to the Spingarn Medal—annually awarded by the National Association for the Advancement of Colored People (NAACP), for outstanding achievement—Graves has also received numerous other awards, including the Entrepreneurial Excellence Award from Dow Jones & Co. in 1992 and the Ernst & Young New York City Entrepreneur of the Year Award three years later. In all, he holds 53 honorary degrees, but as he wrote in the thirtieth anniversary issue of his magazine in 2000, "I have always said that these awards recognize the magazine's role in uplifting African Americans. By showcasing their achievements as well as gaining a forum to address the issues of the day, we helped fuel the aspirations of generations of Black entrepreneurs and business people." In the same issue, he wrote, "We wanted to show our readers a better way and, at the same time, communicate to the business world, from Madison Avenue to Wall Street, that there was a viable Black consumer market. It was my vision to show a more positive side of African American participation in the business mainstream. Along the way, we would carve a path for future generations."

It took Earl Graves nearly 30 years to realize that he could apply salesmanship to social change. "We've made a difference in terms of Black America owning a piece of the economic action." Though he occasionally sells advertising to account executives, that chore is now handled by his oldest son. He, Graves Sr., sells to even tougher front lines: chief executives, congressional leaders, and cabinet members. "I still have to hustle. We've got entire generations of Black kids who are going nowhere. *Who's going to pay the freight later?* It has nothing to do with minorities; it has to do with the bottom line."[8]

For all his success, selling is what drives the man. Part of his secret is believing in his product: "*Black Enterprise* has become America's survival manual for the Black community. We have lived up to, in large measure, the readers' and advertisers' expectations. In the end, nothing serves a salesman better than filling the needs of his customers. *A product is invented only once, but selling is forever.*"

In his book *Wealth and Power in America*, Gabriel Kolko, an economic historian, presented considerable evidence that the reins of power are always held by the controllers of wealth. If this is true, not only does Black America hold the reins to its destiny, *but it is not poor!* Psychologists suggest that our models of thought tend to become our life experience. Those men and women who believe they can succeed tend to succeed. Those who entertain thoughts of failure and self-doubt tend to fail. Plain and simple, your level of wealth and prosperity will never rise higher than your patterns of thought. The greatest fortunes have been built by dreamers and innovators of unwavering faith who believed in their power to accomplish whatever task they turned to. There is no law by which you can attain great wealth without demanding it, expecting it, believing it, assuming it, and thinking it when all that you hope for is not yet visible. Prosperity flows only through channels that are open to receive it.

Quiet as it is kept, there's no need to hire a locksmith; there's no great mystery that unravels riches or abundance. Truth be told, focused thinking has been characteristic of those who have left their mark on the world. There is no changing the principle of a law of wealth. Whatever your business, profession, or occupation, your mental attitude will determine the level of your financial success. A pinched mind equates to a pinched supply. The reason that so many fail to reach their financial goals and the ranks of have nots continue to swell in a land of such promise is that far too many refuse to alter their thinking and commit themselves to the million-dollar habits that lead to financial success. These poor souls lack the self-confidence that never looks back, that burns all bridges behind them. The ever-present tinge of doubt and uncertainty as to whether they will succeed taints their efforts. And this little difference is what spells the difference between poverty and affluence.

If you doubt your ability to do what you set out to do; if you think that others are far better suited; if you fear to step out on faith and assume the calculated risk; if you lack backbone, boldness, and determination; if timidity and a shrinking nature shadow your every move; if you have yet to remove *can't* from your vocabulary; if you lack a daring spirit; if you are constantly held back by caution; if you have yet to get over your love affair with lack and limit; if you have yet to embrace your divinity, that infinite source that knows no failure; and if you're driven by the words "I wish to," "I hope to," and "I'll try"—again, here lies the critical difference that measures the distance between power and weakness, wealth and poverty, and have and have not. Most people refuse to follow the guidelines that eventually could free them from financial insecurity. All it takes is a little discipline and forethought—from your career goals and spending habits to your saving and investment strategies and, most importantly, your attitude. If you make the commitment, wealth will wrap its arms around you throughout your life.

THE MATHEMATICAL FORMULA
THAT GUIDES ALL WEALTH

Wealth creation centers not only on what you know *but on what you do*. And what you do is easier than you think. As eloquently stated by the writer and social commentator George Gilder, "The very process of creating wealth is the best possible education for creating more wealth."[9] Economic security is not attained by the possession of money alone. It is attracted by the service one renders, for useful service may be converted into all forms of human needs, with or without the use of money. Those who have attained economic security have done so not because they control a vast fortune but because they provide employment opportunities, satisfy a need or want, or provide goods and services to society. In short, they *add value*. It is in this manner that all enduring economic security must be attained.

Business philosopher Jim Rohn postulated, "Becoming a millionaire is not that difficult, and it is not the most important thing. The most important aspect of becoming a millionaire is the person that you must become in order to accumulate a million dollars in the first place."[10] Rohn's insight couldn't be more timely. In order to generate wealth, you will be required to alter your mind-set—shifting from the individual who constantly worries about his or her finances to the man or woman who is fortunate enough to concern him or herself with everything but money. You must drastically alter your habits if you are to achieve your financial goals. Or, as one respondent in this study pointed out, "The first million is difficult, but the second million is inevitable."

Writer and worldly philosopher Earl Nightingale shared his formula for compensation. More than 50 years ago, Nightingale explained that the amount of money you receive will always be in direct proportion *to the demand for what you do, your ability for what you do, and the difficulty of replacing you.* For example, in our current economy, highly skilled workers will outearn unskilled employees who in all probability can be easily replaced. This is not to say that any one individual is superior to, inferior to, or more important than another; this formula and example centers on compensation only. Moreover, from a human standpoint, janitors are just as important as brain surgeons. However, the amount of money each will earn will be in direct proportion to the demand for what they do, their ability to do what they do, and the difficulty of replacing them. A person can be trained to clean and maintain a building in only a few days, and replacing that employee is not difficult. A brain surgeon spends many years learning the profession—often at great sacrifice and expense—and he or she cannot easily be replaced. As a result, the surgeon might earn as much money in an hour as a janitor might earn in a month. These extreme cases are used to show the relation of income to demand, skill, and supply, but this principle is as definite as the law of gravitation and just as unerring as the principles of mathematics.

As the result of countless interviews and surveys, I've discovered that wealth is the by-product of a specific mental attitude. There is little secret that society can be divided into three groups: the poor, the middle class, and the wealthy. Not only does each group think differently regarding money, but, as Table 2.1 shows, the haves and the have nots also hold different views on the other eight variables that comprise a well-lived, fruitful life. Call it what you may—the mentality of the rich, a prosperity consciousness, or *the calculus of compensation:* Millionaireship is the outward manifestation of a mathematical formula that is as true and consistent as 1 plus 1 equals 2. For example, bury a pebble, and it will obey the law of gravity. Bury an acorn, and it will obey a higher law and grow; that's the inward nature of each. Just as the source of true success lies within each of us, wealth also emanates from within.

Research suggests that three primary goals can be found in the mind-set of the poor, the middle-class, and the wealthy. The primary goal of the poor is *survival,* the aim of the middle class is *comfort,* and the objective of the wealthy is *freedom and control.* Your personal belief regarding money eventually will define how much money you will earn. If you possess a scarcity mentality, you will seek either

NINE DRIVERS OF WEALTH

	Variable	Have Nots	Haves
1.	Life	Survival	Achievement
2.	Family Unit	Matriarchal	Patriarchal/Legacy
3.	Education	K–12	Lifelong learning
4.	Money	"Act rich," spend, consume	"Act poor," conserve, save
5.	Work	9–5, "necessary evil," hourly worker	5–9, "life work," "self" employment
6.	Time	Present to past	Future
7.	Relationships	Social, party	Networking
8.	Destiny/Fate/Dream	Chance, while sleeping	Choice, conscious, fully awake
9.	Faith/Spirituality	To praise	To practice, possibilities

Table 2.1

comfort or, like the poor, live out your existence day to day. If your outlook revolves around abundance, you will seek freedom. The scripture that admonishes us to "seek and you will find" applies equally to our finances. If you seek to survive, you will. If it's comfort that you desire, you will find it. If your mission is freedom, you will land on its shores. As I uncovered, there is power in long-term positive thinking. This simple act can and will create a fortune if you make it a habit. As the calculus of compensation summarizes, the men and women in this study were rich in mind long before they became rich in life. To further refine your study and analysis of Black America's wealthy, be sure to read, implement, and incorporate the next viewpoints and everyday actions into your financial life. Haves versus have nots will show you how. More important, this chapter will motivate you to try.

Driver 1. Life: Survival or Achievement

When asked "What does money mean to you?" and "What qualities most likely lead to financial success?" the majority of millionaires in this study summed it up well. They cited "freedom and security" and "hard work, goal setting, and perseverance," respectively. When asked about the best aspects of possessing money, virtually none mentioned high-priced toys or the ability to purchase the desires of their heart. Instead, far and away the most common response focused on freedom, self-determination, and controlling their destiny. One female respondent, in particular, felt compelled to share her thoughts. "Somewhere deep within in me, I always sensed that my day would come—yet for me, the path to success was never about fame or fortune. It was about the process of continually seeking to be better, to challenge myself to pursue excellence on every level. The question I ask every day is the same as it has always been: How much further can I stretch to reach my full potential? *Dream big—dream very big*. Work hard. Continue to move in the direction of your goals. And once you've done all you can, stay the course."

Driver 2. Family Unit: Matriarchal or Patriarchal /Legacy

In 1965, when Senator Daniel Patrick Moynihan published "Moynihan's War on Poverty," suggesting that the out-of-wedlock birth rate and the number of families headed by single mothers—both nearly 24 percent—pointed to the dissolution of the social fabric of the Black community, Black scholars berated the author and dismissed his findings.[11] Moynihan, an avowed liberal, was attacked as a right-wing bigot. Now, in all honesty, the Black community would do just about anything to return to those statistics. Today, more than 75 percent of Black infants are born out of wedlock while more than 60 percent of Black households with children are headed by women. Although the U.S. Census Bureau is somewhat foggy regarding the nature of wealth and prosperity, it is quite clear as to the root causes of poverty. Avoiding long-term poverty, according to this federal agency, is not rocket science. The bureau's stance on poverty can be summed up in four steps:

1. Finish high school.
2. Work.
3. Get married—preferably prior to beginning a family; and once you enter into this sacred union, *stay married.*
4. Avoid criminal behavior.

Moreover, the U.S. Census Bureau pointed out that African American married couples are, in fact, better off than those who remain single by nearly every standard. Married couples have higher incomes, longer lives, and better health, and they suffer from less violence and poverty.

No group has taken this directive to heart like Black millionaires, who consistently cite family as the most rewarding aspect of their lives. And although money may create more options, choices, and time to spend with family, the wealthy place family at the forefront of all non-work activities. Nearly 80 percent of the millionaires in this study were raised in homes consisting of both biological mother and father, where the average household income was less than $35,000. More than 70 percent are married, most to their first spouse. Roughly 90 percent are parents, and, as parents, these millionaires are quite clear regarding their expectations of their children. Family wealth is not self-perpetuating. Without careful planning and stewardship, a hard-earned fortune can be dissipated within a generation or two. Although Black millionaires are often proud to have graduated from the school of hard knocks, nearly one-half shared that it is important for their children to attend a "highly selective or prestigious university." They generally feel that such institutions provide quality education that enhances career opportunities in addition to superior peer group connections. Seen in this light, the competitive pressure that Black millionaires feel toward their children's education—whether it is an Ivy League school or a top-rung historically Black college or university—may have less to do with their child's educational foundation than with preparing their offspring for generational wealth. To the doting mother and father, such would be an unparalleled prize.

Driver 3. Education: K–12 or Lifelong Learning

The state of education within the Black community has been the source of much concern—and deservedly so—but the haves in this study view lifelong learning as just as important, or even more so, than any degree they may have earned along the way. Unlike their poor or middle-class counterparts, Black millionaires rate education beyond their time in the classroom highly. The disparity is startling. A Carnegie Foundation report states that the Black high school dropout rate in many urban areas exceeds 50 percent.[12] Moreover, the National Commission for Excellence in Education reported that 44 percent of Black 17-year-olds are functionally literate.[13] African American students are only half as likely as Whites to be placed in honors or advance placement English or math classes and are 2.4 times more likely than Whites to be placed in remedial classes. According to my survey, the overwhelming majority of respondents purchase 20 books per year, and the types of books they read most often are either motivational/self-help or business. For most, reading as a pastime began early in life. Many reported that, during elementary school, they read books independent of any school assignment. As I was told by a respondent whose net worth exceeds $50 million, "Far worse than not reading books or attending seminars or self-improvement courses is not even realizing that it matters. This habit alone will cause you to amend your thinking. If you would commit to becoming a lifelong student—reading the books, attending the classes, networking with like-minded individuals—then today would mark the first day to a better financial future. If you haven't read a single book in the past 90 days, on the surface, this habit doesn't seem to matter. But here lies the danger. Consequently, there's no way for you to enhance your career skills or improve your bottom line. I'm constantly on the prowl searching for ways to advance and grow my business."

When asked for the keys to financial success, Antonio Reid, half of the legendary LaFace Record label, drew on a habit that he has used over his storied career. When Reid began his musical pursuits as a drummer for a local Cincinnati, Ohio–based band more than 25 years ago, he sought a career in the executive suite with a zeal rarely equaled. When asked how others could break into this highly competitive arena, he notes that countless opportunities exist outside of the studio in the marketing, finance, and legal fields. But to crack the code within this industry today, the now-chairman and CEO of Epic Records suggests that all who seek to enter the music business take the necessary steps to polish their management skills as well as their talent. "Gone are the days when you will be given a year to prove yourself," Reid emphatically states. "In order to gain traction, you must make an immediate impact within the first 30 days. Far too many aspiring musical producers often lose sight that music is above all a *business*." To serve as an example to those who would follow, although Reid never attended college, he enrolled in the Advanced Management Program at Harvard Business School while simultaneously presiding over LaFace Records. The program, which required him to devote 60 to 70 hours a week to his studies, prepared him to become the foremost practitioner of his craft in addition to speaking the language of corporate America—a language so few in the music industry, Reid believes, comprehend. "I'm constantly asked why would I relinquish valuable time to dedicate six weeks to this intensive program," he explained. "Easy. I've come to realize that prosperity begins by dedicating yourself to lifelong learning. The moment you cease to grow is the moment you begin to die."

Driver 4. Money: Act Rich/Act Poor

In some ways, I believe we are forced to agree with the twentieth-century writer and journalist Ernest Hemingway, who stated that the rich are different. But Black millionaires are not too different from the middle class in terms of the attitudes, values, and qualities that shape their day-to-day lifestyles. However, they are radically different from the average African American in terms of how much money they possess and, in turn, how they spend their earnings.

The Black millionaires surveyed in this study are distinguished by a belief that wealth is important and that the accumulation of wealth is a desirable life objective. Moreover, they believe in the wisdom of investing part of their earnings for the long haul and benefiting from the rewards of compound interest. They also believe in protecting their wealth by utilizing professional investment advice. And, finally, they believe in spending wisely. They are willing to spend money in order to make money, but they are always in a position to tell their money where to go rather than asking where it has gone.

In a 1996 magazine article titled "Banking on Us—the State of Black Wealth," economist and former college president Julianne Malveaux described an all-too-frequent occurrence. She wrote:

> Everything about the way my friend Carla presents herself trumpets that she is living large. A walking billboard of designer labels, she dresses in $900 St. John knits and carries a $400 Chanel bag as she strides up in $200 Ferragamo pumps to fold her well-dressed self into

a $50,000 Lexus. But, as the saying goes, all that glitters is not gold: Carla's actual net worth—that is, the value of her assets, or what she owns, minus the value of her liabilities, or what she owes—is a paltry $20,000, about $50,000 less than someone like her (35 years old with an annual income of $60,000) should be worth. She also carries credit card debt of nearly $30,000, which amounts to an alarming one-half of her annual income—and that's not including what she owes on her car. If she were to lose her job, she'd be in huge trouble.[14]

Again, the question begs asking: *What does your money mean to you?* What message does it bring? Does it say "Eat, drink, and be merry, for tomorrow we must die"? Does it mean clothes for the naked, bread for the starving, schools for the ignorant, hospitals for the afflicted? Is it a message of generosity, or does it cry out "More, more, more"? Does it bring a message of comfort, of education, of an opportunity to aid your fellow man or woman? Is it filled with promise and purpose, or is its appearance deceiving? Does your money speak to your character, your aims, and your ambitions? Or does it point out your lack of values or shallow standards? Before you offer your response and make the life-changing decision to join the ranks of the financial elite, unlike Carla, I suggest you discard whatever media-driven images you may have about the wealthy. Most people who are hoping to look wealthy are doing just that. An expensive car or designer fashions do not constitute affluence. In fact, the opposite is closer to the truth. Millionaires in general are too often stereotyped by the media, especially in reality television, as possessing not only gaudy, extravagant tastes but also irresponsible fiscal habits. The media also reinforces this perception by focusing on the small percentage of individuals who do live such ostentatious lives. While these people do exist—it is particularly common among those living off inherited wealth—they are the exception, not the norm.[15] We've seen the public and professional misconceptions regarding the genesis of wealth and the mind-sets of the affluent. This, in turn, has led to a slew of myths about how the wealthy dispose of their income.

For starters, Black millionaires are quite serious when it comes to earning and spending their money. Yes, it's true: Some within this income bracket may indulge, both monetarily and socially. However, these gatherings and affairs are few and far between. Events such as these typically are conducted behind closed doors and gated walls, where participants know they will be surrounded by those of similar financial means. Since the length of time people have been affluent will, in some way, determine how they will spend their money and live their lives, there is little need to impress. Although the majority in this study use the services of a financial advisor or seek out expert investment advice, Black millionaires are hands-on when it comes to managing their wealth. When asked to select the phrase that "Describes you best," nearly one out of four said "Disciplined about spending money." Conversely, fewer than 2 percent responded "A bit extravagant." In terms of personal shopping, these consumers could be listed as intelligent shoppers, who scour through newspapers and online Web sites for the best deal. Their spending is dispersed across a variety of outlets, from retail stores to the Internet. Their designers of choice? Typically, Ralph Lauren, St. John, Tiffany, and Louis Vuitton. Where Carla would be attracted to these labels as symbols of status and prestige, value, price, and customer service are the driving factors that influence respondents' purchasing decisions. Eighty percent stated that "they always search for bargains," and 25 percent use coupons. Their stores of choice? Sam's Club, Costco, and Wal-Mart, in addition to high-end retailers such as Nordstrom's and Bloomingdale's. One-third replied that "they rarely finance or buy on credit." With regard to your spending habits, two-thirds replied that they "limit wants in order to fit income." Though their homes are far from palatial—the average appraised value is less than $299,000—Black millionaires are certainly proud of their residences, and they invest considerable time and money in home improvements. One in five shared that their form of splurging is to redecorate their home. The millionaires in this study own between three and four cars, and their garage is more apt to feature a Ford or Chevy than a Maserati or Bentley. Brands of choice include Mercedes, Lexus, BMW, GM, and Ford in that order.

The consumer behavior of Carla and her fellow have nots may be driven by the need to demonstrate that they have arrived, but the wealthy refuse to be guided by such directives. One respondent, a female Detroit-based business owner and a millionaire several times over, was more than honest: "I've got no problem mouthing the words 'I can't afford it.' I've come to know that the art of keeping begins with the art of spending."

Prior to any major purchase, the financial elite are apt to ask three critical questions: *Is this expenditure necessary? Will this purchase add to my wealth or diminish it? Is this an impulse or a planned purchase?* By now, a common thread is apparent regarding the consumption patterns of the affluent. Although the wealthy enjoy the benefits and options that money presents, their spending can be categorized as nothing short of thoughtful and prudent. Plain and simple, their thinking is guided by this maxim: If he or she looks rich, he or she isn't. Living lives of excess, exorbitance, and waste runs counter to their values. Or, as another Detroit-based millionaire who owns a slew of businesses in the Midwest remarked, "The poor keep score by cars and clothes; the middle class keep score by degrees and titles; but the wealthy keep score by their bank account." The monetary benefits of character, faith, and principle are simply beyond computation.

Driver 5. Work: Necessary Evil/Life Work

Virtually every success story mentioned in this book involves someone working longer or harder than his or her peers. As a child, Tyra Banks was drawn to photography and fashion. Radio personality Tom Joyner slaved away for thousands of hours in obscurity prior to being labeled the fly jock (traveling from Chicago to Dallas every day). Perhaps nothing tops Maceo Sloan's ordeal. He ground away for years, perfecting the art of investing, before he ever got his chance. Throughout countless conversations, the wealthy were quick to extol the virtues of hard work. Many told tales of 70- and 80-hour workweeks and spending nights and weekends in the office. Several respondents revealed that their personal road to wealth began "when I took any job that crossed my hand, even a position that paid minimum wage." Their number one rule? "Start earlier, work harder, and stay later." As one respondent blurted, "Whoever can rise before dawn 365 days a year never fails to make his family rich." But beyond sheer hard work, persistence, and grit, other factors are equally if not more important. Not surprisingly, the wealthy love their work. Initially, I mistakenly reasoned that these individuals love money so much they'd do anything to attain it. However, I found the opposite to be true. More than 70 percent of respondents agreed with this adage: "Do what you love and the money will follow." Those interviewed were more apt to be entrepreneurs, professionals, and executives, occupations that require intense periods of focused attention. Several spoke of their contributions in their particular field or industry; they shared stories regarding their employees and customers; seldom, if ever, did they mention the money they had earned. The financial elite seem to realize intuitively that the key to financial success begins by committing yourself to an inspiring cause that impacts others in a positive way. The possibility of their business or work being passed on to their children added energy to their attitude. In short, they were driven by something much larger than simply earning a living. Obviously, they were set on forging a life. They believed in their cause and were committed to seeing it through. Rather than money, their dreams and vision motivated them to reach their financial goals.

The wealthy are ruled by passion and their heart. When it comes to life and their work, they are completely engaged. More than 75 percent replied that "they would continue in their present line of work" when asked, "What would you do if you won one million dollars in the lottery?" And speaking of the lottery, from my survey data, Black millionaires emerge as a unique breed. Driven by solid attitudes and values revolving around work, wealth, and investing, it is no secret that the higher an individual's net worth, the less likely he or she is to ever play the lottery. This is in stark contrast to a 2008 Illinois study that examined lottery sales in the state's six most heavily populated Black zip codes. According to Illinois lottery records for the 2007–2008 fiscal year, Greater Grand Crossing, Chatham, Roseland, and Pullman communities—four areas that feature a Black population in excess of 90 percent—generated lottery sales of nearly $50 million.[16] Ironically, nearly one-half of the residents age 16 and older are unemployed. One of the area store owners stated the obvious: "No one but Blacks come to buy hundreds of lottery tickets each day. And the sad part is that the majority are unemployed. I can see them walk over here from the public aid and unemployment office down the street."[17]

The Black financial elite are more apt to place their solid faith-based values into action with a consistency that is lacking among many of the poor. My data suggest an almost unanimously high value assigned to both work and financial success. Generating an income through devotion to career is the primary manner in which the typical

Black millionaire reaches the goal of financial independence. Sure, everyone wants to win the lottery, and even the wealthy play for fun. But they don't spend half of their paycheck on tickets, and winning the lotto is not their primary strategy for creating wealth. As a number of respondents have openly stated, "It should dawn on people that with the lottery as with any other form of gambling, the house wins and the neighborhood loses."

Driver 6. Time: Present to Past/Future

In his longitudinal study conducted in the 1950s and published in 1964 as *The Unheavenly City,* Edward Banfield of Harvard University studied the qualities that predict upward mobility.[18] He sought to uncover the root causes of wealth and economic success as they relate to the individual, siblings, family, race, and succeeding generations. This highly regarded social scientist studied and compared his findings against the most common factors known for financial success. His ten-year study led him to a single attribute that he concluded was a cause of prosperity, more accurate than any other quality or trait discussed in previous research. He called this variable the "time perspective," defining it as "the amount of time an individual takes into consideration when planning his or her day-to-day activities or rendering important decisions."[19] In short, the time perspective refers to the planning process—either short or long term—an individual utilizes when pursuing current or future goals and objectives. Banfield rationalized that the longer you could project yourself into the future, the greater your chances for financial success. For example, the young newlywed couple that begins to save in order to finance their child's college education practices the "long time perspective." Moreover, the student who graduates from college, enters medical school, and perseveres through years of internships and residency, and subsequently, after nearly a decade of intense training, proudly gains the title board-certified physician is another example of the long time perspective. And, not surprisingly, the millionaires in my study utilized a long time perspective. With regard to saving 15 to 20 percent of their income; participating in retirement plans, 401(k)s, 403(b)s, or individual retirement accounts; or investing in the stock market, either mutual funds or money market accounts, these survey respondents stood in unanimous agreement.

Unlike the average worker, whose version of time perspective lasts no longer than approximately two pay periods, you, the reader, may have a time perspective of 10 to 15 years. The homeless, the unemployed, the addicted, and those who for some reason or another find themselves at the bottom of the social pyramid cling to a perspective no longer than a few days, if not hours or minutes. Millions of individuals who find themselves down and out constantly bemoan the loss of the golden opportunities they allowed to slip through their hands—the weekends, evenings, and downtime they idled away when they could've been laying the foundations for a productive, financial future. Years later, they feel as if they have little to look forward to but old age, poverty, and bitter regrets. Their most valuable commodity is not time but hope. Time is more than money; time is your greatest opportunity. When asked, "Which would you rather possess—more time or more money?" two-thirds of these millionaires replied, "More time."

The question for each of us to decide is not what we would do if we had the means, the resources, the knowledge, the ability, and the opportunity; the question is this: *What will we do with the time we've been given?* It's true—time is money. If you fail to respect this invaluable resource, I doubt that you will respect anything else.

Driver 7. Relationships: Social /Networking

Born on a farm off a dirt road in the segregated South, Lillian Lincoln Lambert believes "Success is a journey, not a destination." Scoffed and ridiculed because she wore burlap-bag dresses to school, she sensed in her bones that there *had* to be a better life beyond the farm. After high school, she moved north. There she plowed her way through a series of dead-end jobs, from maid, to typist, to peddling magazines door to door in New York City before ever realizing that the journey was internal and that education was her ticket out to a new world. Along the way, friends, family, and mentors taught Lambert that she needed the support of others in order to succeed—and that asking for help was not a sign of weakness but of strength and wisdom.

Disillusioned after three years in New York, Lambert moved to Washington, DC, where she found work in a federal typing pool while attending college part time. At age 22, she transferred to Howard

University and studied business. While there, she met the marketing icon H. Naylor Fitzhugh, one of the first African Americans to earn an MBA degree at Harvard Business School. They became fast friends. Lambert worked as Fitzhugh's research assistant at Howard, and he, in turn, not only became a mentor but convinced her to apply to Harvard after earning her undergraduate degree. When Lambert arrived at Harvard in 1967, she didn't realize that she was one of only six African American students—and the only Black female—in a class of 800. During her first year, Lambert and four Black classmates discussed the need to increase Black enrollment in the renowned business program. With the support of Dean George P. Baker, the group persuaded corporate partners and foundations to recruit and increase their funding efforts among African American students. As a result, the Harvard Business School African-American Student Union was formed. Over the next two years, the organization increased the number of Black students sevenfold while significantly improving financial aid and career development opportunities among African American students.

In 1969, Lambert became the first Black female to graduate from Harvard Business School. Her story is that of a poor country girl who was raised on a hardscrabble farm in rural Virginia and became a successful entrepreneur—achieving the American dream on her own terms. For 25 years, she has served as president and CEO of Centennial One Inc., a building maintenance company headquartered in Landover, Maryland, which she launched on a shoestring—$4,000 in savings and a $12,000 line of credit. Built pretty much from the ground up through the power of networking, her roster of clients included ABC News, Dulles Airport, Hewlett Packard, NationsBank, Northrop Grumman, and the one-time consulting giant Arthur D. Little. With initial revenues of $150,000 and 20 part-time employees, she grew the enterprise to $20 million in sales, boasting more than 1,200 employees, before selling it in 2001.

I share Lambert's story to point out that attaining wealth requires more than determination and its accompanying psychological traits. Most people who are wealthy credit a large part of their success to their ability to cultivate and sustain meaningful and prosperous relationships. In a word, Black millionaires network. Many seem to do it compulsively, whether they realize it or not. For the financial elite, networking is a means of reaching a goal, achieving an objective, even if, like Lambert, they initially lack funds or resources. To those blasting forward with nearly nothing, the most valuable and easily accessible resource to draw on is other people.

The most affluent individuals in our society, at every level, are those men and women who know the greatest number of wealthy people. They organize their schedules and daily routines in order to place themselves within their sphere of influence. Once connected, they immediately begin to form new, positive reference groups. They place into action a plan to develop as many good, high-quality, and mutu-ally beneficial relationships as possible within the shortest amount of time. Whereas have nots may be quick to say, "It's who you know," the wealthy would challenge that thinking and reply, "It's what you know about who you know as well as who knows you." Or, as Lillian Lambert shared in her four keys to financial success:

1. *Plan your work but remain flexible. Due diligence is critical. You may be forced to navigate detours, challenges, or a new way of thinking in order to achieve your goal and reach your destination.*
2. *Push yourself out of your comfort zone. Take a risk. You won't achieve anything by staying in a box; it's counterproductive. Never underestimate your skills or strengths, or how much you can accomplish or achieve. Don't worry about the distance, only concentrate on the direction.*[20]
3. *Lean on your network, but be careful with whom you associate. Few choices will influence your future more so than this decision. Surround yourself with like-minded individuals who share your passion, beliefs, and desire. Build a team who shares your commitment and who compliment your skill set. Your net worth will be reflected by your network.*[21]
4. *Stay positive. Look at the bright side. Transforming your life begins by transforming your mind-set. Opportunity often resides in difficult circumstances.*

It's a popular belief that who you know matters most in life, but no group believes this more fervently or works more ardently to cultivate their personal networks than Black millionaires. Nearly two-thirds of respondents agree that networking is the key to financial success.

Moreover, this survey points out that Black millionaires view networking as a way to connect with others to whom you can turn for advice and counsel. They cite networking as a "way of conducting business and a way of life."

Driver 8. Destiny Fate/Dream: Chance or Choice

In his best-selling book *Outliers,* the widely read journalist Malcolm Gladwell postulated that there are two categories of highly successful people: those who attribute their success to the ability to set and achieve personal goals and those fortunate few—or "Outliers," as Gladwell calls them—who find themselves born to perform a specific task.[22] With regard to the fortunate few, these individuals are usually well aware of their life's work while they are relatively young, and their thoughts, dreams, vision, and energies are in complete alignment. "I was raised by parents who instilled in me a strong work ethic and the expectation that I would succeed regardless of my chosen path," explained Debra Lee, CEO of Black Entertainment Television (BET), as well as the highest-ranking African American female executive at Viacom, Inc., BET's parent company. "At an early age, I was taught that my destiny lay within—that a power existed that if I awakened it, aroused it, developed it, and matched it with honest effort, I could literally change the world."[23] With a demanding job and positions on the boards of Eastman Kodak, Marriott International, and Revlon, Lee's days are hectic. But no matter the pace, her calling and purpose fit together like lock and key.

Also joining the ranks is Dr. Benjamin Carson, the famed neurosurgeon. Carson can be seen in the halls of Johns Hopkins hospital pursuing his life's work trailed by dozens of physicians from the wee hours of the morning until late at night. In spite of Carson's countless awards and recognition, during the course of an interview, I was pleasantly surprised at his warmth and accessibility. His only mission is to deliver better healthcare and enhance the quality of life for all those who cross his path. Lee Jenkins, a personal friend and one of the fortunate few, is easily the top Black stockbroker and money manager in Atlanta, Georgia, if not the Southeast. When not working with his clients, he can be found delivering his message on finance and sales to those searching for a better life. Like Carson, he starts early and works late. He loves his work and has built his investment practice to the point where he easily fits into the 1 percent profile within this study. Thousands of men and women in all fields of study could be labeled part of the fortunate few. Early on these individuals identified the star they were meant to follow, and they followed this point of light their entire lives.

At their core, Black America's financial elite know and practice the power of dreaming big dreams. They have long since abandoned the notion that they are powerless over the circumstances of their lives. Nearly 95 percent said that "they live by clearly defined goals," and 25 percent replied that "goal setting is the key to financial success." When asked "How do you view yourself?" nearly 50 percent responded "goal oriented." I have found the wealthy to be consumed by their goals and dreams regardless of day or time. As one Florida-based respondent whose net worth easily exceeds $50 million chided, "It's impossible to do extraordinary things when you are thinking ordinary thoughts." And another seven-figure participant chimed in, "How you think is who you become."

Driver 9. Faith/Spirituality: Praise or Practice

Some readers may remember the highly successful television show called *The Millionaire*. Each week some deserving soul would receive a cashier's check for $1 million from an unknown benefactor. Recipients could keep the windfall and spend it any way they saw fit on the condition that they never revealed the source. As fate would have it, recipients were overcome with joy until they discovered that money could not buy happiness. Ironically, in every episode, the recipient faced a host of challenges to the agreement with the benefactor, and many times the money had to be returned.

Hollywood has produced several movies demonstrating that true happiness does not emanate from material wealth—a lesson that most millionaires have come to know. For example, the movie *Money Grows on Trees* depicts a family that suddenly becomes rich when they discover that a tree in their yard grew, of all things, money. Nonetheless, in the course of the movie, the family faces a slew of difficulties because of their money tree. These are fictional examples of people who failed to find happiness from money alone. *But what of real life?* In accounts of individuals who have become instant millionaires by winning the lottery, more than a handful say that life became more complicated after their financial windfall. In all of these examples, fictional and real, there seems to be a missing link to personal happiness and fulfillment. What is that link? If people have not developed spiritual wealth, no amount of money will make them happy.

The overwhelming majority of the wealthy in this study believe in God. Each affirms that he or she is an integral part of the Creator's divine plan. With this firm belief in the order and ongoing promise of the universe, they've been able to develop a creative imagination, self-esteem, wisdom, goals, and a deep abiding faith. "My greatest inspiration has been and continues to be my faith in God," says Valerie Daniels-Carter, a Black woman who presides over a $95 million fast-food empire.[24] "He is the source of my strength and He gives me the ability to do the things I do. My desire is to create a legacy of giving a hand up. I try to leave my fingerprints on everything that I do—and everyone knows that a fingerprint lasts forever."

Their faith serves as the bedrock—a root system, if you will—that has allowed them to bend and grow with the winds of change without breaking no matter the challenge or circumstance. This ability to adapt is apparent in their unceasing habit of looking at the bright side of even the darkest dilemma. Many of the financial elite credit their strong religious faith as a source of their ability. Case in point, when asked, "How often do you attend church or a religious service?" two-thirds of survey respondents replied "once or twice a week." More than half of the respondents tithe, and nearly 30 percent donate 10 to 15 percent of their earnings to charity. And the size of church that Black millionaires attend? Nothing fancy—fewer than 2,500 members. According to the affluent, faith provides *spiritual* wealth. It is the source of love and nurtures the risk taker with wisdom. Whereas material wealth is dependent on a bevy of factors that sometimes lie outside of our control, spiritual wealth lies completely in our hands.

The type of faith that seems to make a difference in the pursuit of financial success is that which provides inner strength on a consistent basis. That means nurturing the belief system regularly—usually on a daily basis—through prayer and meditation. However, another component is necessary. An old Russian proverb states, "Pray to God, but row for the shore." This type of activist spirituality characterizes the wealthy who express a deep spiritual faith.

NEW RULES OF MONEY

Everything that I have learned over the course of this research suggests that financial success follows a predictable course. It's not the best and brightest who attract great wealth. If that were so, our colleges and universities would be stacked with the Oprah Winfreys and Bob Johnsons of the world. Nor is millionaireship simply the sum of our creativity and the efforts we make on our own behalf. Truth be told, the ability to attract abundance and prosperity is a gift. The haves are those who've been given opportunities—and who have had the strength and presence of mind to seize them. The lesson here is simple but often overlooked. The most common quality that the wealthy share is their propensity to act; they're intensely action oriented. When opportunity knocks, they not only take the initiative, they take charge. Unfazed by the notion that every individual with an idea is a minority of one, millionaires plan their work and work their plan, regardless. They realize that the gifts from such actions are greater than anything imaginable. The affluent operate in a constant state of motion, driven by a sense of urgency as well as a bias for action. As a result, they cover more ground and in less time.

In short, it's one thing to read, study, and clutch to your chest well-worn biblical verses, such as Philippians 4:13—"I can do all things through Christ who strengthens me." It's another matter altogether to exercise your faith—to place it all on the line—and put those words into action. The financial elite in this study not only talk the talk, they walk the walk. Yes, it's true: "All things *are* possible for him that believeth." But your goals and financial objectives will never see the light of day until you put your faith into action.

The ultimate question is, of course: How does all of this apply to you? It doesn't, unless you are prepared to change those habits that continue to lead you down the road to lack and limit. These ideas change nothing unless you are poised to open your mind to the possibilities, to believe that, with diligence, desire, and some proven smart direction, you too can join this elite body of wealth creators. Charles Darwin, the nineteenth-century English naturalist, was correct when he observed, "It is not the strongest of the species that survives, nor the most intelligent, but those the most responsive to change."[25] In other words, it is not so much what you do with your hands as what you do with your mind that counts.

MILLIONAIRE LESSON NO. 3

The poor keep score by cars and clothes. The middle class keep score by degrees and titles. But the wealthy keep score by their bank accounts.

THREE

BELIEVE IN THYSELF WHEN NO ONE ELSE WILL

The Third Law of Wealth

If you can force your heart and nerve and sinew
To serve your turn long after they are gone,
And so hold on when there is nothing in you
Except the Will which says to them: "Hold on!"
If you can fill the unforgiving minute
With sixty seconds' worth of distance run,
Yours is the Earth and everything that's in it,
And—which is more—you'll be a Man, my son!

—Rudyard Kipling

WHAT MIRACLES A STEADFAST FAITH HAS PERFORMED! No philosophy or course of action would allow people to achieve a goal if they believe they cannot. Conversely, who or what can defeat the man or woman empowered by faith? In essence, they can't be talked down, written down, or moved off course. Poverty cannot dishearten them, and misfortune cannot deter them. Faith, it has been said, is the best substitute for friends, pedigree, influence, and capital. It has mastered more obstacles, overcome more difficulties, and enabled more millionaires than any other human quality.

Faith binds the hopeful to their tasks until their deeds are accomplished. Faith is that something within which does not guess but knows.

It knows because it sees what we can only envision. Faith carries in its nature a power that controls and demands, a force that inspires audacity and heroic courage. Faith is the prophet within, the divine messenger appointed to guide us through life, at the very moment when we would lose heart and waver. Faith sees resources, untapped powers, unlimited possibilities, and potential that doubt and fear conceal. Faith is assured and never afraid because it sees a way out and uncovers a solution to every problem. All that endures, everything that stands the test of time, has been carved out of the bedrock of faith. There is no medicine like faith, no elixir so effective, and no tonic so powerful as the positive expectation of a brighter tomorrow. It is this dreaming, this hoping, and this promise for the future that bolsters our courage, lightens our burdens, and clears the way. The apostle St. Paul of Ephesus—who was obliged to fold tents for his daily bread—explained the life-changing power of this spiritual force when he rhetorically asked, "Who can estimate the power of faith?" Faith provides both the power and the glory.

ACCORDING TO THY FAITH BE UNTO YOU

There can be no more striking example of the power of faith than Cathy Hughes. During her journey from teenage mother to corporate executive, Hughes proved that determination, hard work, and reliance on inner strength—a boundless faith—can create success. Founder of the African American radio network Radio One, Hughes has been called the most powerful woman in radio. Since purchasing her first radio station in 1980, Hughes now owns more than 70 stations in a variety of urban markets. She is the first female owner to operate a radio station ranked number one in any major market, and she is the first African American female to head a publicly traded company. Her path to financial success has been a long, arduous climb that most couldn't—or wouldn't—endure. She dismisses her struggles—from homelessness, to life as a single parent, to banks that refused to loan her much-needed capital with a quick laugh. "You survive because you are doing something that you love," she explains. "It wasn't tough on me when I was going through it."[1] And go through it she did.

A native of Omaha, Nebraska, Hughes credits her parents and the hardscrabble Midwestern work ethic for honing her independence and confidence. Although the family lived in a low-income apartment complex, racial pride was set in stone. "During this time, Omaha was a place where you worked and performed at your best or you perished," she recalls. "My mother constantly drilled 'Believe in God; believe in yourself. If you fail, you let your people down.' We were taught to achieve, not in spite of our race but *because* of our race."

Hughes descends from a long line of achievers. Her maternal grandfather, Laurence Jones, launched Piney Woods Country Life School, an acclaimed Mississippi private academy that has served the most promising Black students since 1909. Her paternal grandparents were domestics employed by a prominent family in Chattanooga, Tennessee. Hughes says the family was so taken with their maid and chauffeur that they left their house to them and sent eight of their children through college. This, in turn, enabled Hughes's father, Edgar Woods, to become the first African American to earn an accounting degree from Creighton University. Her mother, Fannie Woods, worked as a nurse when not playing trombone in an all-female swing band called the International Sweethearts of Rhythm. Hughes's love affair with radio runs deep. The oldest of four children, she was given a transistor radio at age eight, hiding the gift under her pillow at bedtime as she desperately tried to tap into broadcasts sent out by White-owned stations in Dallas and Nashville, Tennessee.[2]

TO BEAT THE UNBEATABLE FOE

At 14, Hughes sold classified ads for the African American–owned *Omaha Star* newspaper. She later credited that experience as shaping her philosophy regarding "the responsibility of Black-owned media." Smart and studious, Hughes was the first African American to attend Duchesne Academy of the Sacred Heart, a prestigious Catholic girls' school in Omaha that propelled her on a long list of firsts. Impressed with her ability and self-assurance, a priest had sponsored her admission, raised money to cover her tuition, and defended her actions when she participated in a local civil rights march. Hughes's roots of political activism were nurtured early—a toughness that she would carry throughout her life. By her own admission a somewhat rebellious 15-year-old, Hughes traveled halfway across the country—against her mother's wishes—to witness firsthand the historic March on Washington. Captivated by the experience, she returned to Omaha a different person and was elected president of the National Association for the Advancement of Colored People (NAACP) youth council.

One year later, her mettle was tested again when she discovered she was pregnant. Depressed and in denial, Hughes dropped out of school and married her baby's father. For the next year, she juggled motherhood, a crumbling marriage, part-time employment, and her activist aspirations. Two years later, the couple divorced, making her another sad statistic: a single Black teenage mother with an unfinished education and few prospects. Nonetheless, Hughes finished high school and, in the footsteps of her father, entered Creighton University. After her marriage ended, she continued taking classes and became involved with a financially strapped local Black radio station as both a volunteer staffer and a small investor. It was her first exposure to the communications industry. Then, in 1971, she was offered a chance to join the staff of Howard University's new School of Communications, headed by veteran Black journalist and broadcaster Tony Brown. After a year as a lecturer, Hughes was appointed sales manager of WHUR-FM, the campus radio station. Within a year, she became general manager, giving her, in essence, cabinet-level status despite the lack of an advanced degree. True to form, Hughes's most significant contribution as general manager had more to do with programming than with organization. She had attended a six-week course at the University of Chicago on psycho-graphic programming. "They taught us that you organize a radio station's format to conform to the taste, preferences, desires, and lifestyles of individual listeners," she recalls. "I knew that Washington, DC, featured an impressive population of single Black women who yearned for late-night soothing rhythm and blues, preferably romantic ballads and music."

The result was *The Quiet Storm,* a program of lush "slow jams" by vocalists such as Nancy Wilson, Billy Eckstine, and Dionne Warwick. One song flowed into another as the format mixed female and male vocalists, old and new. In the midst of the disco craze, *The Quiet Storm* rejuvenated the careers of singers who had lost their radio audience. Begun as a weekend segment and hosted by student disc jockeys, the program became so popular that within weeks of its debut it was airing nightly. This innovative format allowed Hughes to distinguish herself by increasing the revenue at the station from $250,000 to $3 million per year. It didn't take long for other stations to notice, and soon "urban contemporary" stations across the country copied the concept. In the wake of its popularity, Hughes urged Howard's administrators to license the now-ubiquitous program. "A licensing agreement," she reasoned, "would've allowed the university to sell the format to other stations. However, unable to see the commercial viability, Howard officials declined." Promising herself that from that moment on she would be in control of her creativity, Hughes left Howard in 1978 to serve as vice president and general manager of WYCB-AM, a local gospel station. But, frustrated by the station's lack of resources, she left after eight months.

"At WYCB, the first 24-hour gospel station, I got the opportunity to build a radio station from the ground up before the owners ran out of cash. They wanted me to obtain a loan. I replied that, if I did secure a loan for them, I wanted a piece of the company. They responded that if I thought I was so smart, I should purchase my own radio station. It was as if a light went off in my head. It was a mess, but a blessing as well. That's when I decided I would never work for anyone again."[3]

ENTREPRENEURIAL PLUNGE

By 1979, Hughes was eager to purchase and run her own station. However, with few resources, her ownership hopes had to wait. For 14 years, WOL had been the voice and sound of DC's Black working class, pumping out a constant stream of soul and rhythm and blues. But when the station became the target of a government investigation, the owners—the Sonderling Broadcasting Corporation (SBC)—placed the station on the market rather than lose the operation outright for allegedly violating its license. SBC was able to sell the station at 75 percent of its fair market value to minority investors as part of a Federal Communications Commission policy meant to encourage minority ownership of radio stations. Using a small apartment building she owned in DC as well as her family home in Omaha as collateral, Hughes placed her bid. She then convinced an assortment of investors, including the city's most prominent Black clergy, to pump in much-needed funding. With their backing, Hughes bought WOL-AM for $950,000.

"At that time, radio wasn't viewed as a good investment. Banks weren't making broadcast loans. Much more daunting was the idea of a creditor lending you $1.5 million—not to mention that the individual hoping to convince you to make the loan is a Black female. Looking back, I made 32 presentations and I was denied each time. Ironically, I gave my thirty-third presentation to a female banker in New York. Before I could finish my pitch, we shook hands on a deal. Chemical Bank loaned me $600,000 and gave me the push I needed."[4]

Once in charge, Hughes and her husband switched the station to an all-talk format, which didn't require the high-resonance quality of FM sound. But more important, the pair felt that the Black community needed information much more than music. Each morning at 7 A.M. sharp, Hughes hit the airwaves offering her take on the day's events. A firebrand who strongly believed in her role as an advocate for the capital's Black community, Hughes was hoping to launch one of the city's most listened to talk shows. For the first 18 months under its new owners, WOL-AM broadcast 14 hours of talk and news each day but not without its detractors; advertisers and lenders weren't keen on the idea. Selling advertising was extremely difficult, and revenues lagged expenses. "We conducted a format search which demonstrated that the one area that no one addressed was news and information for a Black audience," Hughes remembers. "I must admit that I was terribly naive. I was correct in my analysis though I was in the dark in terms of the cost. Talk and news is the most expensive format. I had a 1,000-watt signal that had been through a payola scandal and had to overcome the stigma of the station being dead."

WALK BY FAITH AND NOT BY SIGHT

But the road ahead would grow tougher. Forced to wear a variety of hats, the building that Hughes bought to house the station was a former drug den. She routinely met with neighborhood thugs to keep the peace and swept up used needles from the station's floor.[5] When her eight-year marriage to Dewey Hughes collapsed, she bought out his interest after pleading with bankers to transfer the loan into her name. Still, she was swamped in debt. She lost her car before losing her home, forcing both her and her son to sleep on a cot at the station, bathing in a restroom at the end of the hall. To provide some cash flow, Hughes bit the bullet and sold a precious heirloom for $50,000—a rare white gold pocket watch made by slaves that had belonged to her great-grandmother. She contacted her creditors to update them regularly and paid them off a little at a time. When one of her investors discovered her asleep at the station at 2 A.M., he arranged for consultants to school her on budgeting and management. It wasn't long before her creditors gave an ultimatum: "Talk is too costly," lenders claimed. "Playing records is cheap—change over or lose the station."[6]

Hughes compromised by slowly phasing in music: oldies in the afternoons, go-go music at night, with only the four-hour *Morning Show* surviving as all-talk. Hughes became host by default. "Nobody else would accept $5.50 an hour." She took voice training and read everything she could to stay informed. Yet for all her finishing touches, it was Hughes's candor, her raucous humor, and "down-front, tell it like it is" demeanor—spouting scripture one minute and talking like a home girl from southeast DC the next—that traveled through the airwaves and grabbed listeners. After nearly two years, the tide began to turn. WOL began paying its creditors and staying afloat. Moreover, Hughes was able to return WOL to an all-talk format, and ratings rose, proving once again that Hughes knew her core audience. The station had never been a ratings powerhouse, but competitors said it made money because of its successful appeal to a targeted audience.

Less than one year later, Hughes bought her second station—WMMJ-FM in DC—for $7.5 million and was well on her way to pursuing her passion: cutting deals, building a media empire, and creating jobs while becoming a real force throughout the country. Strong-willed and opinionated, Hughes yearned to devote the majority of her time to the business end and entrepreneurial side of the industry—a role that she relishes. Today, her son, Alfred Liggins, who serves as president and chief executive officer, works alongside Hughes running Radio One, Inc., the largest Black-owned and operated broadcast company in the country. This media giant is the first of its type to simultaneously control several major markets and is the first female-owned radio station to rank number one in any major market. In 1995, Radio One purchased WKYS in Washington, DC, for $40 million, which became the largest transaction between two Black-owned companies in the history of broadcasting.[7] Hughes reached the pinnacle of success when she forged Radio One into a multimedia empire, acquiring more than 70 radio stations in 22 markets—a deal worth more than $900 million—and taking the company public, making it one of the few

Black-owned firms listed on Nasdaq. In 2000, Hughes made history again—she and Radio One purchased Los Angeles' KBBT-FM, "The Beat," for $430 million, and placed actor and comedian Steve Harvey at the helm of the morning slot. Like the *Quiet Storm* nearly 30 years earlier, the decision to bring Harvey on was based on intuition. Hughes studied the L.A. market and determined that the universally known comedian was one of the few on-air talents capable of turning the urban radio market around. Since urban audiences offer unique challenges, in order to keep listeners loyal, stations must forge meaningful relationships with their core listeners and the target audience they serve. Harvey and Hughes made a formidable team. Their philosophy of empowering Blacks in business as well as in life, stopping only to ask for guidance from above, is an outlook that works.

Throughout her life, Hughes's hallmark has been her ability to embrace the calculated risk. True to form, in 2004, she would once again step out on faith and shun nonbelievers by partnering with the cable behemoth, Comcast Corporation, and introduce TV One—a cable network aimed at Black viewers. There is little doubt that Black Entertainment Television, created by media mogul Bob Johnson, dominates—almost monopolizes—Black television broadcasting. Consequently, some market analysts were and remain skeptical. However, Hughes believes there is room for another network targeting African Americans, and she may be right. She has proven repeatedly that her ventures can survive and thrive. To carve out space, Hughes openly states TV One's mission: "to provide quality, wholesome entertainment and information for African American adults." And when asked why her network will succeed, she simply replies, "First and foremost I'm an entrepreneur. But I've gotten bitten by the TV bug in the same way I got stung by the radio bug, and now they can't get rid of me." Today, her cable network reaches 40 million households and is growing, dispelling any doubts about Hughes's business acumen.

A HUGE DREAM REQUIRES HUGE FAITH

In the world of broadcasting, Hughes's claim to fame is what she has been able to achieve at a time when many of her Black counterparts have vanished from the communications landscape. Her success has not come easily. As a Black woman, Hughes has seen the cost of a radio station increase the moment she walks through the door. She has had lenders tell her to play Neil Diamond when she wanted to spin Al Green. Speaking with missionary zeal about empowering her race, she simply responds, "After 30 years of being in bed with my lenders, I've convinced them that I do not believe in programming the easy way, and I do not believe that an owner has the right to program for profit only. It's critical for us to tell our story from our perspective. When the company is Black owned, Black decision makers and Black employees promote their point of view. There has to be some social value."[8]

Hughes's personal achievement is a testament of spirit, hope, hard work, and an incredible degree of faith. Her dedication to women-owned businesses, minority economic development, and entrepreneurial spirit are manifested in every aspect of her work and life. As such, she has been honored by both *Black Enterprise* and *Fortune* magazines. Moreover, her pioneering work has led *Essence* magazine to name her one of "100 Who Have Changed the World." Hughes's is a story of one individual who found her passion early, learned as much as she could, persisted through the tough times, changed plans when necessary, and continued to hold on while there was little to hold on to. While her work ethic continues to drive her, Hughes wants all to understand the power that built her bridge over troubled waters. She advises all who will listen to persevere, be willing to do any job asked of them, believe in God, and work hard. "Through it all there was never a time when I lost faith. Sure, I may have doubted myself or doubted others, but I never lost faith in the spirit that lies at the center of my life. There's a lot in this world that you can't see but still can believe in, such as your hopes and dreams. Just because you can't hold it in your hands doesn't mean it's not there. Faith was the stepping-stone to all that I desired. And a huge dream requires huge faith!"

ROAD TO DISTINCTION IS PAVED WITH YEARS OF SACRIFICE AND FAITH

For those readers who search for abundance, for those who long for financial freedom, and for those who seek the keys to a seven-figure lifestyle and all the benefits this bracket holds, I suggest that you re-read the example of this media mogul. Examine how she confronted her detractors. She did not lose heart when the hisses and jeers rang in her ears. Note her response when her first marriage crumbled, and she was forced to bear the combined burden of being a woman and raising a child alone. We get a hint as to what it means to make the most out of impossible conditions. When faced with similar circumstances, perhaps 99 out of 100 men and women would have ended their march toward prosperity, but not Cathy Hughes. Although her knees did buckle, she rose to the occasion.

Deep within, she knew that a wavering aim and a faltering purpose were not a part of her nature. Her divine faith supplied all the capital she needed. And when fate attempted one last final blow—holding her child and sleeping on the floor of her station, a one-time drug den—without a word or a look of reproach, when others would cringe, she never flinched. She looked her creditors in the eye and refused to abjure her faith. Although she was broke and homeless, no barriers could keep her from her goal. No individual who walks the path of prosperity will tread very far until self-faith is born within; until he catches a glimpse of his higher, nobler self; until she realizes that her ambition, her aspiration, are proof of her ability to reach the dream and vision that consumes her. The Creator would not have mocked us with the yearning for infinite achievement without providing us with the ability and opportunity for its realization. What did Christ care for the jeers of the crowd? The palsied hand moved, the blind saw, the mute spoke, the leper was made whole, the dead rose in spite of the ridicule and scoffs of the spectators. There is nothing attractive in timidity, nothing lovable in fear.

If I was called on to say why so many who began their upward journey with such high hopes that they would create vast sums of wealth fall short of the mark, I would say they lacked faith. There is no redeeming value in people who continually cry out against their condition and stating to an incredulous world what remarkable accomplishments they could achieve if their lots were different. Wrong! You play the hand you are dealt as you exercise your faith. Here lies the Third Law of Wealth. He who begins with crutches will generally end with crutches. Help from within always strengthens, but help from without invariably weakens. And what do we call that help from within? Faith! If you want knowledge, you must work for it. If it is food and shelter you crave, you must toil for it. If you hope for the best that money can buy, these amenities can be attained only by the sweat of your brow.

And how do you increase the level of your faith? Ask James, half-brother of the carpenter from Galilee, who wrote, "Do you want to know, O foolish man, that faith without works is dead." In a world of action, faith is power. Yes, unconquerable faith—even when circumstances are unfavorable—will carve out a way to unexpected success. How many Black millionaires are there who, in their early years, made their greatest strides toward wealth and financial fulfillment and developed their greatest talents and gifts when reverses of fortune swept away every available resource? The Creator may see a rough diamond in you that only the hard hits of poverty, doubt, and rebuke can polish. Have you not been given your marching orders?

As it has been written in Romans 5:3, "Glory in tribulations, knowing that tribulation produces perseverance; and perseverance, character; and character, hope; and hope does not disappoint!" It's true: He who wrestles with us strengthens us. Where faith exists, there is life; where it is missing, helplessness and hopelessness will cloud the day.

Comedian, radio personality, and best-selling author Steve Harvey would never enjoy his millions had it not been for the doubt and ridicule of an elementary school teacher. Tyra Banks was so stung by indifferent and biased modeling agencies that she vowed to all who would listen that her image eventually would be the benchmark by which beauty would be measured. Gospel artist Kirk Franklin and social entrepreneur John Hope Bryant never lamented or grieved over lost wealth. In a down economy, they simply triumphed over difficulties and set out to build their next fortune. Billionaire David Steward was more than $3 million in debt before the tide turned in his favor. Countless viewers now seek his counsel and investment advice through the forum known as Shark Tank, but FUBU founder and branding icon Daymond John has solidified his place within the fashion industry. How did he do it? Success was anything but easy. However, I would wager that John's wisdom would not be sought had it not been for the endless stream of rejection that he encountered from Wall Street's most financially savvy investment bankers. And on the eve of his most trying procedure—separating Siamese twins joined at the base of the brain—Ben Carson, arguably our nation's most celebrated neurosurgeon, had to avoid and sidestep the slings and arrows of colleagues within the medical community who openly questioned whether his hands were truly "gifted" at all.

Our faith is a measure of inner belief. It provides us with a glimpse of our possibilities. The individual who professes little faith reaps little while those who live by a mighty faith receive much. The only inferiority in us is that which we place into ourselves. The persistent thought that you are not equal to the task; that you lack the qualities required of the hour; that you're weak, inferior, or ineffective; that you lack backbone as well as grit; that success and fortune were omitted from your birthright eventually will lower your expectations and paralyze your ability. No one is defeated until he or she gives up. And the point is: Don't give up.

UNLEASH THE DAVID WITHIN

You and I might have winced watching Michelangelo conduct his daily routine. He was barely 26 years old, but his arthritis caused him to walk with a stoop and feeble shuffle. His every move was a painful ordeal. Yet Michelangelo labored for two years on what would be one of his most memorable pieces of art. History tells us that Michelangelo was commissioned by the Medicis, the wealthiest ruling class in Italy during the 1400s, to create a statue in the main square of Florence. This powerful family was renowned for their patronage of learning, literature, and the arts, and such a request could not be denied. For more than two years, the famed sculptor searched for a block of stone out of which he could create the type of masterpiece worthy of such a request. Finally, on a dirt road overrun with weeds and shrubbery, he found a huge slab of marble lying on a wooden pallet. The rock had been hauled down from the Alps in nearby Tuscany years before but had never been used.

In his zeal to uncover the perfect stone, Michelangelo had walked past this rock dozens of times and never given it a thought. But that day something was different. As he moved back and forth before the stone, studying every angle, Michelangelo actually envisioned the statue of David in its entirety. Filled with inspiration, the artist immediately instructed his aides to haul the block of marble to his studio. There, he began the arduous task of hammering, chiseling, sanding, and polishing his life's work. For weeks he stayed holed up in his studio, with chisel, mallet, and drawings in hand, ever ready to obey the call of a new thought. While Florence slept, Michelangelo placed his head, his heart, his faith, and his soul into the marble block before him. On his knees, every day, he prayed for fresh inspiration, new skill. He believed that the Almighty would answer his prayers and direct his hand. When the day arrived for the statue's first public viewing, thousands traveled throughout the region and gathered in the main square. When his masterpiece was unveiled, those in attendance stood in awe amazed at the sheer beauty, grace, and remarkable attention to detail. Here stood the *David*, so plain and yet so convincing. Michelangelo was immediately recognized as the greatest sculptor of his age. But in response, he laid no claim to genius; he said it was all a question of hard work. When asked how he managed to create such a moving piece of art, Michelangelo admitted that he saw the *David* complete and perfect in the marble. All he did was remove everything that was not the *David*.

A host of parallels exist between you and the preceding story. Like Michelangelo's *David*, each of us resembles a masterpiece trapped in stone. But the marble that envelops us is not excavated from quarries or rock pits. Rather it's derived from low self-esteem, lack of confidence, the shadows of doubt and fear, and our inability to exercise our faith. In order to realize our true potential, we must release all limited thinking by dreaming big dreams—establishing huge prosperity goals—while utilizing the miracle-working power of faith. Just as Michelangelo "removed everything that was not the *David*," you and I could benefit by chiseling away those negative confining qualities that were never a part of our inalienable birthright. Cut away the timidity, the inferiority, the lack of ambition, the impossible. Trim away the lethargy, the inertia, the mundane, the indifference, the petty. Nip in the bud the despondency, the discouragement, the misery, the skepticism, the "Oh, woe is me." And, by all means, tear away the pessimism, the cowardice, the impoverished state of mind, the hopelessness, and the lack of faith.

FAITH HAS MADE MORE MILLIONAIRES THAN ANY OTHER FORCE, QUALITY, OR TRAIT

The world always makes way for the individual armed with the sustaining power of faith. Consider Johnnie Cochran, Jr., concentrating his rapt attention first on one juror, then another, going back over the entire line again and again, analyzing every member of the jury until he burned his argument into their souls, until he hypnotized every possible candidate with his purpose, until each member of the jury saw with Cochran's eyes, thought Cochran's thoughts, and felt Cochran's emotions. He never paused until he projected his mind into theirs. There was no escape from his concentration, his persuasive rhetoric, his convincing logic, his undeniable faith in the outcome of the trial. "Carry the jury at all costs," he admonished young lawyers. "Move heaven and earth to carry the jury. Do all that you can the best that you can. But in the end, hold fast to your faith that both judge and jury will see your point of view."[9] This strategy would serve the celebrated defense lawyer well when he led an astute team of legal minds through a racially contentious maze that would be labeled the trial of the century—the O. J. Simpson murder trial. When it came to his earnings and financial well-being, Cochran never deviated from the faith-filled approach that attracted his millions in the first place. "Do your homework prior to making any investment decisions," he told me over dinner. "Locate the best talent—the best money managers, the most astute financial advisors. Make sure that they buy into your fiscal thinking and monetary outlook. As I did in the legal profession, I set a goal to develop a wealth-building dream team and create a network of relationships in the financial sphere. Once my team reviews any and all deals, I just move out on faith."

An overnight success that was 20 years in the making, Terry McMillan might just be as far as you can get from the traditional image of a tweedy novelist. Free-spirited, outspoken, and sassy, she wears stylish clothes, lives in a plush southwestern-style house near Oakland, California, and points out the amounts of money earned or owed to her with the ease of an agent—book advances, paperback rights, foreign publishing contracts, movie options, book clubs, and impending presentations. Her walk-in closets feature rows of designer attire and accessories. The trendy earrings she collects have become her signature, alongside her white sun-roofed BMW that bears Arizona plates, a vestige of her last teaching assignment in Tucson. McMillan, who still holds a tenured post at the University of Arizona, will certainly never be forced to teach again. But reaching financial independence has been anything but easy. Although the top magazines and New York editors routinely returned her manuscripts, suggesting that she stick to her day job as a word processor, it is said that the acclaimed writer turned over entire libraries hoping to ensure that every word, phrase, sentence, and paragraph fit seamlessly, like hand into glove, before she thought her novels worthy of publication.

The oldest of five children, McMillan was born in Port Huron, Michigan, a predominately White, working-class community. Her father, who suffered from tuberculosis and was confined to a sanitarium during most of McMillan's childhood, battled the lingering effects of alcoholism as well. While McMillan was in middle school, her father left the family, which forced her mother to take on a variety of minimum-wage jobs, including as a domestic and an assembly line worker. McMillan credits her mother, widowed when she was 16, with "teaching me and my five siblings the value of faith, taking risks, and resiliency."[10] To assist with family finances, McMillan found a job shelving books at a local library. There her imagination roamed.

Always an avid reader, she became totally absorbed in the classics, particularly Hawthorne, Louisa May Alcott, Henry David Thoreau, and Ralph Waldo Emerson. After studying these prolific writers, McMillan falsely believed that the literary world was reserved for "wealthy whites only." But this perception would soon change.

With only $300 to her name, she moved to Los Angeles, working as a secretary by day and taking classes in African American literature at a local college at night. In this setting, McMillan was introduced to the works of Black writers such as Richard Wright, Zora Neale Hurston, Jean Toomer, and Ann Petry, whose novel *The Street*—replete with its frank, provocative, and open depiction of Black urban love and life—would greatly influence McMillan's writing style. By the time she left Los Angeles for New York City to attend graduate school at Columbia, McMillan had a bachelor's degree in journalism from the University of California at Berkeley and a love affair with writing. Twenty-six credits shy of her master's degree, she left Columbia and joined the Harlem Writer's Guild, where, while working as a word processor and raising an infant son alone, she wrote and published her first novel, *Mama*.

The novel was based on just one of several short stories that McMillan had tried with limited success to get into print. When the Harlem Writer's Guild accepted her into its program and told her that

"Mama" should really be a novel, not a short story, McMillan expanded the manuscript to nearly 400 pages. Highly autobiographical in tone, the book explores the grim and humorous realities of an urban African American family. On a whim she sent her work to Houghton Mifflin—a first-tier New York publisher—hoping that she would at least receive free editorial advice. She was pleasantly surprised four days later when an editor called and mentioned that she loved her story and hoped to publish her book.

McMillan knew the power of publicity and was determined not to allow her debut novel to go unnoticed. When the publisher told her that it could not afford a full-blown media blitz, she decided to promote the book on her own. Using the facilities at the law firm where she then worked as a typist, McMillan wrote more than 3,000 letters to prospective readers and bookstores, who found her approach hard to resist. By the end of the summer 1987, she had attracted several offers for readings and presentations. Next, she coordinated and personally financed an exhaustive media tour—a cross-country odyssey that included nightclubs, hair salons, and churches—proving that she was more than willing to peddle her book out of the trunk of her car to anyone who would stop and listen. Her faith and relentless determination touched a chord with readers, and her success story has become one of the most remarkable in the publishing industry. The novel received positive reviews, and her ceaseless letter-writing campaign and reading tours created a template of how to sell to African American readers. Six weeks after *Mama* was published, the book rushed into its third printing.

Although her first two works enjoyed a welcomed level of success, her third book, *Waiting to Exhale*—which spent three months on the *New York Times* best-seller list and swept the nation's bedrooms, beaches, college campuses, reading groups, and rush-hour subway trains, selling more than 700,000 hard copies in the process and nearly 4 million more in paperback—made her a millionaire. Not since Alice Walker's *The Color Purple* had there been so much discussion about the state of relations between African American men and women. The fact that a Black female author was profiling vivid characters with whom many Black women could identify had the added effect of proving to booksellers that there is a sizable, previously ignored market for Black fiction—just as the $67 million for the film version proved there is a sizable market for Black movies.

Regardless of the size of your dream or the state of your resources, nothing lies beyond the reach of faith. This divine force looks past obstacles that would discourage most. This spiritual connection backs all achievement, sees triumph beyond temporary defeat, and carries the day. Faith is the locksmith that opens all doors; that no obstacle can bar, no difficulty or disaster can dishearten, or no misfortune can swerve from its intended purpose. Faith is a friend and willing ally to the down-and-out, the have nots, those who complain that the door to financial success is locked and gated. If they only knew that each of us receives in life what we concentrate on with all our might. There's no need to wait for luck, for outside assistance, for capital, for a boost, or for anything or anyone other than ourselves. Here lies your helping hand. Although our level of financial attainment—whether we are rich or poor, wealthy or penniless—may rest in our hands, any enduring change begins with our own ability to exercise our own faith.

After speaking before 1,000 followers at a Washington, DC, gathering, McMillan was cornered by an aspiring writer seeking to gain inside advice. The young admirer proudly shared that she had recently spent six days on a poem she hoped to publish. Unimpressed, this esteemed author lit a flame under the would-be hopeful and urged her to polish her craft. "Oh, really?" was McMillan's response. "I've never spent less than six months on any material that I hoped would make it to a publisher's desk. Nothing is denied to anyone who is willing to pay the price. Though some of my readers may view me as a rock star, I can recall the days in which I was a struggling writer who was trying to find an audience for my voice. Whatever position I have attained is due to my faith. God gives us what we need when we really need it."[11]

A ZEST FOR LIFE

Self-made millionaires approach every activity with inner belief and fervor. Their friends and associates often speak of their incredible energy and zest for life. If these qualities don't describe you, I suggest that you begin to develop the habit of embracing each day as an exciting new adventure.

At the conclusion of a Sunday service, a member of the Dallas, Texas–based Oak Cliff Bible Fellowship Church approached the celebrated pastor, Tony Evans, with the following question: "Dr. Evans, what would you do if you knew you would die tomorrow?"

"Just what I do every day of my life," he responded calmly. "I would end my day with prayer only to wake up in glory."[12] As the senior pastor and one of the most respected leaders in evangelical circles, Evans has not only taken his congregation from 10 believers who met weekly in his home to more than 8,000 members, but he has also revolutionized the traditionally conservative role of Christianity in the community. Without this sublime faith, a fierce commitment to his mission, how could this once-unknown preacher build such a ministry? Here's a clue. With regard to the pastor's divine self-confidence, Henry Van Dyke, the nineteenth-century educator and writer provides the answer: "Where you find a flower, you know there must've been a seed. Where you find a river, there must've been a spring. Where you find a flame, there must've been a fire. And when you find a man beloved and blessed of God, you know there must be faith." Whether it was Abraham going out, not knowing whither, or Moses contending with Pharaoh, or Paul proclaiming the gospels, or Dr. Evans saving the least, the last, and the lost, in the end, men and women of faith win. When asked to explain how he achieved his mission, the pastor replied, "The secret and source of all wealth, success, and heroic achievement, has been and will forever be faith!"[13]

SWEET TASTE OF SUCCESS

A careful look at the sources of history's greatest fortunes not only exposes the futility of trying to speculate your way to billions, but also refutes a common misconception regarding the connection between original ideas and great wealth. It is true that new ideas have given birth to many immense fortunes, but the original thinkers have not generally been the ones who made the fortunes. A more dependable strategy is to learn how to make money from ideas, and then be prepared to capitalize on an original notion dreamed up by someone who is more skilled at that sort of thing.[14]

If this sounds like a jaded notion, consider the story of Michele Hoskins. During the winter of 1983, Michele Hoskins knew she had hit rock bottom. A mother of three, she was jobless and had just survived a bitter divorce. "When I leave," her ex-husband boasted defiantly, "you won't be anything." Try as she might to prove him wrong, she ended up on welfare. "It was humiliating," she recalls. "But those 18 months on government assistance motivated me to strive for a better life."[15] Thanks to a dogged work ethic, years of sacrifice, an undeniable faith, and an old family recipe for breakfast syrup that was first created by her great-great-grandmother, a slave in Mississippi, Hoskins has found her fortune. The Chicago native now supplies Michele's Honey Creme Syrup—a sinful confection of cream, honey, and churned butter—as well as a line of gourmet pancake mixes to 10,000 stores across the country, including Kroger, Safe-Way, Winn-Dixie, and Wal-Mart.

What Hoskins, president and CEO of Michele Foods Inc., markets isn't just any pancake syrup or batter. This recipe and secret blend is part of an astonishing story—a set of instructions and combination of ingredients that was passed down through the generations. The original syrup was comprised of churned butter, cream, and honey. America Washington, her great-great-grandmother and a slave who created the recipe for her owner, had stipulated that the recipe could be passed only from mother to daughter, and not any daughter—the third daughter of each generation, a stipulation that puzzles Hoskins to this date. Her mother won the prize recipe, but she had only one daughter, Michele, who managed to persuade her mother to share the recipe. Moreover, she stated that she wanted to pass the recipe on to Michele's third daughter, Keisha. Thankfully, after eight years of prodding, her mother relented. This beloved family recipe would become Hoskins's saving grace.

In 1982, Hoskins took inventory. With little financial security and three small children, her dreams were the only asset she possessed. But her life was about to change. After preparing breakfast one morning for a few close friends, her guests raved over her pancakes and syrup. A heart-to-heart talk with her family led her to believe that a recipe for success might literally be at her doorstep. Two years later, she went for broke. She resigned from a part-time teaching job and sold her condo, car, furniture, and jewelry to raise $150,000 to launch her business. She and her children moved in with her parents, where Hoskins and her youngest daughter made batches of syrup on an old stove in the basement and bottled the product. "My family thought I had lost my mind," Hoskins remembers. "Each night my girls and I would painstakingly fill bottles of syrup by hand. It took nearly one hour to fill 12 bottles as our feet stuck to the floor. But deep down inside, I knew it was going to work."[16] She took the recipe to a chemist who formulated the ingredients into a marketable product suitable for mass distribution. Next, she figured out the nuts and bolts of the business, including finance, accounting, and other crucial aspects of running a company. Finally, she attempted to break or circumvent racial and gender barriers to get her product on the market.[17] Little of it was easy. Within a year, however, she had contracts with two major chains in the Chicago area. Three years later, her syrup was featured in 300 stores.

But Hoskins was hoping to branch out nationally. To make the transition easier, she developed two new flavors—butter pecan and maple cream—and was making gains marketing her syrups in St. Louis, Detroit, and the Midwest. "But I was still struggling," she shared with me. "Sometimes I was forced to barter syrup in order to pay the rent. The frustrating part was failing to comprehend the ins and outs of the food manufacturing industry in addition to being a Black woman who, far too often, was not taken seriously. In 1991, I caught wind of the racial discrimination lawsuit that was about to impact the Denny's restaurant chain. Needless to say, I immediately saw an opportunity. I realized that Denny's and its competitors were seeking to address their diversity needs. Without any contacts or letters of introduction, I personally called Denny's headquarters every Monday morning at 10:30 for two years, in an effort to convince the chain to carry my product. My faith and persistence paid off."[18] In 1993, Denny's awarded Michele's Foods a $3 million contract.

Nearly all the millionaires surveyed for this study indicated that a major component to their financial success and their ability to overcome fear and low self-esteem is a direct function of faith. Those men and women who are destined for success believe that—sooner or later—they are going to be successful. They believe that whatever occurs, either positive or negative, is part of the grand plan that will lead to their financial windfall. They refuse to entertain, dwell on, or discuss the likelihood of failure. The concept of failure never occurs to them. Or, as Michele Hoskins revealed, "My fortune has its roots in the belief that a good idea can't be stopped—and in the single dollar that got me started."

The men and women in this study know how to defeat fear and worry, primarily by unleashing their inner self-confidence and a firm belief within their own abilities. Here are the values that Michele Hoskins used repeatedly as she made the leap from fear, worry, and despondency to the life of which, at one time, she could only dream:

- *Giving back.* Of those to whom much is given, much is required. If you possess love, hope, or graciousness in abundance, offer your gift to those who need it. When you serve others, that form of service returns to you in the form of compassion and gratitude. And as you reach out to others, you'll realize that your struggle, your challenge is neither enormous nor insurmountable. One of the primary reasons that such a small percentage of African American households have attained millionaire status is because so few seek to own and operate their own businesses. Hoskins took advantage of programs that encouraged and supported minority and female-owned companies, rode the wave of expansion of these types of businesses in the late 1980s and early 1990s, and gradually built a network of colleagues who assisted and supported her. Hoskins launched a nationwide mentoring program, "From Recipe to Retail," to aid, uplift, and support entrepreneurial hopefuls who desperately seek to follow in her footsteps.
- *Let the spirit move you.* To honor her ancestor's gift, the Chicago native introduced the marketplace to a life sweetened with success and triumph and leavened with challenge and toil. Through it all, she carries a great deal of respect for the gift that was graciously passed down to her. "It's ironic and humbling," she explained, "that this legacy begun by a slave—my ancestor—would eventually pave my road to financial independence. I felt as if my great-great-grandmother was calling out to me. It's as if she reached out from the past and said 'I have been waiting for someone to accept the challenge and step out on faith.' I thank God each day that I heard the call."
- *Leaving a legacy.* Hoskins's parents told her, "Anything that the mind can conceive can be achieved." When Hoskins endured an emotionally draining divorce, not to mention

working one part-time job after another, she read an article highlighting women business owners who managed to reach their goals and thereby control their own destiny. It forced her to think, Why not form a company and sell my great-great-grandmother's syrup? In true entrepreneurial form, Hoskins began to visualize her enterprise replete with bottles, labels, and packaging, as well as the stores that would carry her product. She decided then and there to join the mix of these high achievers and leave a legacy for her three daughters.

- *Faith.* "One of the greatest fears that each of us faces," Hoskins points out, "is the fear of failure. Whether I was mixing product or presenting before a distributor, the fear of failure always seemed to fester—the nagging insecurity that I wouldn't succeed or that I was not good enough. Fear is an emotion that wealth requires you to conquer. The longer it lives within you, the stronger it lives within you. Thankfully, my foundation centers on the man above. Crisis prayer is okay, but daily prayer is better. In His eyes I am always 'good enough.'"[19]

TRUE NATURE OF WEALTH

Now open your wallet and take a good, long look at the currency inside. Regardless of the amount, as you gaze into each compartment, try to see these shapes, forms, and objects for what it really is: a collection of green strips of paper and metallic coins of various sizes. Ask yourself whether this is the true definition of money. Reading your monthly bank statement might suggest that money is nothing more than a succession of random numbers printed on the letterhead of a lending institution. But how is it truly defined? As oversimplified as this may sound, money is the best indication of who you really are. No one states this concept more aptly that the pioneering psychologist William James: "In its purest sense, a man's self is the sum total of all that he can call his, not only his body, but his home, land, bank account, wife and children, and his psychic powers as well. If they wax and prosper, he feels triumphant; if they dwindle and die away, he feels cast down."[20]

Abraham Maslow, founder of Third Force psychology, believed there is a tendency in our lives for "self-actualization." Maslow referred to self-actualization as "the clamoring of capacities to be used, a restlessness for self-development, accomplishment and esteem."[21] Your full potential emerges not just when you develop skills but when you first unlock the door to the internal resources of the mind waiting to be tapped. Unlocking that door simply comes by altering your pattern of thought. Maxwell Maltz, the renowned plastic surgeon, underscored Maslow's point. He theorized that imagination plays a far more crucial role in life than one is led to believe. According to Maltz, "Creative imagination is not something reserved for the poets, the philosophers, the inventors. It enters into our every act. Imagination sets the goal picture that our automatic mechanism works on. We act, or fail to act, not because of will, as is commonly believed, but because of imagination."[22]

Harvard psychologist William James, in his *Principles of Psychology*, defined genius as "little more than the faculty of perceiving in an unhabitual way." In his essay on behavior, he referred to habit as "the enormous flywheel of society, its most precious conservative agent. It alone is what keeps us all within the bounds of ordinance and saves the children of fortune from the envious uprisings of the poor."[23] Every fortune has its start in the mind of a single man or woman. The affluent take to heart Dr. James's definition of genius by making note of their surroundings—particularly in their work and environment with new eyes, the eyes of possibilities and no limit. Millionaires form the habit of seeing things not as they are but as they perhaps will be, as they could be, as they insist they be. To the wealthy, sight is a quality of mind, a mental perception, not just a physical process. As the wealthy strive to reach their objectives, they train their thinking and beliefs to correctly capture what lies in their view.

Through mental habits and practice, the affluent cut a path where none existed before. Seeing well is essential to seizing well. To an extraordinary degree, wealth creators do both. Seeing their ultimate goal in their mind's eye, they bring together ideas from different contexts to construct a completely new entity. These men and women view their surroundings not as material but as ideas in action. Unlike most of us, they focus not on circumstances but on opportunity.

What effect has the traditional outlook of Black America had on their community? With the possible exception of the American Indian, no group has suffered more, endured more, or been impeded more than African Americans. Most immigrants came to this land of hope and promise with their culture intact and bolstered by strong self-esteem, both of which have resulted in an ever-regenerating entrepreneurial spirit. Blacks, however, were broken down physically and emotionally and systematically denied opportunities to be either employee or employer. Since the dawn of American history, at the hand of government and private enterprise alike, African Americans have been forced to run faster and dig deeper just to enjoy the most basic of human necessities. *And the result?* A misapprehension of the fundamental codes and concepts of capital and markets and a cynical view as to the root cause of wealth and prosperity. This distorted mind-set has taken a severe toll. As this is written, in 2012—with the first Black president in the White House—race relations have made enormous strides over previous decades. However, the statistics regarding Black wealth still remain quite dismal. So dismal that far too often, we Black Americans fail to grab hold and utilize the third law of wealth—*faith*—to lift ourselves out of our financial doldrums.

It is doubtful that any other law has proved to be the turning point in more lives. Faith has been the miracle worker of the ages. The third law has rallied and motivated more millionaires, sending them back to their dreams and visions that they had abandoned in moments of discouragement. This one word has kept scores of businessmen and women from failure after they had given up hope. Personally, I have listened to story after story from participants in this study who shared how this quality aroused their ambition, changed their ideals, and propelled them to the successful undertaking of what they before had thought impossible. No one can become prosperous while he or she expects to remain poor. You cannot exceed the limits that you set for yourself. Before you can lift yourself, you must first lift your spirits—and "spirit" is another word for *faith!* If anything, this text is replete with examples of ordinary men and women, of average ability, who have seized routine occasions in order to reach their financial goals.

Although it's true that African Americans have cleared many of the steepest hurdles and gone far in a short period of time, why haven't we seen more wealth creators? *Why haven't Black Americans developed a larger and more prosperous wealth identity?*

The core reason, according to the eminent Black sociologist E. Franklin Frazier, is that Blacks "lacked experience in buying and selling, which are at the heart of the spirit of business."[24] Others, such as the famed historian Carter G. Woodson, believe the reason goes much deeper. Woodson theorized in his seminal tome, *The Mis-Education of the Negro,* that "if you can control a man's thinking you do not have to worry about his action. When you determine what a man shall think you do not have to concern yourself about what he will do. If you make a man feel that he is inferior, you do not have to compel him to accept an inferior status, for he will seek it himself. If you make a man think that he is justly an outcast, you do not have to order him to the back door. He will go without being told; and if there is no back door, his very nature will demand one."[25]

"This attitude," warned economist Walter Williams on the editorial pages of the *Philadelphia Inquirer,* "droned on year after year, not only undercuts youthful initiative, but affects the mind-set of those teetering on the brink of giving up all hope of cutting a huge slice of the American economic pie."[26] But Black America is currently living in the middle of a revolution, one that is as earthshaking a change as was the Industrial Revolution, in which humans shifted from horse-drawn carriage to supersonic travel. What lies at the core of this revolution is not manual dexterity; it is information—the marriage of learning and creativity—and knowledge. Knowledge is no longer a source of power; it is *the* source of power. Prosperity and its antithesis, poverty, are based on formal ideas, knowledge, and a limited belief system—not on class, culture, or race.

With regard to Dr. James's reference to psychic powers, one of the most important behaviors utilized by today's Black wealthy is the habit of faith and belief. It seems that most successful and wealthy individuals are men and women of faith. By *faith,* I am not implying that millionaires believe or follow a dogmatic doctrine of inflexible codes of conduct. On the contrary. The habit of faith requires simply that you believe that there is a higher power in the universe that desires a spiritual relationship with you and wants the best for you. The greater your faith, the greater your confidence that everything occurs for a reason and equally for your benefit. Throughout this research, I uncovered perhaps the most important faith-filled mental and spiritual principle that the wealthy hold dear: You become what you think about. In other words, our outer world is a mirror image of our inner world. What occurs on the outside of our lives is often the reflection of what is going on inside of our lives. According to the high-net-worth men and women in this study, you can discern the inner condition of an individual by looking at the outer condition of his or her life.

People are often puzzled as to why the wealthy and affluent continue to build on and increase their resources and why the impoverished or unsuccessful tend to remain in poverty. This refrain resembles the old saying, "The rich get richer and the poor get poorer," which is largely true. The poor do not, as a rule, get poorer, but they do tend to remain poor, while the affluent tend to become even more prosperous.

One reason for this phenomenon is the hopelessness and despair that restrict poor people's lives. Their inability to dream, to encapsulate aspirations beyond their current circumstances, to envision positive results is just as much a cause of their lack of financial success as is their poverty. Why is this such a problem? Because we are all creatures of habit. People at the bottom of the economic scale are as bound by the habits that have resulted in their lack of prosperity as the successful are bound by theirs. There is a conservatism of the poor that is every bit as strong as the conservatism of the rich. People, in general, tend to avoid anything that smacks of change. One would think the unsuccessful or poor would welcome any kind of change, but they don't. They have grown used to their way of life and feel that change might be for the worse. Affluence in life is not so much a matter of talent or opportunity as it is of concentration, persistence, and hope.

The converse of this proposition is equally as important. A self-limiting belief system can almost be damning. One of the great moments in humanity's long evolution occurred when people discovered that they could be free, that they could control their destiny. This didn't mean—nor did people think it meant—that they could control the elements or the giant beasts lurking in the world. However, this did mean that people could take charge of their own affairs and somehow alter the conditions surrounding their lives by changing their thoughts and belief system.

HOW MILLIONAIRES USE THE
POWER OF FAITH AND BELIEF

Best-selling author T. Harv Eker wrote in his book, *Secrets of the Millionaire Mind,* that we live in

> a world of duality—up and down, light and dark, hot and cold, in and
> out, and fast and slow. These are but a few examples of the thousands
> of opposite poles. For one pole to exist, the other pole must also exist.
> Consequently, just as there are "outer" laws of money, there must be
> "inner" laws as well. The outer laws include concepts such as busi-
> ness knowledge, money management, and investment strategies. These
> are essential. But the inner game is equally as important. An analogy
> would be the quality of a carpenter's tools. Using top-of-the-line tools
> is imperative, but being a top-notch carpenter who masterfully uses
> these tools is even more critical.[27]

Eker goes on to share that "it's not enough to be in the right place at
the right time. You must be the right person in the right place at the
right time."[28]

So who are you? How do you engage in critical thinking? What
are your beliefs? What are your habits and traits? How confident are
you? Do you truly believe that you deserve wealth? What is your ability to act in spite of fear, anxiety, inconvenience, and discomfort? Your
character, your thoughts, and your beliefs are critical aspects of what
determines the level of your financial success.

The financial elite have long since recognized that financial independence should be one of life's major goals. Thankfully, financial independence is easier to achieve today than at any other point in human
history. There are literally thousands of examples of men and women
who started with nothing or found themselves buried deeply in debt
and still managed to build financial empires. We live in one of the
wealthiest countries in the world in a time of growth and prosperity.
We are surrounded by more economic well-being and affluence than
ever before. By mastering the laws of wealth and adjusting their mind-
set, the wealthy and affluent make it their business to gain their fair
share of abundance. They've come to know that the roots of wealth
grow from seeds of thought—seeds that only they can plant.

QUESTION YOUR BELIEFS

The law of belief states, "Whatever you believe, with feeling and conviction, becomes your reality."

People, millionaires included, act in a manner consistent with their deepest and most intensely held beliefs, regardless of whether they are true. Our beliefs largely determine our reality. Secretly, if not overtly, nearly everyone desires to become rich—in other words, to enjoy the fruits of a prosperous life. So, if the desire is there, why do the vast majority fail to achieve financial success and its attendant rewards? Simply put, far too many have nots believe they are incapable of reaching such positions. Consequently, they've never developed a blueprint for altering their financial status, nor have they created a plan to gain access to those who have actually reached the level they wish to attain.

For example, take the typical day in the life of the average worker. So many give one-third of their day to a job they don't particularly enjoy. Moreover, after arriving home from "a hard day's work," they spend the remainder of their day engaging in various activities hoping to ease the frustrations heaped on them during the day. This displeasure with their chosen career path affects relationships with their spouses, children, and friends and stifles thoughts and desires of improving their lives. And yet, they forge on, believing they must. Most people unwillingly drag themselves to work on Monday while fixated on the clock until Friday, when they can finally free themselves of the shackles they believe they are forced to endure for five, long, painful days. They receive exactly what they expect from life: boredom, frustration, roadblocks, and meager earnings. He can who thinks he can, and he can't who believes he can't. This law is inexorable and indisputable. We are what we believe ourselves to be—nothing more, nothing less.

So many people are quick to believe that those men and women who have accrued wealth and influence are highly favored by fortune. But it is closer to the truth to say that their success is the result of expectations—the sum of their creative, positive, habitual thinking. The riches they enjoy are nothing more than the manifestation of their attitude and mind-set. They have wrought—created—what they possess out of their constructive thought and their unquenchable faith in themselves. As it is the fierceness of the heat that melts the iron ore and makes it possible to weld it or mold it into shape, as it is the intensity of the electrical force that dissolves the diamond—the hardest known substance, so it is true that the law of belief attracts prosperity to those who think it is possible.

We do not believe what we see; rather, we see what we believe. Millionaires seem able to pick up signals that others miss. Wealth creators see a pattern that spells opportunity or impending danger. This sensitivity to cues may emanate from previous knowledge, intuition, or belief systems. We can possess life-enriching beliefs about ourselves that promote happiness and optimism, or we can foster negative beliefs regarding our potential that eventually will surface as roadblocks to the realization of all that is truly possible. As one respondent shared as I quizzed him on potential and possibilities, "If you're not a millionaire or bankrupt by your thirtieth birthday," he explained, "you're not really trying. I've never begun anything with the idea that I couldn't succeed, and I never had much patience with those who were ready to explain why I couldn't." Another survey participant was a bit philosophical, choosing just the right metaphor to convey his point: "Wealth is a by-product of your thinking. I can't make you wealthy by giving you a handout, but I can place you on the road to prosperity by teaching you what I know." He then gave a stunning interpretation of the oft-used quote from Benjamin Mays, president emeritus of Morehouse College: "Not to reach one's goals is not nearly as bad as having no goal to reach."

Law of Cause and Effect

Since economic thought first became formalized more than two centuries ago, two different schools of reasoning have revolved around wealth and its creation. One view, espoused by the English mathematician Thomas Malthus, contends that wealth is primarily physical and therefore finite and limited. However, the second view, defined by the French economist Jean-Baptiste Say and later clarified by the Scottish economist and moral philosopher Adam Smith in his seminal work *The Wealth of Nations,* states that wealth is essentially metaphysical. As it is the result of ideas, imagination, innovation, and individual creativity, it is therefore unlimited. This outlook not only lies at the heart of the law of cause and effect but is so powerful, pervasive, and all-encompassing that it affects everything we think, say, or do. Black millionaires embrace no other mental law, at an ever-increasing rate, than the law of cause and effect. This law simply asserts that wealth and prosperity are the direct effect of specific causes and actions. By adhering to this fundamental principle, the wealthy shatter many cherished, time-wasting myths, including the widely accepted belief that financial independence is the result of some mysterious, carefully guarded secret. Countless respondents have clearly demonstrated that achieving major financial objectives is a matter of developing and consistently practicing the same simple habits that all millionaires employ—and that these habits work 100 percent of the time. Moreover, anyone willing to put forth the necessary effort can learn and develop these habits. In the application of this law, I have found the wealthy to possess an intense desire to grow—to outperform not only their competitors but their own previous results as well. They keep score; they measure their progress. Moreover, they don't permit the lack of money or resources to constrain them. Black millionaires believe it is better to hold fast to a workable plan and lack money than to possess a fortune and aimlessly drift.

"Wealth begins in the mind," one respondent stated as we conversed during a focus group. "Forty years ago, I was dead broke without two dimes to rub together. But I was just as prosperous then as I am today. Why? Because in my mind I held grander visions. I sought out and emulated those who achieved financial success. I learned there is nothing as sad as the man or woman who prevents his own success by programming himself with thoughts of failure and mediocrity."

One Washington, DC–based entrepreneur whose income is in the seven-figure range has an outlook on life that is exactly what I expected it to be: "Very happy and fulfilling." Yet fulfillment wasn't something that had come early to him. In advising young people who may want to follow in his footsteps, he said, "You must be sure this is something you really want to do. You must be committed and focused. If the passion is not there, find something else to do."

He then placed a high premium on setting the right priorities. "Forget the drive for the dollar," he said. "Go where your heart and mind take you. Then make sure your words, actions, deeds, and thoughts are congruent to your goals and desires."

It was on his road to millionaireship that another member of the Black financial elite discovered the paradox of wealth. Over lunch in his resplendent Greensboro, North Carolina, home, he shared the following thoughts: "Wealth and poverty are literally states of mind. True wealth lies within the human spirit and is attitudinal. It stems from the ability to sacrifice today for the sake of tomorrow and consists not chiefly in things but in thought. More than two decades ago, I launched my business with less than $1,000 and today I'm part owner of several enterprises, including a 380-room Columbus, Ohio, hotel; a string of day cares; and real estate holdings in Hilton Head, South Carolina. Though my parents never owned a car, I own several luxury models. Realizing ever-present opportunity is your greatest gift. By assuming responsibility for the quality of your thoughts and actions, you can drastically alter your life. You've heard it before, but it bears repeating: 'Change the thought and you change the experience.' But there are still mountains to climb. While our race has finally achieved basic freedoms, there's still the critical issue of uncommon freedom that is more or less economic in scope. Pursuit of this next level must be won by tightening our grip on individual freedoms and initiative. Civil rights must give way to 'silver rights.'" In other words, financial and fiscal initiative.

Finally, another interviewee who also insisted on anonymity sat back in his creaky old swivel chair shaking his head in disbelief as he pondered Black America's spending habits. "As a people, we're three times the size of Sweden and damn near three times as wealthy. They produce a car and sell it across the globe. We don't even make a lousy pair of gym shoes. Why sugarcoat the truth? Though we can't change the color of our skin, we can sure change the color of our thinking."

Through their words and deeds, the financial elite have proven that wealth is not a function of the matter or physical resources we can measure but of the ideas, action steps, and behavioral patterns we can't calibrate or quantify.

Law of Control

If you asked a handful of men or women caught in the grips of a midlife crisis and barely making ends meet why they fell short of capturing their fair share of the American dream, you might be shocked by their responses. With regard to reaching clear and delineated financial goals, some would offer that they never had a chance, that fortune eluded their appeal. Or that they were held in check by circumstances; they lacked opportunities, contacts, connections, or proper schooling. Probably nine out of ten would sing this sad refrain or plead some similar excuse. Yet probabilities suggest that opportunity did visit these individuals more than once in their youth or adulthood, but they failed to see that wealth consisted of conducting their affairs in a prompt and professional manner.

As young adults, they failed to view every errand or chore as a chance to display a work ethic that exhibited promptness, energy, and professional behavior or their lessons in school as the cornerstone to lifelong success. They did not conceive that, during the demoralizing idle hours of leisure, yawning, and boredom that they wove into the fiber of their lives, others were seizing opportunities and improving the lives of their fellow man. They did not envision that their slipshod methods, their careless attire, and their negative attitude would hinder future success. As a rule, people who unlock the door of opportunity and make their mark in the world do so because they have found a way to elbow their way to the table. What others do and have done for them has no comparison to what they have done for themselves. The child who has been brought up in luxury and not obliged to work, whose talents and skills are never called into question, rarely walks through the door labeled "World's Richest." All too often the man or woman who is crowded out and even kicked out turns out while those who are pampered fail to come out. The habit of depending on the self, a determination to uncover inner personal resources, develops strength as well as wealth.

No, it is not opportunity, chance, luck, and influential friends that create abundance or prosperity. Wealth will always be found within the individual, or it will not be discovered at all. The golden opportunity that so many seek is completely within your control—just as the Creator planned.

A female respondent who launched a New York–based public relations agency views financial independence as a matter of self-sufficiency. Her early days in business were marked with struggle and self-doubt. But now, as she puts it, "I think I've got a handle on things." She represents a number of top-shelf clients and is highly sought after in her field. Still, wealth doesn't end here. There's an inner dimension involving spiritual growth, inner peace, and emotional stability. "Prosperity goes beyond the dollar sign," she states. It encompasses the total package—harmony, comfort, and emotional well-being. "I deal with a lot of people who society would label 'successful'—those who have all the outward signs or material trappings. In a few cases, I wouldn't be so quick to agree. While chasing the brass ring, inner control of their lives has slipped through the very hands of those we parade as models of success. There is only one success: spending your life in your own way."

When asked for her formula for wealth, a 50-year-old-plus female who goes to battle each day on Wall Street replied in rather traditional, objective terms: "Continuous hard work, stubborn determination, faith, and a fierce desire for independence.

"Is that all?" I asked.

"Sure, there's other factors," she replied, "but wealth creation, for the most part, doesn't deviate or vary its requirements. These are the four main qualities that have served me well throughout my career."

A highly successful Boston, Massachusetts–based entrepreneur struck the same note. She spoke meditatively about the sacrifices she had made in the process of launching her technology firm: "My struggle to outrun poverty has done more to develop my character than anyone will ever know. Had I been born with a silver spoon in my mouth, there would've been no necessity for me to work, to build, to dream, or to provide a much-needed service. As soon as I decided to step outside of my self-enclosed cocoon, I immediately began to benefit from the scope and breadth that wealth demands. And my story applies to my peers as well. Had the bulk of millionaires been born wealthy, we would still be in the Dark Ages. Our vast resources would be untapped and our cities underdeveloped. As human beings, we are wired to make our greatest effort and perform at our best while struggling to attain the desires of our heart." Although financial independence has not come easy, this self-made woman now clearly seems to be in charge of the direction of her affairs.

Isn't it strange that so many of our children—born and bred in the midst of luxury—who have always leaned on others, who have never been obliged to elbow their way to the table, and who have been coddled and fitted with crutches from infancy, void of the strongest possible motive for the development of their power, rarely develop in any aspect of life, whether financial or otherwise. Then consider how many immigrants—young, old; male, female; and nearly all poor—come to this country uneducated, ignorant of the language, friendless, and penniless and yet have risen to positions of distinction and wealth, putting to shame millions of native-born children who possessed every advantage of wealth, education, and opportunity but have never been heard from.

As a college professor, I see this scenario all day long. Consider one young man who arrived on these shores a short time ago on the lowest rung of the economic ladder but has already risen to a position of importance wholly unaided. He is a fine example of a self-educated, self-trained, and self-disciplined individual. He has brought out his latent qualities and strengthened his weaker traits. He has pruned out of his thoughts and habits those words and images that would embarrass his culture and hinder his progress. He has gained such momentum that there seems to be no limit as to what he is likely to become. His is an inspiring example of the possibilities in this country, one that explodes all excuses and myths of poor children who believe they have little to no chance of advancing in this world.

When asked for his thoughts, George Fraser, CEO of the Cleveland, Ohio–based *Success Guide,* a networking journal, took a page from the behavioral psychologist Abraham Maslow, who coined the phrase *internal locus of control.* Fraser says, "The happiest and most contented people are those in pursuit of their dreams or ideals. How would I define wealth or prosperity? I'm doing what I want to do. It's not monetary; it's not work; it's all of the above. Prosperity isn't measured in numbers, fame, or money—it's not a line drawn somewhere just above the million-dollar mark. Prosperity involves choosing your own destiny and living out your potential in your own way." Fraser discovered this definition and its meaning firsthand once he left an $85,000-a-year post with the United Way nearly 20 years ago to chase brighter rainbows.

Faith and self-help have built nearly all the grand fortunes in Black America. Education, capital, and contacts may indeed awaken and arouse you, and perhaps uncover hidden dangers along the way, but these qualities cannot move you a single step on the road to wealth and prosperity. It is your own legs that must perform this task.

A moving picture of belief, trust, and patience was that of Farrah Gray, who was buried in poverty and struggled with hardship for nearly

20 long years before capturing success and amassing his fortune. Many a man or woman facing a situation like his would have been depressed, daunted, and demoralized. But not Gray. On the contrary, he embraced his challenges, learned the difficult lessons that his circumstances taught, and persevered in the face of failure. How does a young man who grew up on the South Side of Chicago end up shaking hands with the president of the United States? How does a person who once lived in a car with his family get invited to spend Christmas at the White House? How does this young boy mingle with high-powered CEOs of Fortune 500 companies and make it onto the cover of *Black Enterprise* magazine at sixteen? The story of Farrah Gray's genius has been told many times, and the lesson is always the same. It is a tale of how Black millionaires reach their lofty status through a combination of ability, opportunity, and a heavy dose of faith. If your faith is of the right sort, it will sharpen your faculties, quicken your energy, heighten your self-esteem, strengthen your character, and provide clarity and meaning to your goals.

Born in 1984 to a single mother and the youngest of five children, Gray grew up in the projects of Chicago dreaming of the day his entrepreneurial wings would take flight. That day didn't take long. Precocious and easily bored, at age six, he began pursuing his pot of gold by peddling door-to-door homemade body lotions and his own hand-painted rocks as bookends and paperweights. Gray was hooked when he earned his first dime. One year later, he decided to forecast his future by printing business cards that read "21st Century CEO." By age eight, hoping to create an entrepreneurial explosion, Gray launched the Urban Neighborhood Enterprise Economic Club on Chicago's South Side; it became the forerunner of the flagship organization he opened on Wall Street at the ripe age of 15—the youngest ever to do so. As a child, Gray constantly questioned adults. He vowed not to be in the same position as his mother—working like crazy from job to job with little to show for it. While his mother couldn't give him much in the way of material possessions, she did give her son a strong faith and a deep sense of curiosity. "He wanted to know everything about everything," his mother recalled. "No subject was off base, especially money. Regardless of the topic I explained as best that I could and, when I couldn't, I told him to go figure it out for himself." With no one to guide him but his mother and his faith, Gray became the perfect example of the self-made man.

"As to how I reached my financial goals," Gray told me and a New Orleans audience, "some people call it conscience, but I prefer to call it the voice of God. If you listen and obey it, then it will speak loud and clear and guide you with little obstruction. But if you turn a deaf ear, or disobey, then that voice will fade out little by little leaving you in the dark. Your life depends on heeding that still small voice."

I sat in attendance at the gathering as Gray doled out in a constant stream advice and counsel as to how anyone could attain a seven-figure income:

1. *Don't give up on your dreams: Great ventures start with small ideas. Don't be afraid to experiment; keep your eyes open, your mind working and your body ready for work. There's no need to hit a home run your first time out, but you will never hit a home run if you don't learn to swing. I only made nine dollars on my first "business," but it was probably the most important nine dollars I ever made.*

2. *Sacrifice is necessary for long-term success. I've taken pride in celebrating my food-stamps-to-finance journey. Some people don't like to talk about being poor. I don't mind, it keeps me grounded. I'll never forget what it felt like to be an elite member of the "have nots." I understand weeping, and I understand joy. Whatever I've achieved is due, in part, to any number of sacrifices that I have rendered.*

3. *Hard work and persistence pay off. The wealthy work harder and sleep less than average men and women. But because they're passionate regarding their chosen field, they're less likely to view their labor as a chore. In the annals of success, we see the same story: We are told that it is lesson after lesson with scholar; brick after brick with the mason; crop after crop with the farmer; painting after painting with the artist; and note after note with the musician that secures what so many desire. Never take "no" for an answer.*

4. *In the words of my grandmother, "Qualify to justify." Give others reason to support you; prove yourself worthy. The best reasons are honesty, integrity, respect, and a strong work ethic.*

Finally, one of the nation's top Black contractors—someone who has built and controls real estate developments from New York to Phoenix, Arizona—offered a common sentiment. Whether it was delivering newspapers, working on the family farm, or mowing lawns, Black millionaires don't just fantasize about becoming wealthy, they exercise their faith and begin the long slow march toward their future. "The greatest task that anyone can perform," he shared, "is to make the most out of the resources you've been given. This is wealth, and there is no other. Prosperity comes not from doing the *impossible* but by doing the *possible* every day. We only need to perform single acts of success each day in order to create a prosperous life."

NEW RULES OF MONEY

How is wealth created and maintained by seemingly "average" men and women with few special skills or talents? What do the wealthy do on a consistent basis? What disciplines have they developed or followed that allow them to achieve their dreams? Over the course of my research, I've stood toe to toe with hundreds of Black millionaires, and I've found this constant trait: They hold fast to an abiding faith.

All too often, those who hunt for wealth and abundance never find it. For example, many of the most profitable gold and diamond mines were abandoned time and again before their hidden wealth was discovered by the more persevering and faithful prospectors. Dissatisfied with superficial drilling, these men and women ventured down into the very core of the earth until they found their treasure. As a result, they became enormously wealthy while other miners, who quit, surrendered, or wandered from claim to claim, never giving their time or energy to a single stake or exercising enough faith in their possibilities to dig deeper, died in poverty. Millions of down-and-out men and women held possibilities that would have made them leaders in the field of commerce and industry, masters in their chosen endeavor; multitudes of employees could have become employers. Instead, they grow complacent while struggling in inferior positions all because they lack the *faith* in their ability to move to the front of the line.

The channels by which Black millionaires reach their financial goals are clear and straightforward. When your thoughts are clearly and confidently centered on a desired outcome, all that is good and right will be drawn to you by your own thinking. This is the spiritual law of the universe that you will encounter as you hope to join the financial elite. While some might believe that suggesting that thought controls every aspect of your life is too simplistic, constantly check your habits as well as any self-limiting beliefs. Each of us is a living magnet, constantly attracting results, people, and circumstances that are in accord with our thoughts. Financially speaking, you are where you are because of your past deeds, actions, and thoughts. I believe you have been drawn to this book by the aforementioned mental laws. It could just be that *The Wealth Choice* is an idea whose time has come in your life. People never reach heights above their level of thought and belief. By controlling your thoughts, not only will you transform your own life and financial condition, you will begin to impact the lives of those around you. As of this moment, you need only to step out on faith.

After a decade of heartbreak and disappointment, setback and defeat, playwright and producer Tyler Perry may have said it best when he emphasized the third law of wealth—Believe in Thyself When No One Else Will. When asked how he rose from living in a car on the streets of New Orleans to become one of the highest-paid filmmakers in Hollywood, he unapologetically leaned on his faith. In a nutshell, Perry said, "Nothing but the grace of God. You must never stop believing."

MILLIONAIRE LESSON NO. 4

When you make up your mind that you are done with poverty; that you will have nothing more to do with it; that you are going to erase every trace of it from your appearance, your manner, your speech, your actions, your home, your associates; that you are no longer going to tolerate poverty or put up with it; that you have charted a new direction—centered squarely on competence and independence—and that nothing on earth can turn you from your goal, you will be amazed to discover a newfound power replete with confidence, reassurance, self-respect, and prosperity. Resolve within that wealth is your divine destiny.

FOUR

TO THINE OWN SELF BE TRUE

FIND YOUR UNIQUE GIFTS

The Fourth Law of Wealth

Don't follow where the path may lead. Go instead where there is no path and leave a trail.

—Ralph Waldo Emerson

CREATING AND BUILDING ONE OF THE FASTEST-GROWING technology firms in the country—a company that currently nets more than $200 million per year in sales and has been valued at more than $1 billion—not only required Amos Winbush III to master the fourth law of wealth but forced him to call on and utilize gifts and talents that he never knew he possessed. Barely 30 years old, his business acumen and savvy have earned him numerous awards, including *Entrepreneur* magazine's 100 Brilliant Companies award and *Inc.* magazine's 30-Under-30: America's Coolest Young Entrepreneurs.

Ironically, it took Winbush less than two years to sense that a college degree was not for him. Although he enjoyed the collegial atmosphere and his business management classes at Louisiana State University, climbing the corporate ladder and dancing to someone else's drum was less than appealing. After dropping out and moving to New York, what began as a hobby soon became his main source of income. If his last name sounds familiar, it should: Rhythm and blues singer Angela Winbush is a cousin. Most of Amos Winbush's family found fame and fortune in the recording industry, and, in 2007, he was poised to do the same, landing a record deal after releasing a series of promising singles. But before his music career could advance any further, fate would play a role.

During a recording session, Winbush noticed that his iPhone had gone completely black, resulting in the loss of critical information and contacts. Frustrated and with nowhere to turn, he spent the better part of a week trying to recover the lost data. The experience led him to quiz other cell phone users as well as their mobile carriers. Baffled that no one had addressed what he believed to be an avoidable problem and angry that his mobile provider had not warned him of such a possibility, an idea was spawned. "I could barely sleep," he recounted. "I literally dreamed about launching a company that would solve an industry-wide problem. The next morning I called my business manager and asked 'How do I start a tech company?'"

Winbush was intuitive and had a keen instinct for making technology user friendly; his creativity as a musician also served him well. After consulting with a software engineer and a host of technology developers, Winbush took the plunge and bootstrapped his company out of his Manhattan apartment. With limited funding and no office, his small team worked from home and local coffee shops. Over the course of the next five years, Winbush skirted bankruptcy and began to frame what would become one of the hottest technology start-ups: CyberSynchs LLC. His goal was to design and build a universal wireless platform that allows users to store, synchronize, and transfer electronic data on the Web to and from virtually any media device—including cell phones, cameras, and personal computers—regardless of where the data are generated. The CyberSynchs Web service is accessible worldwide and stores subscribers' contacts, text messages, voicemails, notes, photos, videos, ringtones, calendar content, GPS, and e-mail. Moreover, even if the device is broken, lost, or destroyed, users who have synchronized their mobile data with CyberSynchs can access their information. Although the company began with mobile synchronization only, the synchronization of all electronic devices will soon be available.[1] Upon agreement, users can download an application that will send their content to a secure account. This technology allows information to flow among operating systems, manufacturers, and cellular networks. Hoping to avoid the experience of so many Silicon Valley start-ups that never made it beyond the new venture phase, Winbush seized the rare opportunity to partner with major high-tech firms, such as Sun Microsystems and Samsung, which enabled CyberSynchs to expand its market penetration exponentially.

Not only does CyberSynchs continue to ride the crest of almost uncontrollable growth, but the future for this innovative firm is full of high-tech possibilities. For example, the company will soon release a product that integrates software into televisions and allows users to avoid purchasing hardware. As of this writing, this New York City–based firm boasts 30 employees and more than 60 million users worldwide. Amos Winbush has been highly successful in executing his pathbreaking idea. But what can you learn from his example? During a personal interview, this young, hard-driving innovator quickly pointed out the key:

> It was only by chasing my dream, overcoming obstacles, and pursuing this course to the end did I ever realize that I had a gift for leading a team and motivating others. I'm not your typical high-tech chief executive. I launched my firm at the height of the recession. We were the ultimate bootstrap company with limited capital and no office. My employees worked from home and, if necessary, we met in local midtown coffee shops. I was forced to wear a number of hats: from staffing, to designing software, raising capital, forging key corporate partnerships, and strategic planning—all of which required me to polish my communication and financial skills, qualities that lay dormant within my personality. At the end of the day, I had to fight for my dream and demonstrate that I could manage a fast-paced technology company.
>
> So to aspiring small business owners, I suggest that you tap into your inner reserves and search inside to find your true gifts, your unique talents. Not everyone possesses the ability to navigate life without a paycheck. I don't care if you earn $5 a week or $5,000—regardless if the economy is on an upswing or ailing—you must look inside and ask "What is my purpose? What are my true gifts? Never allow what you *can't do* to stop you from doing what you *can do*."

Like his peers, Winbush adheres to the two qualities shared by nearly all successful men and women:

1. They know who they are. They possess a keen sense of what makes them tick; they understand their own motivations, and most have mastered the difficult task of deciphering their unique gifts, talents, and abilities. They know that personal assessment is the first step to amassing great wealth.
2. They are obsessed with playing to their strengths. In short, they are driven by tightly crafted goals matched only with the discipline and skill set to achieve their objectives.

The difference between the haves and have nots does not rest with possessions or lack thereof. *No!* Their disparity can be found in their individual talents and abilities as well as their goals and what each group is willing to do to attain them. How can you apply this fundamental truth? By understanding that *you* are different and then by capitalizing on your differences.

THE IT FACTOR

You can sense a special something in the skilled self-confidence of corporate rainmakers such as Ken Chenault of American Express, Ursula Burns of Xerox, or Rita Mack, a Black woman who at the height of her corporate career left a cushy job to seek her destiny under McDonald's Golden Arches. Three franchises later, Mack's nimble fingers rest on the switch of the most powerful economic engine within the Black community: the National Black McDonald's Operators Association (NBMOA). As chief executive officer and chair, Mack oversees the mission of the 37-year-old organization while ensuring the success of McDonald's 1,400 African American franchises and supporting the communities that they serve. This is no small task. The revenue from the NBMOA franchises exceeds $3.2 billion. Mack's very presence exudes self-assurance. "The main business of life," she mentioned during an Atlanta, Georgia–based focus group, "is not to do but to become."

We saw it in the early 1990s in R. Donahue Peebles, at that time a powerful player in real estate development in Washington, DC. As told by a writer at *Inc.* magazine, while on a family vacation in

Miami, Peebles decided to purchase and renovate the majestic but aging Royal Palms, a 417-room resort at the end of South Beach's tony Ocean Drive, an undertaking that would require six years to finish. This project allowed Peebles to break new ground—the Royal Palm Crowne Plaza became the first Black-owned resort in the United States. And just as important, the project cemented Peebles's reputation as an aggressive and politically savvy businessman and one of the most powerful real estate brokers in South Florida.[2] Today, Peebles's Atlantic Development Corporation portfolio includes hotels, apartments, and office space in Miami Beach and Washington, DC, in addition to 13 acres of prime Las Vegas land adjacent to the famed Encore casino. As a result, Peebles's corporation is the largest African American–owned development firm in the nation, with real estate holdings valued at approximately $500 million. But for those of you who hope one day to replicate Peebles's success or at least to conduct business with this real estate mogul, I offer the following advice: His strategy and personal philosophy are even more aggressive than the facts suggest. Peebles's strength of character as much as his smarts has made him successful. It's a combination of hard work and good judgment and having the disposition to go with your call regardless of whether it's popular. "I take being a minority businessperson as a responsibility," he shared with me during an interview. "My grandfather was a doorman for 40 years at a Marriott hotel in DC. I'm the product of a single mother who worked as a secretary during the day and pursued her real estate license at night. I make it my business to provide opportunities to minorities and women, both of whom are underrepresented in my industry. But all too frequently people come up with excuses as to why they can't succeed. They say it's too difficult, and they relinquish their goals before they have a chance to fulfill them. I could have made a lot of excuses in my career, but the number one ingredient to financial success is to focus on the task at hand. Though each of us is gifted, unfortunately, some of us fail to open our gifts."

LIVE THE LIFE YOU WERE DESTINED TO LIVE

I personally felt *it* the moment I shook the hand of John Hope Bryant. In 1984, the celebrated social entrepreneur was a homeless teenager living out of the backseat of his car. Eight years later, he was running a successful financial services firm with 40 employees and a $5 million budget. But soon it would all come to a screeching halt. In 1992, although Bryant's life finally seemed under control, his beloved city—Los Angeles—was ripped apart by racial strife due in part to the Rodney King verdict. After the violence and chaos subsided, Bryant saw that his community was not only in shambles but desperately needing a hand up, not a handout. More than willing to fill the leadership void, Bryant solicited the support from bankers, investors, and corporate America— basically anyone who was interested in rebuilding South Central Los Angeles. Refusing to ignore the pain and horror each new day brought, he launched Operation HOPE, an organization dedicated to providing just that, hope—uplifting the economically disadvantaged while broadening the financial empowerment in those declining areas through increased fiscal awareness. The organization's primary mission was to connect those areas hard hit by the riot to private-sector opportunities. No stranger to hard work, Bryant went knocking on doors attempting to secure financing for those whose businesses were damaged or destroyed or financing would-be entrepreneurs who dreamed of launching new enterprises. Since inception, Operation HOPE has served more than 1.2 million individuals, raised more than $500 million, while creating 1,000 new homeowners within those areas affected by the riot. As of this writing, this economic good Samaritan is sought the world over for his leadership and ability to transform once-blighted and neglected communities into wealth-creating and stable oases of hope.

These examples both frame and illustrate the essence of the wealthy mind-set. The wealthy are driven by the skills and unique talents like those of John Hope Bryant—gifts that wipe out disappointment and embolden the heart for future conquest; abilities that encourage and motivate as well as provide direction. The Black financial elite have an internal drive for self-discovery. They operate under a sense of urgency and a passion for achievement. Anyone who desires the key to joining the seven-figure club and enjoying all that life has to offer should clutch these profiles to his or her heart. By choosing to define life on your terms, you take the first step toward success. But *you* must *choose*.

Unfortunately, so many of us awake each morning with dread in our hearts and fear in our minds. We face the monotony of another day with its hopeless toil and ceaseless pressures. More and more of us are being hammered into a lifestyle we cannot endure, cannot afford, or can barely tolerate. We have forgotten one of the basic tenets of the prosperous life: We have been given dominion over this world. We each chart our own course. It was never the intention of our Creator to chart a course for us. That would place us all under His bondage. Instead, He bestowed on each of us talent and gifts and the ability to think and envision our own way in any manner that we choose.

But the key is *choice.* Bryant had no doubt that the jury in the Rodney King trial—a court case that would infuriate so many in our nation—would return a "guilty" verdict. He believed that, between the national media and the irrefutable videotaped evidence, it would be impossible for the verdict to *not* be guilty. As it turned out, Bryant was mistaken, but he refused to allow the verdict and its violent aftermath to destroy his essential optimism; to the contrary, the riots gave this visionary the impetus to start an organization focused, literally, on providing hope for the future.[3] With regard to our lives, each of us has been given options. We need not spend another day in poverty, self-pity, or fear. Why is there so much needless pain and grief? Why are there so many unnecessary failures? The answer is obvious. A maxim states: "Success in life comes not from holding a good hand but playing a poor hand well." Too many of us have never dared to find our talents, strengths, and gifts. The indigent who guide their pushcart through the alley to gather bottles and aluminum cans will remain between the shafts of their rickety cart as long as they believe that they lack the talent for anything else.

Why have we permitted the plague of doubt, fear, and poverty to infect us? Why can we cure some of the most dreaded diseases, circle distant planets, transplant human organs, and even create life in a test tube and yet make so little progress in elevating our opinion of ourselves and our many talents?

To underscore the above, Bryant used the following analogy:

If I gave a homeless man $1 million, the odds are three to one that within one year, he would be broke and homeless once again. Unfortunately, so few understand that his problem is not that he is *broke* but rather that he is *poor,* and there is a difference between the two. Being broke is a temporary economic condition, but being poor is a disabling state of mind and a depressed condition of the spirit, and you must vow to never be poor. The word *capital* is derived from the Latin root *capitis,* or, simply put, knowledge in the head. Consequently, if you are poor in your *thoughts and mind,* you will be poor in your *pockets.* The alternative is also true. If I can convince you that you are valuable, wealthy, important, and that you've been given a place in this world, and then equip you with the tools to succeed in this market-driven economy, then you will be given a real shot at opportunity and sustainable financial success. But you must be prepared when your moment of opportunity arrives. That means you must be twice as smart, twice as aggressive, twice as assertive, twice as creative and enterprising, and twice as talented. This is the only way that you can tip the scale in your favor. If you don't uncover your gifts, it's because you fail to realize that gifts have been given. To sum up, you don't get money—money gets you![4]

WHAT THEY TEACH AT HARVARD
BUSINESS SCHOOL

You may have read or heard of the Harvard study to be discussed in this chapter. It's worth citing as you dedicate both time and energy to designing the financial life you want to lead. In his best-selling book *What They Don't Teach You at Harvard Business School,* the highly regarded sports agent Mark McCormick noted a ten-year study conducted at Harvard University in the 1980s. In 1979, graduates of this renowned MBA program were asked to set clear goals for their future as well as specific strategies to accomplish them. After analyzing the data, only 3 percent of these graduates actually wrote their goals, 13 percent developed goals and objectives but had not committed their plans to paper, and 84 percent—aside from "a May graduation and enjoying the summer"—failed to set or clarify any goals at all.

Ten years later, in 1989, a follow-up study was conducted where researchers interviewed members of that same graduating class. To their surprise, they discovered that the 13 percent who set goals but failed to write them down earned, on average, twice as much as the 84 percent of students who had no goals at all. Furthermore, the 3 percent of graduates who set clear, specific written goals earned ten times that of their classmates. The only difference between the groups was the clarity of goals they had set (and spelled out) for themselves on graduation. In the context of this book, what does this study mean?

Black millionaires do what they do best. When I asked survey respondents to identify specific strengths, they were quite clear as to the skills, talents, and abilities they held in abundance. Moreover, they were aware that to excel financially in their chosen field and to find lasting satisfaction in doing so, they had to become efficient at finding, describing, applying, and utilizing their innate talents. In short, Black millionaires shift their focus and utilize any special gifts. Refusing to be miscast in their vocation, they shun any personal weaknesses or tasks that don't pique their self-interest no matter how minute or trivial and, instead, explore the intricate detail of their unique talent.

Throughout my focus groups, nearly three-quarters of respondents cited that they "strongly agree" with the statement "I am doing what I do best" in terms of their profession, title, role, or economic status. Practically speaking, here lie the two assumptions that guide the thinking of Black America's financial elite:

1. Each of us has been given talents and gifts that are enduring and unique.
2. Individually, your greatest opportunity for financial growth lies within your greatest strengths, talents, and gifts.

These two assumptions explain why Black millionaires continue to think outside of the box; with regard to their career and life's work, they break all the rules of conventional thinking. Realizing that no individual can be ideally successful until he or she has found his or her true place, they refuse to be a square peg in a round hole.

During the course of this research, I had the good fortune to hear Carla Harris, the managing director of global capital markets for the industry leader Morgan Stanley and one of the highest-ranking Black women on Wall Street, address a group of bankers, analysts, investors, and members of a little-known Black millionaires roundtable. Harris's words were typical of the motivating and insightful presentations that she has delivered to similar audiences throughout her career. A room full of ambitious, highly skilled wealth creators and their supporters eagerly awaited her remarks. Her delivery was fast and breezy, and it was tinged with her own personal down-home philosophy. I sat glued to my seat and watched her work her magic. The Wall Street vet grabbed the edge of the podium and leaned forward. Before she uttered a word, she shot her listeners the kind of stare an adult gives a child when he or she is about to explain one of life's innermost secrets. But instead of offering her assessment on the current state of the market or which blue-chip stock to buy, her words were centered on what I interpreted to be the bedrock of prosperity and abundance as well as the fourth law of wealth.

Surprisingly, this fourth law remains unknown to the masses as well as to most educators and the so-called learned among us. I urge you not to follow their example. For any number of reasons, they chose not to open this door. If they could, they would have done so. For example, though the possibilities of life are open to all, why do so few of my race manage to climb among the ranks of the wealthy, particularly in a country where financial independence is available to anyone who comes calling? Case in point, when reviewing the U.S. *Statistical Abstract*—a collection of statistics on social and economic conditions tabulated by the U.S. Census Bureau—I discovered that fewer than 3 percent of Black males 65 years of age and older boast incomes of $75,000 per year. Furthermore, more than 80 percent of all Black men 65 and older have incomes below $50,000 per year, and nearly 75 percent have incomes between $5,000 and $50,000. Today, the majority of men and women launch their working careers when they are in their twenties, often earlier. These individuals are fortunate to live in a free world—in the most open society on the face of the earth. Each person is given more than 40 years in their chosen line of work to make the grade financially. Yet, according to the data, very few do so. *Why?*

Conduct your own survey. Stroll through your neighborhood and ask your friends and family members two questions:

What are you doing to increase your current income?
How much money will you be worth at age 65?

Canvas your community—ask 50 men and women, 100, 1,000, everyone you know—until you are completely convinced that the reason that people don't earn more money, and the root cause as to why so few are financially stable as they approach retirement, is that they seldom, if ever, engage in any constructive thinking on either subject. To prove this analysis, ask yourself the same thought-provoking questions. Prior to reading this chapter, what were *your* plans for increasing your income? How much money do *you* want to earn? How much money have *you* decided to be worth by age 65? In your estimation, what does this question have to do with the fourth law of wealth?

The answer is simple. People who earn impressive incomes are not lucky, nor do they possess a monopoly on talent or ideas. Nor are they endowed with more intellect than their friends or neighbors. Most individuals who earn handsome incomes began in the same fashion as you and I. The only difference between those who earn large incomes and those who don't is that at some point the financial elite utilized this fourth law and made a conscious decision to change their lives for the better.[5] Those who have reached seven-figure status have been noted for their power of focus and concentration, which makes them oblivious to every challenge, circumstance, or roadblock. If you are to walk among the financial elite, you must alter your habits, refine your thinking, develop key relationships, embrace the unlimited possibilities that lie within your reach, and take control of your life. However, these basics alone will be of little value and will fail to place you within shouting distance of your financial goals. Without a fixed purpose—the ability to focus your faculties on one dominant objective—these attributes will be of little use in navigating the road to affluence. What prosperity demands, what millionaireship calls for, is the man or woman who, when opportunity knocks, can move immediately; who, when times are tough, turns neither to the left nor right; come hell or high water, can hang on as long as it takes; when they can't catch a break, can lay it all on the line; and when down to their last dime, can proceed on faith. These are the men and women who step to the front, who make their mark, and who earn millions in the process.

THE WAY TO WEALTH? LIVE
YOUR LIFE ON PURPOSE

By any measure, Carla Harris boasts an impressive resume: from bestselling author, to sought-after lecturer, gospel singer, and board director of eight nonprofit organizations. Harris, who squeezes those activities into a calendar that also includes her responsibilities as managing director for Morgan Stanley's investment management business, clearly is someone who understands how to concentrate—to stay focused and sane amid a multitude of claims on her time and attention.

If you wish to test whether this peak performer is capable of turning the *impossible* into the *possible,* just mention that she can't do something. Earn an MBA from Harvard? No problem. Become a managing director at Morgan Stanley Dean Witter, one of Wall Street's preeminent investment banks? Done. Record a gospel CD in the same year that she executes one of the largest initial public offerings (IPOs) in U.S. history? All that and more. To drive this point home, when Harris was a senior honors student at Bishop Kenny High School in Jacksonville, Florida, her guidance counselor advised her *not* to apply to any Ivy League schools. Not only did she apply to several, she was accepted to each institution and ultimately chose to attend Harvard University. When her mother wondered aloud how she and her husband would foot the bill for tuition, Harris responded, "I don't know, but I'm going." She worked her way through school to make it happen.

In Harvard's core economics course, a professor told Harris, then a freshman, that she lacked the aptitude for economics. "You can't think," he said dismissively. She, of course, promptly chose to major in economics and went on to graduate magna cum laude after producing a senior thesis of such high caliber that her paper is housed in Harvard's archives alongside the work of such iconic alums as John F. Kennedy, Jr. "It goes to show you," she said of the moment, "never second guess yourself. And never consider giving up. If there's something that you care about, don't give up; keep pressing on, and you will definitely reach your goal."[6] Count on Harris to defy the odds, whenever and wherever they're stacked against her.

Harris's name was first written in the annals of Black capitalism when she arrived at Harvard with the intention of pursuing law. The summer after her sophomore year, however, the economics major decided to take on an internship in investment banking, courtesy of Sponsors of Educational Opportunity, a mentoring program geared for minority students. "I fell in love with Wall Street," she recalls, "and the idea of taking on an enormous amount of responsibility at a relatively young age."[7] At Morgan Stanley, which she joined right out of Harvard Business School, Harris leads the equity private placements effort in global capital markets and covers the retail and consumer industry as well—only one of a few Black women to do so. In 1999, she managed the execution of the IPO for the United Parcel Service, at the time the largest public offering in U.S. history, with more than 100 million shares raising $5.47 billion in the process.

So what was the message that Carla Harris—the most powerful Black woman on Wall Street—shared with these wealth creators? What rule holds such a dominant position in the creation of wealth?

A CAREER IS WHAT YOU'RE PAID FOR, BUT A CALLING IS WHAT YOU ARE MADE FOR

Who is the most celebrated actor? Though some may disagree, arguably Denzel Washington, who would devote a lifetime, if need be, to refine his character. *Who is the greatest writer?* Many would cite Alex Haley, who gladly spent 20 years in an effort to find his race a home and deliver to humanity one of the world's seminal texts.

Who is the greatest entertainer and musician? Being ridiculed, mocked, and jeered couldn't dim Beyoncé Knowles's intense desire to use those gifts planted in her soul by the Almighty. For the better part of her childhood, poverty pinched her hard in her humble Texas home. Twenty years ago, no one outside of her tight-knit circle had ever heard of her name. For years she had toiled in anonymity, but at last her opportunity arrived, and she was equal to the task. Knowles had made up her mind that hers would become a household name. Although she had gone to various performing arts schools and participated in singing and dancing competitions as a child, Knowles rose to fame in the late 1990s as the lead singer of Destiny's Child, one of the world's best-selling female R&B groups. Following the trio's breakup in 2005, Knowles released her first solo album, which debuted at number one on the *Billboard* charts. Her third CD was released in November 2008 and included the immensely popular "Single Ladies (Put a Ring on It)," which earned her six Grammy Awards in a single year, the most honors ever won by a female artist.

Ask music lovers to count the most influential African American musicians of all time on one hand and most would say Wynton Marsalis long before they ran out of fingers. It has been said that Beethoven probably surpasses all other musicians in his painstaking fidelity and persistent application. There is scarcely a bar in his music that was not written and rewritten at least a dozen times. This is also true of Marsalis. Talent, it has been said, is simply the constant desire to practice.

Who is the greatest athlete? Take your pick. But remember it was Michael Jordan who was required to shoot more than 300 jump shots each day after he was deemed unfit to join his junior high school basketball team. Oblivious to everything outside of his goal, in little more than a decade, Jordan would guide his college team, the University of North Carolina, to the National Collegiate Athletic Association championship before capturing the title "world's champion" six times in the professional ranks. With all the vigor and tenacity in his nature, Jordan concentrated on his ambition, and the world has seen the result. Those who know him best have stated that his entire soul was focused on acquiring a championship ring.

There is no grander sight than that of a young man or woman endowed with a great talent dominated by a single purpose marching straight to his or her goal. Defeat only gives them additional power, opposition only doubles their effort, dangers only increase their courage. Regardless of what comes—whether sickness, poverty, or disaster—they never turn their eyes from the objective: to use their great gift and to monetize their talent. It is the discovery of your personal strength that not only gives meaning to life but adds value to your bank account. Say what you will of genius, the fact remains that no amount of intellect has ever won out unless it is reinforced by the nerve to overcome the obstacles that appear. Was not John H. Johnson the son of a domestic; Herman Cain, of a chauffeur; Willie Gary, of a sharecropper; Shawn Carter, of a clerk; Stanley O'Neal, of a farmer; Bob Johnson, of a factory worker; David Steward, of a mechanic; and Michele Hoskins, the great-great-granddaughter of a slave who didn't win her freedom until age 13? Affluence demands—no, requires—that all who seek to join its circle be guided by the inspiration of a great mission to lift them beyond an ordinary life. Again I ask: *Have you discovered the elusive fourth law?* Here's another clue.

"Why do you lead such a solitary life?" an admirer asked of Mary J. Blige. "Performing on this level leaves little room for anything else," was Blige's short reply. "This art form requires my entire soul. It's the one thing that I do." Blige dropped out of high school one year short of graduating. Her mother urged her to work in the coastal seafood industry near her Savannah, Georgia, home earning minimum wage like so many of her peers. But her love for music could not be suppressed. Nature had locked in her spirit a treasure that eventually would bless millions.[8]

Blige's future may have played out in a numbingly predictable—and bleak—pattern of poverty and hopelessness had she not tapped into her early years of singing in her Pentecostal church. Years later, she recorded a cassette of Anita Baker's "Caught Up in the Rapture," which she played for a friend. That friend happened to be Sean "Puffy" Combs, then a producer for Uptown Records. Moved by what he heard, he signed Blige to his label in 1989. She was 18 years old. Today, Mary J, as she is affectionately called, continues to gain momentum as an R&B artist, capturing multiple Grammys, American Music, and *Billboard* Music awards. Her latest album, *Stronger with Each Tear,* sold more than 330,000 copies in its first week. As of this writing, she still works, still tours, and has ventured into acting. And she has no desire to slow down. Coasting is not a part of her DNA. "I can't," she states emphatically. "I just can't. It would be selfish to coast. I didn't go through so much hell to coast."

As chronicled by a *Fortune* magazine article, in 1962, Harvey C. Russell did what no other Black man had done before. He became a vice president of a Fortune 500 company. The firm was Pepsi-Cola, and Russell, then age 44, had been a standout salesman in its "Negro Sales Department." But widespread rejoicing did not greet this milestone and Russell's eventual financial windfall. When it caught wind of Russell's promotion, the Ku Klux Klan called for a national boycott of Pepsi products. The group flooded the country with handbills that read, "Don't buy Pepsi-Cola and make a nigger rich."[9] Undaunted, Russell knew that history is full of such examples. Fortune smiles on those who roll up their sleeves and pursue their calling regardless of what others may think, say, or do. What would force this skilled marketer to risk life and limb? Adept at product placement and blessed with the gift of gab, Russell knew that the pursuit of any vocation other than sales would be akin to being a fish out of water.

Frustrated by her inability to find beauty products that met her needs, in 1990, New York native Lisa Price began adding oils and fragrances to unscented lotions. Although she held a lucrative position as a writer for the immensely popular *Bill Cosby Show*, she knew she didn't belong there. Other ideas burned inside of her. Price continued to experiment with her concoctions and eventually began producing a limited line of items for family and friends. She could have easily focused her time and attention on her writing career in such a sought-after and visible field, but when this talented screenwriter saw an opportunity for financial freedom, she ran with it. When word of her products spread and demand grew, Price began marketing outside of her inner circle. After taking her moisturizer and fragrance oils to a church flea market, Price sold out in a matter of minutes. For the next nine years, her apartment was packed with inventory including jars, labels, lotions, and creams.

Her business began as a modest mail-order operation in 1999, but Price soon opened the first Carol's Daughter store, named in honor of her mother, in Brooklyn's Fort Greene neighborhood. It was her mother, Carol, who had urged her to turn her hobby into a business. Soon magazines such as *Essence* and *O*, the Oprah magazine, featured her products, and celebrities such as Halle Berry, Angelina Jolie, Shawn Carter (Jay-Z), and Jada Pinkett Smith became loyal customers. The following year, Price was named the National Black MBA Association's 2000 Entrepreneur of the Year and received *Working Woman* magazine's Entrepreneurial Excellence award. "I'm not special," Price admitted. "I wasn't born with a lot of money. I'm just an average woman who listened to the universe when it told me to believe in myself. Your most important task is—and will forever be—to stay focused and uncover your talents and gifts. At the end of the day, you will be the individual who will breathe life into your dreams."[10] Maintaining her focus paid off when an advertising executive caught wind of her spirit and brokered deals that placed Carol's Daughter, which includes more than 300 products for the face, hair, and body, in Dillard's, Sephora, and Macy's department stores as well as the Home Shopping Network. Price's company is now a multimillion-dollar business with seven stores and 85 employees.

HOW ONE MAN WAS DRIVEN TO USE HIS GIFT

Seven years ago at the National Black MBA conference in San Diego, California, I shared the dais with one of America's most prolific motivational speakers. For years, Les Brown has inspired and ignited audiences around the globe. It has been said that Brown's message resonates because he sprinkles warmth, humor, hope, and much needed information into every presentation, especially in a society that is void of such values.

I, like the nearly 300 conference attendees, was perched on the edge of my seat as this world-class orator shared his story. Once Brown grabbed the microphone and began to work his magic, everyone within ear-shot of his voice was hooked. Within a forty-five minute period, he took his listeners to the source of his roots and how he was driven to use his gift. His tale began six weeks after his birth in the loving arms of his adoptive mother, Mamie Brown, the only parent Les and his fraternal twin brother Leslie have ever known. Mamie Brown, a 38-year-old single woman who worked tirelessly as a cook, maid, and nursing home caretaker, raised her two adopted sons in a two-bedroom shotgun house on the outskirts of what is known as Liberty City, one of the poorest sections of Miami, Florida. "When she took us in," Brown explained, she had no idea as to how she was going to support us. She wanted a family, and she proceeded to do whatever it took to clothe and feed us. She was a woman of tremendous determination and courage."

But Brown's story does not end there. He spoke in glowing terms of the one individual who is equally responsible for his success—Mr. LeRoy Washington, a high school speech instructor. Admittedly, as a child, Brown was a poor student. Though he possessed a quick and sharp tongue, written material was beyond his grasp. Moreover, because of his hyperactive nature and poor classroom performance, as early as the fifth grade, the Miami school system labeled him "educable mentally retarded"—a burden and stigma that not only weighed heavily on his spirit but forced him to flounder throughout his grade school years. Mr. Washington was not only the drama and speech teacher at Booker T. Washington high school, but he was a figure of note. He prided himself on finding and developing character and talent in his students.

From the moment Les Brown met Mr. Washington and heard him speak, a seed was planted. He wanted to become one of Washington's star pupils. One day, during a speech class, Brown was asked to step to the blackboard and diagram a sentence. When Brown responded that he couldn't because he was classified as educable mentally retarded, his teacher stopped him in his tracks. "Don't you ever say that again,"

Washington demanded. "Someone's opinion of you need not become your reality!" This event was the turning point in Brown's life.[11]

"Most people die broke because they fail to uncover their true calling. They drift from one idea to the next, and, as a result, they set their aim too low. They stop dreaming, growing, believing, pushing, and striving. In this global economy, that mind-set is no longer an option. Each of us must begin to understand that either we expand or we will be expendable. Although I was humiliated that my teacher shared my shortcomings with my classmates, I was liberated. Mr. Washington looked at me with the eyes of Johann Goethe, who said, 'Look at a man the way that he is, he only becomes worse. But look at him as if he were what *he could be,* then he becomes what *he should be.*' A seven-figure income does not require IQ," Brown told his audience, "only 'I will.'"

In that one moment, Mr. Washington forced Brown to realize that there is something special inside of each of us, a basic goodness that we must choose to manifest in every possible way. "Thanks to my mother and, later, Mr. Washington, I grew up with the conviction that I was going to be somebody. Where my peers may have envisioned only a life of minimum wage or even life on the street, I dreamed of greatness. And those dreams propelled me to pursue my gifts."[12]

Les Brown has a dream, and he is living it. In 1986, broke and sleeping on the cold linoleum floor in his office, he began to pursue a career as a motivational speaker. By the early 1990s, he was one of the highest-paid public speakers in the nation. His company, Les Brown Unlimited, Inc., generates millions of dollars per year from his speaking tours and the sale of motivational products. Brown's audience is wide—from Fortune 500 companies, to assembly-line workers, to prison inmates, to special education classes. His mission is to promote a message that will help others become uncomfortable with mediocrity. "A lot of people are content with their discontent," Brown explains. "I want to be a catalyst to enable the average man and woman to see themselves having more and achieving more."[13]

"In order to do something you've never done," Brown pointed out,

you've got to become someone you've never been. Financial independence is a choice, not a destiny. Each of us has the potential to reach our monetary goals, but reaching those goals is up to you. Had I not lost my job in broadcasting as a disc jockey, I would have never experienced a remarkable string of events. I would've never run for the Ohio Legislature. I would've never pursued the goal and dream of becoming a talk show host. I would've never seen myself as an individual who could make a difference in the community. My advice to all is to shoot for the moon, because even if you miss, you'll land among the stars.[14]

It is men and women like Les Brown, who trample on impossibilities; like John Barfield, who don't wait for opportunities but make them; like Cathy Hughes, who keep at it when others give up; like Chris Gardner, who, when faced with disaster, turn neither to the left nor the right; like Michele Hoskins, who, when others drop to the rear, lean on the well-worn scripture "According to your faith be it unto you"; and like Carla Harris, who, during her moment of truth, as she stood before admirers, colleagues as well as college students, when asked for the key to wealth and prosperity, openly shared, "I am really no different than you. I may have made more money than you, but money doesn't really explain the difference. Everything that I've achieved during my career has been the result of knowing my particular strengths and talents combined with precise goal setting strategies and discipline. I have learned long ago from those far more wealthy than me that goals and objectives are great, but understanding your gifts and purpose is imperative. If you follow this simple plan, financial success will take care of itself. This is the theme that I live by; this is the one thing that I do. When you get excited about life—life, growth, and money will get excited about you." Here again is the fourth law of wealth: Regardless of the difficulties, no matter how unpromising the circumstances, Black millionaires are drawn by an irresistible impulse to the vocation for which they were created.

FINANCIAL ADVICE FROM THE MOST POWERFUL BLACK WOMAN ON WALL STREET

On the surface, Carla Harris's remarks may sound like simplistic mother wit that you tell others after you've already banked your first million. But Harris is sincere. She loves what she does, and she genuinely believes that her reputation as one of the most successful Black women operating in the capital market arena is due to her ability to carve out a role that plays to her unique strengths. But surprisingly, her talents are not those you might expect to see in a successful investment banker. Today's global marketplace is fast paced, extraordinarily complicated, rife with internal politics, and, at times, less than moral. Therefore, you would think that the individual best suited for this environment would be blessed with urgency, operate with a take-no-prisoners approach, and be skeptical regarding the motives of both potential clients and investors.

Harris cannot claim any of these strengths. By all accounts she is patient, compassionate—trusting of other people's motives—and deeply spiritual. So how does she succeed? Like so many of her wealthy peers who are both successful and fulfilled, she found a way to cultivate the talents and gifts that she does possess and put them to work. With a disdain for wasted time, she turned her natural patience into long-term goal-setting plans of action—a skill that is sorely needed on Wall Street. "One of the keys to *long*-term financial success is to think *short* term," she explained during an interview. "At the beginning of each year, I list my goals in two columns. On the right, I state the type of person I want to be; and on the left, I list more definitive goals, such as 'to generate $50 million in revenues within this calendar year.' Furthermore, every day I prepare a to-do list that I know will undoubtedly change throughout the course of the day. Any change will eventually impact my week, months, and year. It is only in this manner that I am reminded that the future begins this very moment. That is an aspect that you cannot lose sight of in this business. Millionaires never ask 'if,' they only question 'when.'" Next, she put her trusting nature to good use by developing key relationships both inside and outside of her company, relationships that have blossomed into a bevy of high-profile IPOs, including Martha Stewart Living Omnimedia, Burger King, and Digitas.

If patience and compassion figure into Harris's work, so, too, does a good measure of faith.

If you had asked me 22 years ago what drives you, what makes you successful, I would've been unable to answer your questions. My faith was there, but I wasn't conscious of it nor did I know how to call on it. Understanding the source of my power—all power—and how to call on it and harness it and use it is the greatest lesson I've learned. I learned it through trials and errors, through hitting a wall and questioning myself; through losing my confidence and then regaining it; and through realizing it was the prayers, it was the faith, it was the expectation of achieving my goals that got me through. That's why, every year, at the top of my to-do list is my objective of establishing a deeper abiding faith. Because every year I learn a little bit more about how powerful I can be with Him out in front.[15]

Carla Harris has used her patience, compassion, and spiritual approach since she first walked through the doors at Morgan Stanley. She has honed it, perfected it, and stuck with it even when superiors and colleagues called her management style into question. Her distinct outlook is the cause of her professional and financial success and, to hear her tell it, also the cause of her personal happiness. She is a world-class investor and capital markets player because she deliberately plays to her strengths and utilizes her gifts. In this sense—and perhaps this sense alone—Harris is correct: She isn't any different from you and me. Her story is relevant not because of what she has attained but because she has uncovered laws and lessons that can serve as practical guides for each of us, specifically the have nots among us. The majority of millionaires in this study realized early in their careers that they possessed certain talents and gifts as well as limitations. They accentuated their own positive traits, talents, and innate skills. Moreover, they refused to permit what they *couldn't do* to interfere with what they *could do*—what they were uniquely gifted to do. Nearly every member of the financial elite in this study was quick to uncover his or her strengths and eventually capitalize on his or her niche while minimizing any shortcomings. As one survey participant was quick to state, "We may be born equal but, thankfully, each of us different. And here lies the starting point to success. It's a lot easier being you than trying to be someone else. I found my niche. I selected a vocation based on my abilities, aptitude, and strong desire to become financially independent. No amount of positive or wishful thinking can make you something that you're not." Another member of the seven-figure club made a play on words and said, "I decided long ago to live my life on *purpose*." And yet another respondent adeptly summed up this chapter when she stated, "A career is what you are paid for, but a calling is what you are made for."

Best-selling author and magazine publisher W. Randall Jones dispels a host of myths regarding wealth and success and offers new evidence in his book *The Richest Man in Town*. He reflects on Andrew Carnegie's well-worn refrain as being only somewhat true. In 1889, Carnegie, the steel magnate, wrote, "There is a power under your control that is greater than poverty, greater than the lack of education, greater than all of your fears and superstitions combined. It is the power to take possession of your mind and direct it to whatever ends you may desire." Jones goes on to share that while each of us may possess incredible personal powers as well as an optimistic, can-do spirit, our potential is limitless only when we find and use those powers to identify our talents, strengths, and purpose. Wealth creation is predicated on finding your perfect niche.

Prosperity does not dictate *what* you should do, but it does demand that you do *something* and that you excel in your efforts. There is no grander sight than that of people in their right place struggling with might and main to make the most of what nature has provided, determined that not an ounce of their potential should go to waste. Go to the bottom if you aspire to reach the top. Be master of your calling in all its details. "Study yourself," wrote Henry Wadsworth Longfellow, the nineteenth-century poet, "and most of all, note well wherein kind nature meant you to excel."

THIS ONE THING I DO!

This one thing I do! Oh, the power of a great purpose. Does anyone doubt that such a mighty resolution adds power to the ordinary man or woman or that it inspires individuals to accomplish what they've undertaken? Neither ridicule nor caricature—neither dread of enemies nor desertion by family and friends—can shake the indomitable will of the man or woman who can mouth such a statement. No two words in the English language stand out any bolder than "I will." Strength, power, faith, and trust characterize their delivery. These words speak to you of triumph over difficulties, of victory in the face of discouragement, of lofty and daring enterprise, and of unfettered aspirations. Just as a photographer could never capture the elegance of Naomi Campbell or Tyra Banks on paper with an unsightly image in his mind, so, too, the ending balance in your checkbook will never be greater than your self-confidence, than your ability to execute your plans. The ability to set specific goals with clear plans of execution has created more millionaires than any other trait, and it has changed the face of the world.

This age of specialization calls not for the merely educated or for the talented or the jack-of-all-trades but for men and women who have been trained to gather their abilities and complete a task as well as it can be done. Mere energy is not enough, and education is of little value unless it is concentrated. In the game of life, the most mediocre students will often outstrip valedictorians simply because what little ability average students possess are focused on a specialized skill. Scholars, replete with college degrees and heads full of knowledge—and impressive resumes—never concentrate their powers. As a result, the scholars never find their way. They lack individuality; they are absorbed within the masses, lost in the crowd, weak, wavering, and drawing an average day's pay for an average day's work. What is more common than the unsuccessful genius or average men or women with commanding talents? Unrewarded genius has become a proverb. Hundreds of thousands of educated and talented men and women are now labeled down and out.

HOW THE WEALTHY DISCOVER THEIR GIFTS

What are the questions we constantly ask the rich? *Where do you live? How big is your home? Where did you attend school? How did you earn your millions?* We naively assume that the answers to these questions will explain or provide the root cause of their financial success. Within the countless biographies published every year, not to mention the tabloid journals that circulate throughout mainstream media, the story line is always the same: Our unassuming hero is a hardy soul born of modest means and, by virtue of his own grit, hard work, and fired by a lofty purpose, fights his way to wealth and riches. Let me assure you that these oversimplistic explanations of wealth creation are sorely lacking. The rich and powerful who find their names written on biographies and tabloids may seem to have accomplished their dreams independently of anyone else. But, in fact, they are, according to Malcolm Gladwell's *Outliers,* "invariably the beneficiaries of hidden advantages and extraordinary opportunities that allow them to make sense of the world in ways that others cannot."[16] Yes, which side of the tracks we are born on does make a difference, as does who our forebears were and the type of legacy they left. Furthermore, many times the lack of a formal education and household income is a constant. But asking the wealthy where they live, what type of car they drive, or how they earned their money is not enough. Answers to those questions are fairly useless. Only by asking what their unique strengths and gifts are and how they uncovered those talents do we begin to unravel the critical difference between the haves and have nots.

Valerie Daniels-Carter stood her ground and fought every step of the way over obstacles that would have stifled lesser people to build her $95 million franchising empire. She had been part of the Burger King fast-food chain for only two years before her ability was recognized and her place conceded. Whoever is armed with a dominant purpose is an army of one. But, fortunately, the Creator is the judge and jury in this game of life where only the most focused and fittest prevail. In 1982, Daniels-Carter left her banking career for fast food when Burger King created a program to attract more diversity to its franchisee ranks. Convinced that she belonged in this arena, she jumped into the business with her brother, John, a Harvard law school graduate who was more than pleased to stay on the sidelines and serve as an investor and advisor. Today, they own and operate 113 restaurants throughout the Northeast and Midwest regions, including 36 Burger Kings, 68 Pizza Huts, 6 Auntie Annie's pretzel bakeries, and an assortment of Coffee Beanerys and Häagen-Dazs ice cream parlors that have made the siblings owners of the largest black-owned fast-food holding company in the United States. She has also become a fixture in her community, so much so that the Green Bay Packers football team elected her to its board of directors, making her the first African American female to hold such a position. Daniels-Carter's rise in the industry is due to her two-pronged approach that never waivers: identify your talents and gifts, and play to your strengths.

Although many watched her corporate career with interest, Daniels-Carter had other plans. Prior to launching V & J Holding companies, she spent nearly ten years in finance, first as a management trainee at First Wisconsin National Bank (now U.S. Bank) in its retail and commercial lending department, and then at Mortgage Guaranty Investment Corporation (MGIC) as an auditor in the underwriting division. While there she began to connect the dots. Mergers and acquisitions had become the rage, which undoubtedly meant that corporate downsizing would not be far behind. Before someone else could determine her fate, Daniels-Carter decided to make her move. Nearly two years later, in 1984, after completing her MBA, she was ready to strike out on her own. Together, she and her brother invested in a single Burger King in the heart of downtown Milwaukee. A combination of personal savings, investor contributions, proceeds from the sale of her car, and a bank loan provided the duo the $900,000 in start-up capital that made the deal possible. After enrolling in the franchise's store management training program, she immediately rolled up her sleeves and went to work. One year later, the team used the profits to add another store before buying four more franchises in 1987.

Daniels-Carter's entry into the fast-food industry was hardly a spur-of-the-moment decision. Driven by an intense entrepreneurial spirit, she had been mapping out a plan to run her own shop since the beginning of her college career. "Banking and finance," she told me, "provided a strong foundation so that I could piece together a business plan, learn the ins and outs of financing, and understand how to create a long-term strategy. While climbing the corporate ladder, I made a conscious decision to enhance my skill set. My brother suggested the fast-food industry, and we researched a number of opportunities before arriving at Burger King. I eventually knew that one day I would operate my own business."[17]

Initially, succeeding in a difficult business and in her hometown of Milwaukee, Wisconsin, which lacked an encouraging environment for minority business development, seemed daunting to Daniels-Carter. And falling into two categories—Black and female—would be not only a test of endurance but a trial that required her to match responsibilities and tasks with strengths. Even today, with the demands on her time—an overcrowded schedule that frequently begins at five in the morning and often extends past nine at night—and with more than 3,500 employees and annual sales that are swiftly approaching $100 million, you would think that she could easily lose sight of what she does best and be pulled into numerous directions. Not so. Daniels-Carter does not need to shift her focus in order to play to her strengths. Instead, like Carla Harris, she remains true to what she already knew about herself, despite many temptations to change tack. Daniels-Carter continually carves her role in order to capitalize on the gifts and talents that became apparent when she was a child of five. The company training director and a close friend who has known her boss for more than two decades remembers growing up in Daniels-Carter's neighborhood. "We were interested in dolls, but not Valerie. She was busy making Kool-Aid and selling it up and down our block. She could get her brother to rake leaves and *she* received the money. Later, she started a business walking neighborhood children home from school for a modest fee. That early entrepreneurial drive, along with an MBA, has served her well."[18]

Carter-Daniels emphatically states her secret in a nutshell: "There is nothing standing in your way to do what you want to do provided *you know what you want to do.* You must come to grips with what you want and what you are capable of doing. *What's your passion?* Will you be an employee or employer? Owning a business isn't for everyone. Not everyone can tolerate 18-hour workdays. Each of us must take a look inside and identify our strengths. Decide what fits your personality, skill set, and God-given directive. Odds are you will never be broke, unsuccessful, or unhappy when you find your true place. But your heart must be in your business, and your business must be in your heart. Fortunately, I knew what I was designed to do: serve others." If the current generation of African Americans who find themselves struggling against cruel circumstances to make their mark could only understand that 90 percent of what is labeled as genius is merely the result of persistent, determined industry as well as the exploitation of a single strength, they would inch even closer to prosperity and reach their financial goals. Unfortunately, millions of have nots flit about from one occupation to another, from one business to another, from one trade to another, pursuing one idea today and another tomorrow; rowing upstream, chasing someone else's dream because it was the "proper thing to do"; or choosing a career simply because a friend, family member, or associate instructed them to do so. When you attempt to pursue that for which you are unsuited, not only will you neglect your strengths but you will fall prey to your weakness, and any chance of wealth and prosperity is diminished because you are out of place. I urge you to follow your bent. If you wage war against your aspirations, you will surely lose.

There is a sense of power in the spirit of the individual who has reached the point of efficiency, the tip of productivity, the place where his or her skill and prowess adds to the bottom line. It is here where those who will eventually be categorized as wealthy begin to work in harmony with their purpose. The fourth law of wealth obligates men and women like Lisa Price, Carla Harris, Les Brown, and Valerie Daniels-Carter to—once they uncovered their unique gift—move immediately, fight it out as long as it takes, devote themselves to a single financial goal, live hand to mouth if necessary, and not care about the opinion of others.

THE DIFFERENCE THAT MAKES THE DIFFERENCE

Eddie Brown took a little longer than Daniels-Carter to uncover his calling, but he found it nonetheless. He struggled to get there, but he knew his "right place" rested in the world of finance. One of Black America's most successful investors discovered one of the top tenets of wealth creation: *Know thyself.*

There's a huge difference between possessing a gift and being truly gifted. Your ability to attain and amass wealth does not depend on innate powers regardless of how talented or gifted you may be. On the contrary, it is your willingness to exercise your faith, persevere, and, above all, be diligent and engaged in your pursuit of your financial goals and objectives. These qualities and these qualities alone make up the it factor. Each of us must search within to answer three critical questions: *Why are you here? What is your strength? And what is your unique gift?* This exercise is not as simple as it seems. Recognizing our true strengths also means highlighting what we lack and relinquishing perhaps unattainable and unreachable dreams. With regard to Brown's financial prowess, consider the following quiz, which serves as a frame of reference for his talents and gifts.

What if the bottom fell out of the stock market and, as a result, your portfolio plunged by 10 percent in a single week? What if one stock, in particular, had seemed like a sure bet when you bought it last month? The company markets a product that consumers need, is well managed, and boasts a consistent track record of growth until it missed the latest Wall Street earnings expectations and dropped like a brick.

Would you:

1. Sell it and question yourself for buying the stock in the first place?
2. Sit tight and do nothing until you recover your loss?
3. Smile and purchase more assuming that everyone else is dead wrong?
4. Study and reconfirm your assessment of the company, then buy more?[19]

If you answered 4, you and Eddie Brown are probably kindred spirits. This shrewd investor is renowned for his ability to uncover stocks that increase in value even when it seems as if the sky is falling and the market is in decline. This strategy has not only helped him become one of Black America's wealthiest and most generous philanthropists, but it has also made him the most watched and emulated investor outside of Wall Street. And while he is perhaps one of the leading authorities on managing risk and mutual funds, he built wealth for himself and others by keeping things simple and sticking to his knitting, hallmark traits that undergird Brown Capital Management, the investment firm he founded in 1983.

Although his company offers an array of mutual funds that require a minimal investment, foundations and pension plans must meet a $5 million requirement in order to garner his service.

At first glance, there is little reason to think that Brown Capital, specifically its founder, Eddie Brown, is one of Baltimore's wealthiest—regardless of color or ethnicity—and one of Black America's richest. To set the record straight, Brown is a self-made man. Born in 1940 in Apopka, Florida, then a small rural town 13 miles from Orlando, Brown was raised in a world where your food was fried and everyone you knew was Black and Baptist. His mother was 13 years old and unwed, so her parents raised Brown as their own. His grandparents lived in a one-story frame house without hot water or indoor plumbing. The Great Depression still had its hands around the throats of struggling Blacks in the South, and Jim Crow's iron heel remained firmly planted on the necks of Black men and women throughout the region. Almost intuitively, his grandmother sensed that her grandson was smart and restless; besides, she wanted to show him there were better ways to earn a living than raising plants and picking oranges. Orlando offered a slew of opportunities, and the warm-weather resort town exposed the young boy to life far removed from dusty roads and farms, a life where businessmen handled daily affairs dressed in suits, starched shirts, and ties. "If you go to school," his grandmother coaxed, "and get a good education you, too, can sit behind a desk and wear a white shirt and a tie."[20] Even then, Brown loved school and dreamed of being the first in his family to attend college.

Brown's grandmother died when he was 13. Unable to care for him, family members sent him to Allentown, Pennsylvania, to live with his mother, who by then worked as a domestic. Although Brown's grades were stellar, instructors at the local high school tried to convince him that college was beyond his reach. Driven and locked on every word, this one-time shy boy graduated among the top in his class a year ahead of schedule before enrolling in Howard University, where, four years later, he would gain a degree in electrical engineering.

After a stint in the army, Brown took a job with IBM while attending graduate school at night. Once he received his MBA, he left the technology firm and shifted careers. He worked for a small money management boutique in Columbus, Indiana, and then, in 1973, he found himself at T. Rowe Price, the global investment powerhouse. It was there, at Price, where Brown realized his strength. His career switch from engineering to finance was an easy transition. He said of the move, "Engineering was very significant in my career preparation. What I gained in terms of analytical skills and rational thinking translates well into the investment world."[21] Brown worked with a team of money managers who invested hundreds of millions of dollars for corporate pension plans, endowment funds, and foundations. A colleague who worked with Brown for nearly a decade in the trenches stated the obvious: "He's smart as hell and he keeps his cool under fire. He's a perfect fit for this industry."[22]

My interaction with the Black financial elite reveals the same wealth-producing habit that holds true regardless of vocation—from former teachers to accountants, from one-time fashion models to electrical engineers who may have found themselves toiling in obscurity behind a desk for a Fortune 100 high-tech company: The millionaire's key to wealth lies in his or her ability to discover and organize strengths in order to apply gifts and talents. Brown's strength and temperament lie at the heart of his company's balance sheet. A tireless researcher and an unshakable optimist, he peers into the future partly by attempting to calculate the current value of a company's expected future cash flow. As a result, his expertise as a savvy investor rests in his uncanny knack to identify companies with a good chance of continuing their success 25 years down the road. Not only is he exceptional at his chosen line of work—Brown Capital boasts $6 billion in assets—but he is a steady and calming force in an environment rife with chaos and uncertainty, a quality he learned at the feet of his grandmother as she tended the orange groves on her family farm in central Florida.

This profile reveals a precious secret that's most effective if uncovered by you, the reader. Eddie Brown had a specific plan, and he conditioned his mind so thoroughly that nothing was going to block him from making his mark. By age 42, he had reached the pinnacle of his corporate career. At industry leader T. Rowe Price, he flourished. He was promoted to vice president and received bonuses paid in stock options in addition to a handsome salary. But in spite of his success, he was well aware of his unique gift and held a vision of striking out on his own. The individual who knows where he or she is going and is determined to get there will find or make a way to arrive at his or her destination.

NEW RULES OF MONEY: FORGET PASSION, FOLLOW YOUR STRENGTH

For more than two hours, I sat in Steve Harvey's spacious corporate office north of Atlanta, Georgia, and listened intently as the actor, comedian, talk show host, entrepreneur, and best-selling author explained how he came face to face with the fourth law of wealth. At the least likely of moments, Harvey—an innocent nine-year-old child at the time—stood in his fourth-grade class and, without an ounce of timidity, shared his goal of one day starring on television. And what was the response? Ridiculed by his classmates and chided by his teacher, a young and impressionable Steve Harvey bore the brunt of jokes for the balance of the academic year. Twenty-nine years later and with an ever-expanding fan base as well as a career that has yet to plateau, the joke is no longer on him.

The youngest of five children born to a homemaker mother and a coal miner father whose life was cut too short because of black lung disease, Harvey left college short of a degree as well as direction. He spent his early twenties working at a number of jobs—from insurance salesman, to letter carrier and even professional boxer—without finding anything remotely linked to his true calling.[23] In 1985, after performing stand-up comedy for the first time, he eventually found his gift. By honing his craft through years of thankless engagements in small obscure clubs, he came close to hitting the big time by the end of the decade, advancing to the finals of the Second Annual Johnnie Walker National Comedy Search. From there, Harvey's career took off. In 1993, he served as the host of *Showtime at the Apollo,* the famed syndicated talent show produced at the legendary Apollo Theater in New York. Three years later, he was approached by a cable channel teetering on the edge of bankruptcy, the WB network, with the idea of headlining his own sitcom: *The Steve Harvey Show.* Geared toward an African American audience, the show also created a unique bond between Harvey and a younger comic, Cedric Kyles—nationally known as Cedric the Entertainer—who played Harvey's best friend on the show and later joined him on a groundbreaking national stand-up tour.

The tour, aptly titled "The Kings of Comedy," featured Harvey, Cedric the Entertainer, Bernie Mac, and D. L. Hughley. Together, this four-man barnstorming road show became a nationwide hit. In 1999, The Kings of Comedy became the nation's highest-grossing comedy tour, raking in more than $19 million. Harvey and his three sidekicks became national celebrities, a status only heightened by the release of Spike Lee's documentary, *The Original Kings of Comedy,* which captured highlights of a two-night show in North Carolina before a hugely enthusiastic audience. The film, which cost only $3 million to produce, earned more than $38 million at the box office.

In 2000, in the face of much industry-wide skepticism, Harvey launched a daily talk radio show, *The Steve Harvey Morning Show.* After initially testing in Los Angeles and Dallas, the show eventually gained national syndication and a New York City flagship. It now airs weekly, reaching nearly 9 million listeners in more than 60 markets nationwide. As Harvey's radio show heated up, one daily feature called the "Strawberry Letter" caught fire. Cohost Shirley Strawberry would routinely read a letter from a female listener seeking relationship advice. She and Harvey would then offer their thoughts. Though Harvey was quick to confess that he never pretended to be a behavioral expert, he leaned on his experience from numerous failed relationships and decades of mistakes to inform with his brief but amusing commentary. A publisher soon pitched him to write a relationship book. Skeptical at first, Harvey knew that such books are a dime a dozen. But his book, *Act Like a Lady, Think Like a Man,* was a revelation. Growing out of a segment on his radio show in which he served up hilarious advice to women callers frustrated in their relationships, the book laid out clear-cut advice, providing women with insight into a man's mind. While critics dismissed Harvey's advice as little more than a collection of overblown stereotypes, fans took to his comedic approach to self-help for the lovelorn.

"When I first wrote this book," Harvey shared, "people laughed. 'What does he know?' They countered. 'He's a comedian!'" With his radio show as a promotional tool, he was able to sell thousands of copies before word of mouth fueled more sales. Oprah Winfrey heard of the book and gave him her sizable platform. By the end of 2009, Harvey had sold more than 2 million copies, and perceptions shifted. He wasn't just a comic, now he was a relationship advisor.

The dramatic story of Steve Harvey's fierce determination and quest to find his unique gift is a perfect illustration. His example is not just impressive in itself but valuable as a metaphor. Arguably one of the wealthiest individuals in his industry, Harvey knows a thing or two about finding your calling, identifying your gifts and talents, and leading with your strengths. His point is clear: "I wanted to be on television since I was nine years old but I didn't make it until I was 38. When my classmates laughed at my dream, it wouldn't be the last time that skeptics would doubt my talent and abilities. But I'm here now. Make your own choices before life makes them for you. Decide now to utilize your talents and gifts. Lose the misconception that you cannot be anything you set your mind to. Instead, lead with your strengths. When I look back over the course of my career, I know there was nothing else I was born to do. I was made to lift the spirits of others, and television and radio were the media that allowed me to do it. It took a while, but that's what I do. I really can't imagine doing anything else."

If you truly desire it, the revelation in this chapter can mark the turning point of your life. You've been entrusted with God-given gifts, and now you have been commissioned to do something far from the ordinary. If there is any doubt that you were born in order to create wealth, I suggest that you abandon it at once. If you are going to possess a new future, you need a new beginning. If you are going to realize a new destiny, you will need a point of origin. Your progress toward wealth and prosperity begins with the self-assessment that follows. Failure to address these questions has proven to be a major stumbling block for the have nots. Study and complete the exercise. Look within, and try to identify your strengths. As you engage in this effort, do not allow any self-limiting beliefs to cloud your thinking or sabotage this activity.

- What will be your legacy? What will be your crowning moment? What is your life's purpose?
- What were you born to do?
- What is the dream or vision that sets the course for your life? Share the one idea that you will definitely pursue.
- What do you wish to occur within the next five years? What will you accomplish?
- Where will you be financially?
- What keeps you up at night? What gets you out of bed each morning?
- What are your skills, talents, and gifts? Why are you unique?

Where are you going? The fourth law of wealth is the starting point of all financial success as well as the stumbling block for those who fall short of the mark. Each of us desires the finer things in life— fame, fortune, and respect—but few go beyond just hoping and wishing for them. The easiest thing to do, whenever you fall short of the mark, is to blame lack of ability or circumstances for your misfortunes. The easiest thing to forget, especially when fate has been unkind, is that you were *born to succeed, not fail.* Unfortunately, our nation has a growing number of individuals who have already sold themselves on the idea that they just don't measure up, that they just can't cut it. They are already dead in spirit, aimlessly parading through life with no sense of meaning or purpose. You will never rise above your level of belief and self-esteem. Decide where you are going; begin from where you stand. If you know what you want, if you are determined to get it to the point that it becomes an obsession and you back that obsession with continuous effort and sound planning, then you have awakened and stirred the coals of this most important law. And if your name is to be found on the roll of our nation's Black millionaires, it is *you* who must identify and utilize your gifts and talents. It has been written that a fish cannot drown in water, a bird does not fall in air, and each of God's creatures must live in his or her own true nature. Success in life comes not from holding a good hand but from playing a poor hand well. Perhaps Shakespeare said it best: "To thine own self be true."

Now, have you found your calling? If so, you have completed the fourth step to financial fulfillment.

MILLIONAIRE LESSON NO. 5

Millionaires understand that they possess innate talents and gifts. They accentuate their positive strengths and skills. They refuse to permit what they can't do to interfere with what they can do—what they are uniquely gifted to do.

FIVE

HOW MAY I SERVE THEE?

The Fifth Law of Wealth

Dr. King and I integrated the lunch counter, but we never integrated the dollar. And to live in a system of free enterprise, and yet not to understand the rules of free enterprise, that's the definition of slavery.

—Andrew Young

MARTIN LUTHER KING, JR. WAS NOT A WEALTHY MAN— at the height of his career spearheading the civil rights movement, he never earned more than $10,000 a year. At age 35, King was the youngest person to receive the Nobel Prize. When notified of the honor, he announced that he would give the prize money—$54,123—to further the cause for justice and equality. Nonetheless, like so many of the financial elite profiled within this study, King was more than aware of the force and logic behind the fifth law of wealth.

King was in many ways an unlikely leader of an unlikely organization—the Southern Christian Leadership Conference, a loose alliance of 100 or so church-based activist groups. At the time, he had neither the quiet brilliance nor the sharp administrative capabilities of Roy Wilkins of the National Association for the Advancement of Colored People (NAACP). He had none of the corporate contacts or business connections of the National Urban League's Whitney Young. He did not have the sharp tongue of James Farmer of the Congress of Racial Equality, the youth and raw militancy of John Lewis of the Student Non-Violent Coordinating Committee, or the bristling wit of best-selling author James Baldwin. Furthermore, King did not make his mark in sports or entertainment, where so many people of his race have long been prominent. Nor was he an imposing figure. In his stocking feet, he was five foot seven inches tall, and he weighed barely 170 pounds. His dress? Conservative at best. He owned six suits—four black and two gray. Although he wasn't much of a social butterfly, after graduating first in his class from Pennsylvania's Crozer Theological Seminary, King could converse with the best of them on the social impact of Thoreau, Hegel, Kant, and Gandhi. But all that would soon change.

In the early evening of Thursday, December 1, 1955, a Montgomery, Alabama, City Lines bus rolled through Court Square and headed for its next stop in front of the Empire Theater. Aboard were 24 Black riders, seated from the rear toward the front, and 12 Whites, seated from the front to the back. At the next stop, six Whites boarded the bus. The driver, as he was trained to do, walked to the rear and asked Black riders to vacate their seats. Three complied, except Rosa Parks, a seamstress and secretary for the local chapter of the NAACP. "I really don't know why I didn't move," Parks later explained. "There was no plot or plan. I was just tired and my feet hurt." Parks was arrested and, in due course, fined $10 for violating Alabama state law.

Overnight Parks's encounter flashed throughout various Black neighborhoods: *Support Rosa Parks—don't ride the bus Monday.* Parks was not the first African American rider to break the law in this way, but for some reason, this incident triggered the frustrations of Montgomery's disenfranchised Black community. Countless African Americans had suffered worse indignities, but hers was the single act that the South would long remember. In Montgomery, 80,000 Whites generally believed there was no problem with the 50,000 Blacks who lived within the city's boundaries. Working mostly as farmhands or domestic servants for $15 to $20 a week, Blacks who called Montgomery home had neither geographic nor political unity. However, within 48 hours of Rosa Parks's arrest, mimeographed leaflets and handwritten signs were posted and distributed in every nook and cranny within the Black community, calling for a one-day bus boycott. That Monday, Blacks walked, rode mules, drove horse-drawn buggies, and traveled to work in private cars. The hastily organized boycott was more than 99 percent effective and took a toll on Montgomery's bus line before economically crippling this vibrant southern city.

On the day of the strike, some two dozen Black ministers decided to push for continuance of the boycott. Their original demands were minor: (1) Blacks would still be seated in the rear, but seats would be handled on a first-come, first-served basis; (2) Blacks would be treated with courtesy, dignity, and respect; and (3) Black drivers would be hired to navigate routes throughout Black areas. To direct the protest, the boycott committee soon became the Montgomery Improvement Association (MIA), and it selected Dr. King, a 25-year-old preacher from Atlanta, Georgia, to lead the organization.

MARKETING 101

Looking at King's game plan, one would think that the young minister was a polished entrepreneur bent on closing one big deal after another. After his morning coffee, a glass of orange juice, and an hour in prayer and meditation, King made his way to his office at the Dexter Avenue Baptist Church in Montgomery. Once there, his first stroke of business was to draft a sophisticated marketing plan—akin to a full-scale product launch—focused on sharing the story of the boycott not only in Montgomery's local juke joints and pool halls but across the nation as well. To measure his reach, King immediately called a state-wide meeting where more than 5,000 followers offered to help. With that type of support, he quickly shaped a network where 200 volunteers offered the use of their cars, and nearly 100 pickup stations were positioned along frequently used routes. Church and mass-meeting collections kept the improvement association afloat, but King took his message global by tapping supporters as far away as Europe, India, and the Far East. In less than one year, he raised nearly $600,000. But fundraising was only part of the picture.

At every turn, King orchestrated and outmaneuvered Montgomery officials. For example, when city and state authorities went to court in order to freeze MIA assets, King had funds scattered around the country in out-of-reach northern banks. With a sound cash flow, he bought 20 new station wagons earmarked for the car pool and had the vehicles insured by Black insurance agents backed by the financially stable Lloyd's of London. He doubled his staff to keep up with increased communication demands, pounding out nearly 100 letters and press releases daily. Much like a Madison Avenue marketing executive attempting to craft a precise message, King insisted that whoever marched with him had to wear their Sunday best. That was the image he wanted splashed across the airwaves and collective conscience of America: peaceful, law-abiding Black Americans, as they walked home from church, being hounded and harassed by Whites armed with rifles and water hoses and barely restrained vicious dogs. It wasn't long before that picture began to take hold. Mimeograph machines in the cramped headquarters worked around the clock. By now, the MIA agenda had spread to include voter registration and equal employment. And, if this were not enough, with ever-increasing funding, King and his staff created a credit union before considering a savings-and-loan association to provide capital for Black businesses and sorely needed mortgages for would-be Black homeowners who were denied traditional financing outlets.

Fourteen months after Rosa Parks sat down, a race stood up; Black patrons, the city's number one consumer group, had made their point. Dr. King and his team met with a slew of lawyers and city officials in Montgomery's administrative offices to announce the end of the boycott. The MIA was jubilant, Whites breathed a sigh of relief, and the young leader turned marketing strategist made the cover of *Time* magazine.

That evening, December 21, 1956, Dr. King addressed an emotionally charged church gathering where he admonished his followers not to gloat but to take their victory humbly. "We've come a long way, and we've got a long way to go," he told those in attendance. "I would be terribly disappointed if any of you go back to the buses boasting." Then he began to share a biblical verse that serves as the cornerstone to his ministry: "It is not this way among you, but whoever wishes to become great among you shall be your servant."

It is my hope that this story of the man who is now immortalized in stone will be used as a reference point regarding the impact of the fifth law of wealth. I share this historical tidbit not to analyze King's marketing or organizational prowess—though his management skills are worthy of emulation—but to show how he used the fifth law to literally change the racial, economic, and political direction of our world. By now, you should have a deeper understanding of the fundamentals of wealth and prosperity. It should be encouraging to note that the fifth law is well within reach of those who care to embrace it. It is by this method that you can transform the little that you possess into much. *How?* By thinking differently; by not only serving others but by adding value. We live in a world where products and services are no longer marketed; the art of marketing *is* the product or service. In other words, if it is wealth that you seek, begin to make a difference in the lives of others. When you do, you are well on your way to building your fortune.

HOW THE FIFTH LAW OF WEALTH
BUILT A MONUMENT

In 1983, four fraternity brothers sat around a cluttered kitchen table debating the finer points of what was thought to be an improbable idea—whether a Black man would ever be memorialized in the nation's capital. Over the next three decades, the fraternity—Alpha Phi Alpha—to which that Black man, Dr. Martin Luther King Jr. belonged—battled government commissions over location and design, kicked in $4 million in good-faith money, and led a public campaign to justify why King deserved a place in the most revered section of the National Mall. Just when it appeared as if the project would collapse, a beacon of hope broke through the clutter.

In 1996, the U.S. House of Representatives passed Joint Resolution 70 giving the fraternity the green light to build the memorial. Although the fraternity was overjoyed, Congress still doubted that the organization could complete the project. As one member who was close to the negotiations recalled, "They were saying 'Here's the plan, here's the site, now go raise $120 million or you're going to be the folks who failed. Your credibility is on the line.'"[1] Watching from the sidelines with checkbook in hand were executives from General Motors. Moved by the idea of a memorial to Dr. King, the automotive giant promised $10 million if the fraternity could identify someone to spearhead the project. That task fell to Houston, Texas, attorney and businessman Harry E. Johnson. Despite a preacher's zeal and personal charm, the project that Johnson and his colleagues initially thought would take no more than 18 months lasted nearly a decade.

Once in place, Johnson leaned on the practices and skill set that enabled him to develop several million-dollar businesses across the country. He quickly put to rest any debate as to why King deserved his place among America's most esteemed leaders. "We don't build memorials to men," Johnson explained to his critics, "we build monuments for the ideals they shared. I was eight years old when Dr. King gave his 'I Have a Dream' speech. As a child he taught me that anybody could lead because anyone can serve."[2] Next, Johnson quickly galvanized a team and set out to attract major corporate sponsors. He rallied VIPs around the potential site, stood for interviews, shook hands, and forged partnerships. For nearly ten years, before the first shovel of dirt was lifted, Johnson pushed and pitched, all in an effort to sell the memorial.

"When you're starting off," Johnson pointed out, "and you approach corporations or individuals, and you mention 'Hey, we really need your help,' the response sometimes resembles, 'Yeah, right, come back later.' Those are the moments when you begin to think, 'All right, nobody really believes this is going to fly.' But I never went in asking for a handout. My entire approach centered on making a difference as well as promoting Dr. King's values. I told each donor that their support was a gift to the world. King was more than an African American—he was a global citizen."[3]

"Or, when you must convince a potential donor that Dr. King really deserves a spot on the Mall," Johnson continued. "When you've got to convince people, it's really disheartening. This should not be a hard sell." But corporate convincing was an integral part of his campaign. Thankfully, Johnson weathered all of the initial complaints—from the selection of a Chinese sculptor, to the depiction of the image, to the accuracy of Dr. King's quotes.

Eventually he pulled in sizable donations from Boeing, Ford, Tommy Hilfiger, Coca-Cola, and Exxon Mobil. The logos of 89 companies and foundations are prominently displayed on the project's website, and million-dollar contributors are listed on a donor wall. But Johnson worked just as tirelessly to receive small checks from average Americans across the country. When millions of people visit the King

Memorial, they will see listed the names of multibillion-dollar corporations. But they will also see the names of churches that sacrificed funds for something that is bigger than their local congregation and community. "The King Monument," Johnson explains, "was financed by average men and women, Black and White, who felt compelled to give a $70 gift."

On October 16, 2011, as the world watched, the national memorial to the iconic civil rights leader—48 years after King delivered his "I Have a Dream" speech—was dedicated. The historic moment was the pinnacle of Harry Johnson's decade-long effort. Over the course of time, millions of visitors will reflect on the controversial likeness of the man, his legacy, and the significance of the first non-president—and the first African American—immortalized on the National Mall. But ironically, most probably won't know who built it. They will find little about the pivotal role played by the Black fraternity of which King was a member. The organization is more than a century old but largely unknown to those outside of the Black race. However, this matters little to the man who made it all possible, to the individual who stood motionless at the base of the site soaking in this once-in-a-lifetime experience. When asked how this day came to fruition, Johnson took a moment or two to set the record straight. I can now report that it wasn't Johnson's fundraising skills or corporate contacts that played a major role. Nor was it the team effort between Johnson and his beloved fraternity. Far from it. In his own words, Johnson revealed the force behind the fifth law of wealth: "At those very moments when I contemplated throwing in the towel and allowing someone else to handle the headaches, I thought about Dr. King. I mean here was a man who, when given a choice, didn't think twice. For my and future generations, here was an individual who chose to endure the beatings, undergo the hardship, turn a cheek to the degradation, put up with the indecency, tolerate the inequities, and withstand the oppression in order that I could possibly enjoy a better life. The least I can do is to try to make a difference—to try to leave this world in a better condition than what I found. I owe it to Dr. King to continue the struggle forward."

Of all the questions asked by those who dare to walk under the banner of millionaire, only a handful stand above the rest: *How will you serve your fellow man? How will you add value?*

CHANCE OF A LIFETIME

Have you ever considered the possibility of thinking in different directions? Think about how you could create something new—in your business or in your chosen vocation. Remember, nothing is done to perfection; nothing is final or complete. Regardless of what you desire, if it is in the realm of reality, you can obtain it through imagination and creativity and apply it to your line of work. Today, throughout the field of enterprise, nothing is being done the way it can be or will be done in the future. Change is the norm. The status quo is dull, boring, and obsolete. If you are to join the millionaires' club, you will be forced to add value—that is, thinking in different, bold, and unique ways.

Nearly one year ago, in 2011, during an entrepreneurship conference in the Bahamas, I shared the stage with Michael V. Roberts, the highly successful St. Louis–based real estate and hotel developer. Throughout our remarks, Mike and I intentionally emphasized the role that creativity and vision play in not only growing a business but in snatching opportunity whenever it exists. Once we concluded our presentation, the floor was opened up for Q and A. It wasn't long before a smartly dressed woman walked down the aisle and asked this question: "Given the current recession and the depressing state of affairs, what can a small business person, such as myself, do?" Since I relish the moments that I spend with the financial elite, I take every opportunity to soak up their insight and rich wisdom; this conference in the Bahamas was no exception. I quickly shifted my eyes in Mike's direction. His response did not disappoint. With regard to the process of sidestepping the routine and the status quo and adding value, his response quickly set the tone for the conference.

"For openers," Mike replied, "the current economic state is not depressing. Interest rates are super-low, industries are being reinvented, and the housing market is wide open. Right here on this tiny island, your countrymen and women have launched social movements, learned new skills, and built billion-dollar enterprises. Trust me, the current recession will end, and each of us will be forced to answer the question: *What did you do when interest rates were at their lowest in 50 years, when technology was going through the roof, when corporations were fighting over talented employees, and when society was searching for the next big thing?*

"I admonish you," Mike continued, "not to answer those questions like the average individual, who will be forced to say, 'I spent my time whining, waiting, worrying, wishing, and complaining,' because that seems to be the norm. We still live in a world that's filled with opportunity. In fact, we have more than an opportunity—we have an *obligation*. An obligation to spend our time doing great things, to find ideas that matter, and to share them. To push ourselves and the people around us to demonstrate gratitude, insight, and inspiration. To take risks and not only make our world better but make it amazing.

"Are these crazy times? *You bet*. So stop thinking about how crazy the times are, and start thinking about what the crazy times demand. There has never been a worse time for business as usual. Business as usual is sure to fail, sure to disappoint, sure to numb our dreams. The marketplace is searching for something exciting, something to feel passionate about, something to connect to. Those of us who live in the more enlightened part of the world are so fortunate. There is an entire world crying out for our gifts, our ideas, and our endless products and services. You get to make a choice. You can remake that choice every day. In fact, it's never too late to choose optimism, to choose action, to choose excellence."

I suggest that you heed the words of Mike Roberts and become a person of deep value. Take stock of yourself. What is the special mark that only you can inscribe? To walk among the Black financial elite—those who've earned seven-figure incomes—remember, wealth is not an amount, but a habit, an act, an attitude. If you expect to become an important figure in the world of commerce, I suggest that you devote yourself to the idea that anything can be improved. If you envy and admire your employer—his or her independence, financial power, freedom from restraint—it will pay you to inquire as to the methods by which he or she rose to this position. Perhaps you will discover that the ascent to financial well-being began when this wealth creator committed him or herself to do the right thing, at the right time, in the right way, and with the right people. In short, to be a problem solver and not a problem; to do what needed to be done, never waiting to be told what to do.

"MY FOCUS WAS TO CREATE AN ENTERPRISE THAT WAS BUILT ON MAXIMIZING SHAREHOLDER VALUE"

By his own admission, Robert "Bob" Johnson got into the cable television business through total serendipity. "To be honest," Johnson recalled during our interview, "I got the idea for BET [Black Entertainment Television] while advising a client who wanted to create a channel for elderly viewers. I said, Hmm, let me see. So I looked at his plan, and wherever he specified the term *elderly,* I altered and wrote *Black*. Black viewers comprise an impressive demographic. However, they are poorly depicted on television as well as the media." Amazingly, what Johnson has achieved since founding BET in 1980 has been based on anything but dumb luck. Armed with only a $15,000 bank loan and a $500,000 investment from cable magnate John Malone, Johnson created a 24-hour programming service aimed at the top television-viewing segment: African American viewers.[4] His idea began turning a profit in less than five years. By 1991, BET had risen to become the first Black-controlled company on the New York Stock Exchange. The enterprise later went private, before being sold to media giant Viacom in 2001 in a deal valued at nearly $3 billion. And, at the end of the day, Johnson was handed a $1.8 *billion* check while retaining his position as chairman and chief executive.[5] The move also made him one of the nation's first Black billionaires and provided the seed capital to launch a handful of ventures, from hotels, to banks, to a National Basketball Association team, all of which are led primarily—if not entirely—by Black executives. Not bad for a boy who grew up the son of two assembly-line workers and the only sibling among ten who would attend and graduate from college. How did this media mogul get his start?

In 1973, while working as a lobbyist in the cable industry, Johnson recognized the obvious need for increased cable programming. He understood that cable programming was going to be made available to the public, and he realized the limited offerings for African American viewers. Johnson resolved to make his move. This void in the cable marketplace was a large untapped market, and his solution was to create a new cable network: BET. But investors, particularly Madison Avenue, were skeptical. For years, the proverbial door was slammed in

Johnson's face, and he often walked away from meetings with potential advertisers on the brink of tears. By all traditional business rules, Johnson should have fallen on his face or failed to get his plans off the drawing board. From the beginning, he had little money, less marketing clout, no distribution channels, and an untested product. The toughest part of his plan, he discovered, was not securing capital but convincing reluctant advertisers of something that he already knew: Black America's wide viewing habits.

Johnson recognized that he had a huge task before him. He knew it was expensive to launch a cable company, so he began seeking financial support from industry contacts and individual investors. Next, he was brazen enough to approach the nation's top advertisers bolstered by data too significant for them to ignore. Each year, the Nielsen Media Research Group releases results of its annual survey on U.S. viewing habits. Since Black households are the largest demographic subgroup targeted by advertisers, they are researched independently. Based on 1980 data from 2,500 households, Nielsen concluded that, surprisingly, African Americans watch 23 more hours per week of television than comparable households. Moreover, Black children ages 17 and under view 11 more hours of television per week than their nearest counterpart; daytime viewing in Black households is 55 percent higher than in non-Black households; and programs featuring positive Black characters are among the most popular programs.

Johnson was not to be outworked. Twice a month over a two-year period, he traveled to Oak Brook, Illinois, home to the fast-food powerhouse McDonald's, with the hopes of signing up the corporate giant as a sponsor.

Johnson didn't recognize when all the pieces were in place. As an untutored lobbyist, the moment seemed so far beyond his entrepreneurial expertise that it made him nervous. In a frenzy of detailed negotiations, financial haggling, and managerial coordination, Johnson managed to overcome each bottleneck in turn. After working obsessively and securing a slew of resources, BET went on the air on January 25, 1980, with a two-hour movie titled *A Visit to the Chief's Son*. The 1974 adventure centers on a father and his teenage son who draw closer together when they travel to Africa to study the rituals of the Masai tribe. "It was uplifting and pro-social," Johnson recalled. "The right kind of thing for us in the early days."[6]

Ultimately, Johnson built BET into the largest minority cable channel in the country, reaching 66 million U.S. households. His rationale was a no-brainer. A major part of his formula: Keep costs low and find inexpensive ways to provide programming. With ad rates substantially lower than those of his cable rivals VH1 and MTV, Johnson knew he couldn't create high-minded original programming. To fill the void, he aired sitcom rerun staples, such as *The Jeffersons* and *Benson,* in addition to late-night talk shows, comedy, and edgy videos. In his own quiet way, the persuasive entrepreneur made his pitch to dozens of corporate types who eventually bought into his ideas. And, as a result, BET exploded. After two consecutive years of red ink, the stream of viewers began to grow, more cable companies began to broadcast the station, and by 1989, BET was able to repay its investors and start on the road to sustained growth. Two years later, BET made history as the first African American–owned corporation to be listed on the New York Stock Exchange. Ad receipts skyrocketed, and Johnson found himself a multimillionaire media executive. He was 45 years old.

HEART OF THE ISSUE

As a businessman, Johnson has broken through doors that should have never been closed. After netting more than one billion dollars in the sale of BET to industry giant Viacom, the man who worked longer, worked smarter, and lived more austerely than his detractors made a bold announcement—he would sell his flagship enterprise. When Johnson decided to sell to Viacom, the global mass media giant, he was openly criticized within the Black community for relinquishing African American ownership of the network. Unmoved, Johnson was quick to assert that BET is different from most Black businesses. Outside shareholders were always a vital component of the company, and besides, though others loved the idea of a Black-owned television network, the bold and resourceful entrepreneur never viewed his groundbreaking enterprise as a family heirloom. "I never saw myself running a family business for my benefit only," he elaborated. "My focus was to create an enterprise that was built upon maximizing shareholder value. The fact is, Black people don't have much of a history creating wealth in this country. As a result, we are sought primarily for our physical or artistic talent. Sad to say, when it comes to building value in companies or managing the money of others, we are nowhere to be found."[7]

And he didn't stop there. "As African Americans," he continued, "we must develop a culture that appreciates wealth. There's a tendency among our race to avoid any discussion of generating or retaining wealth simply because it's perceived as being boorish or narcissistic. We need a fresh outlook, a new mind-set, a philosophy that praises wealth creation as much as we elevate those who work in our neighborhoods and communities. The social activist mold that was developed for Al Sharpton and Jesse Jackson was not created for me; nor was the artistic mold that was set in stone for Oprah Winfrey and Jay-Z. That is not a part of my DNA. The recipe that was developed for me is the same formula that was created for Ken Chenault, Richard Parsons, and Stanley O'Neal. I create wealth and I add value. That's what I do."[8]

Since walking away from BET, Johnson has remained true to his mission. He has created the RLJ Companies, a holding company that represents a variety of business ventures, including a record label, more than 100 hotels—although a board member within the Hilton umbrella of properties, he is the number one hotel operator in the Marriott chain—a private equity fund, and, of course, the Charlotte Bobcats basketball team. Which brings me full circle to Johnson's opening statement.

New York Times sportswriter William Rhoden was quick to point out when Johnson was introduced as the new owner of the NBA's expansion franchise in Charlotte, North Carolina, there was a mad scramble to determine whether the media mogul was the first African American to become principal owner of a major sports team. That depends on the definition of *major*. Robert Douglas, known as the father of Black basketball, formed the revered Harlem Rens in the 1920s. The Rens were a *major* team, winning world championships in the next decade. In baseball, Rube Foster founded the Negro National League in 1920 and owned the Chicago American Giants. But in the context of our contemporary multibillion-dollar sports culture, Johnson's purchase was unprecedented. No African American before him had owned a majority stake of a team in a major sports league. As the number of Black athletes increased, the lack of Black ownership became a noticeable blemish.[9] During his presentation to league officials, two traits came through loud and clear: Johnson is a businessman above all, and all other financial matters are relegated to the bottom line. This billionaire owner is a perfect fit for the NBA, where literally everything revolves around marketing and promotion. When the 29 owners met to vote on Johnson's bid and management team, they were quick to welcome him aboard.

But the purpose of this profile is not to debate whether Viacom is a good corporate citizen and whether they will hold to the same interests of the previous owner. Nor is this example rendered to gauge whether Bob Johnson is truly the *first* Black owner of a *major* sports team. No, the focus centers on a never-failing prosperity principle—the fifth law of wealth—that's most effective if uncovered by you, the reader. Bob Johnson held true to a specific plan while conditioning his mind so thoroughly that nothing could deter him from stamping his mark. In his own words, Johnson stated, "I wanted to create a business that is built on maximizing shareholder value."

Your financial future, like a block of marble, stands untouched before you. In your abilities, talents, gifts, as well as this fifth law, you hold the chisel and mallet. The world has the right to expect a work of art—a masterpiece. You need only to utilize this fifth principle, which gives you the right to ask the universe for increased compensation. What will you hammer out? Given the resources at your command, society expects you to join the ranks of the financial elite—those who are deserving of earning seven-figure incomes. Great advantages bring great responsibilities. Will you shatter the marble into an unsightly piece of stone or, like Dr. King, will you call out a monument of wealth, untold riches, and abundance—a symbol to future generations as well as those trapped by poverty and ignorance? The dramatic story of the man who created the fifteenth largest television network in the United States, creating eight Black millionaires in the process, is a perfect illustration of the power and reach of the fifth law.

IT'S NOT ABOUT THE MONEY

The purpose of sharing Bob Johnson's message is not to discuss the challenges of wealth creation with regard to the Black community or to point blame or single out those who constantly struggle to attain wealth. No, this story runs far deeper than just a few pages or any one individual. Contained within his passage is a principle that you would do well to know. Somewhere in this profile, you will recognize your-self. This truth, sublime in its simplicity and powerful in its profundity, is the bare essence of abundance and prosperity. "It's not so much about what I do," Johnson professed, "it's about what I help others to do. I'm not concerned about what I've built; I'm more concerned about what I've helped others to build."

Johnson's entrepreneurial drive to create BET arose from a fear that someone of equal talent and equal ability would beat him to the punch. "If that would've happened," he confessed, "I would've hated myself for the rest of my life. In all honesty, the entrepreneurial path that I traveled came about because I never really embraced the idea of working for someone else. It was never about the money—I was really forced to pursue this path because I don't enjoy taking orders. In other words, it was never my intention to work for the man. I wanted to *be* the man."

In virtually every discussion I had with the Black financial elite, each would underscore Johnson's remarks: "*It's not about the money.*" But this, I found, is one of the romantic fibs that so many of the wealthy tell themselves as well as anyone who will listen. This belief—*that it's not about the money*—somehow makes the ultra-affluent feel better about themselves. Perhaps it helps assuage misplaced guilt. At least it makes them feel humble. After nearly seven years of similar discus-sions with these extraordinary men and women, I can tell you un-equivocally that it is indeed *very much* about the money. But it's even more about making an impact, influencing others, and taking the road less traveled. Money is only a barometer—a scorecard, if you will—of their ability to add and deliver more value.

Those surveyed within this text are staunch in their belief that you must first create substantial value—products or services that enhance the well-being of others—before money will flow from any commer-cial enterprise. How will you attract more money? *By creating more value.* This is not simply a semantics issue; this is a completely different philosophy, mind-set, and approach to the money that you currently possess. Instead of asking "How can I increase revenue?" begin to ask *How can I increase the quality of my service?* Instead of asking "How can I expand my business?" ask *How can I make a difference?* Rather than asking "How can I become *wealthy?*" ask instead *How can I become more valuable?* I suggest that you begin to alter your mind-set regarding this all-important principle within your life.

What is the crux of Bob Johnson's message? Money is only a tool to exchange value. The only way to generate a seven-figure income is to deliver seven figures' worth of value. If people fail to perform more service than they are being paid for, then obviously they are receiving all the income to which they are entitled. In order to hold their position or maintain their sources of income, regardless of how they earn it, people must deliver the value for which they are being compensated. Every position, regardless of the task, level, or stature, provides each worker with the opportunity to advance his or her livelihood based on this often-used principle. You may disregard or ignore this law if you so choose, but you cannot do so while simultaneously enjoying the fruits of enduring financial success.

UNIVERSAL LANGUAGE OF MONEY

To underscore this point, one early spring day, Operation HOPE founder John Hope Bryant stood before a handful of my business students and explained his philosophy.

> It became obvious to me as early as 2006 that we are not only experiencing an economic crisis but a crisis of virtues and values. Somewhere along the way we lost our storyline. We moved away from the concept of capitalism and free enterprise as something that builds or enhances the quality of life of society and reduced it to "that vehicle" that simply makes money for me. For nearly 100 years, America has been that place where the power of an idea created amazing value for society, for customers, workers, shareholders, and yes, the entrepreneur who created it all. The problem is, in the past 10 to 20 years, American capitalists have confused value for money, effectively making the by-product (money, power and position in the world) the product instead of making a difference in the lives of others or adding value.
>
> You ask anyone today, "Why are you in business?" and nine times out of ten they will reply "I'm in business to make money." "Why are you a basketball player?" "I play ball to get paid." "Why are you on Wall Street?" "*To make money.*" And on and on. This is the only time during my lifetime when a broker, investment banker, and the hustler

in my old neighborhood share the same mind-set and sink to the same level. We've lost our storyline. When a Wall Street investor "shorts" a stock of an otherwise healthy company and for no other purpose than "to get paid," we must understand this investor not only neglected his obligation to his client, but he created nothing, and we, as a country, have lost our storyline.

The entire game has revolved around money, which is wrong, and, as a result, as a nation, we have lost our storyline. Ironically, responsible subprime lending, which is actually a good thing and arguably has done more to lift poor people out of poverty than any other financial program over the past 50 years, has turned into predatory subprime lending, which is not a good thing at all. Again, we have lost our storyline. But rainbows always follow storms, and people do not change in good times, they change in bad [times]. They do not change when they are comfortable but rather when they are uncomfortable. Well, it's time for a change in our community. This is my cause and my life's mission: To teach the world's poor, underserved, and the struggling middle class the universal language of money and spread the precepts of financial literacy.[10]

THERE'S NO SHAME IN THE PURSUIT
OF THE ALMIGHTY DOLLAR

But even if those surveyed and interviewed for this study would privately, if not publicly, admit that money was their primary motivation, the world would still benefit from their efforts and endeavors. Say what you will, but money—the almighty dollar—is the catalyst that primes the pump of worldly exchange. The want of money is a power strong enough to keep the world in balance.

Money is one of the great principles of moral gravitation. What will humanity *not* do to satisfy this all-absorbing passion? What will humanity *not* risk or do in order to make ends meet? There are men and women born with a genius for capital who possess the instinct of accumulation. Their talent and inclination to convert dimes into dollars by bargains or shrewd investments are as strongly marked as the ability and inclination of Romare Bearden and Henry Ossawa Turner to produce memorable works of art, or Scott Joplin to compose piano rags, or Garrett Morgan to make life so much easier due to his inventions. It would be a gross dereliction of duty, a shameful perversion of gifts, had these people disregarded the instincts of their genius and shunned their talents by channeling their energies into other areas.

I wish I could fill every adult who reads these pages with the utter dread and horror of poverty. I wish I could make every man or woman feel its shame, its constraint, its bitterness, to force them all to vow never to be poor. Without financial independence, no one can reach his or her true calling. No one can perform their best work when want and woe are tugging at their heels, when they are tied down and forever at the mercy of circumstances or on those upon whom they depend for employment. If people have to pay that much for existence, they are paying too high a price. What can be more humiliating than the sense of being but a day's march ahead of lack and want? Poverty is a condition that no one should choose willingly.

We see the evidence of pinching, grinding, debilitating poverty everywhere. We see it in prematurely depressed faces. We see it in grown, able-bodied men—with cup in hand and earthly possessions in tow—navigating busy street corners and intersections while pleading for spare change. We find it in our women, trapped in a sea of hopelessness; single mothers who wish to make their lives and homes a centerpiece for their children but, unfortunately, can't seem to make ends meet. We've uncovered it in our children, tender souls who've grown up too fast, too soon. Robbed of their childhood and facing life short on skills and values and long on hardship, they're unable to cope, unable to find a shoulder on which to lean. They can be found fostering despair and doubt where love and hope should rule. Enticed by the lure of the streets, too many of our children get into crack before they get into Christ. Too many find gangs before they find God. And far too many are trapped in prison because they knew not the power of prayer.

Praise it if you will, but poverty is a curse that will dwarf you mentally and spiritually. It invites disaster. There is scarcely a redeeming feature about it, and those who extol its virtues are generally the last to accept its conditions. It is difficult to be a man or a woman while living in extreme poverty. Why? Because the poor are forever at the mercy of circumstances. They cannot be independent, they cannot command their time, and they cannot afford to live in the homes or surroundings of their choosing. It is difficult for a man to be a man or a woman to be a woman—proud and true—when want and lack stares him or her in the eye. Hampered with debt, bound in bondage to those on whom he depends, and forced to make a dime perform the work of a dollar. It is nearly impossible to preserve the dignity and self-respect that enables a man or woman to look the world squarely in the face. The lesson is clear: Poverty stifles ambition and thwarts brilliant plans. It is the duty of every man and woman to exert every effort to escape from its clutches.

Though some may take exception, the pursuit of wealth is not only legitimate but a *duty*. If people gain their fortunes through the honest sweat of their brows, the struggle to satisfy their own selfish instincts will increase their influence and multiply their power. This perpetual progress to attain wealth, if they are careful to guard against any narrowing, demoralizing, and negative influences—and if they understand that their possessions should not own them—will develop their intelligence, sharpen their skills, add to their energy, increase their thrift, and stabilize their character. No force has done more to promote and propel society while safeguarding any chance of civilization slipping back into chaos. *Everybody* and *everything* thirsts for the almighty dollar.

Pride seeks it. What else besides pride can render power, position, and influence to those who possess it?

Vanity yearns for it. What other force could make status-hungry people purchase fine clothing, sumptuous housing, fancy cars, and a host of material possessions that they cannot afford to buy?

Love hopes for it. What loving parent doesn't want the best for his or her children?

The church prays for it. Don't you hear it every Sunday: Send me your tithes and offerings?

And even death gropes for it. After all, who wants to die poor?

Empty pockets never held anyone back. Only empty heads and hearts can do that.

Without the urge, this tremendous push for power, influence, and advantage that wealth provides, how could nature develop our best attributes? Without this infinite longing, from where would the discipline, faith, and perseverance that industry commands come? Without this constant struggle, what would motivate self-improvement, self-sacrifice, bold daring, and the need to take the calculated risk? Perhaps Orison Swett Marden said it best: "It is very difficult for the rich to be so selfish that the poor cannot enjoy their wealth. Whether they rear it into architecture or place it into elegant carriages; whether they spend it in costly banquets, rare diamonds and precious stones; or build costly churches, summer residences, however they spend it or use it, thousands of others will see it, enjoy it, and carry away with their eyes a large share of the real value."[11] So condemn the rich, berate the affluent, bemoan the well-to-do, but recognize that our values are based on our greenbacks more than our reputation. Our place in society is determined more by our assets than by our education and social graces. Even the pew to which the usher seats you in church is too often chosen with reference to your ending balance rather than your deity and reverence. The respect that attends wealth is as old as the Bible, which states: "If a man comes into your assembly with a gold ring and godly apparel, and there comes in also a poor man in vile apparel, and ye have respect to him that weareth the gay clothing, and say unto him, 'Sit thou there,' are ye not partial?"[12] The most successful African Americans, especially those who are self-made millionaires, give us a great gift: the gift of hope—hope that we too can join their ranks, that we can, with proper diligence, also enjoy the American dream.

HOW TO MAKE YOUR MARK

It should come as little surprise that the tiny battered farmhouse seems to be the birthplace of so many great men and women. Hundreds of examples could easily be cited to warrant this assertion, from A. G. Gaston to Alonzo Herndon, John Merrick, Charles Clinton Spaulding, S. B. Fuller, Eddie Brown, Maggie Walker, John H. Johnson, and, yes, Herman Cain. Where a lowly start would have a numbing effect on most, these people are representative of individuals of strong constitution and even stronger self-esteem who toiled for long hours at low pay in fields they would eventually master. The story of John Wesley Dobbs provides an example. One day Dobbs, known to friends and family alike as the "unofficial" mayor of the famed Auburn Avenue in Atlanta, Georgia—the centerpiece of Black economic development and, at the time, just a handful of promising storefronts and gravel roads—was greeted with derision by a visitor from the ever-expanding northeastern region of the country. Dobbs's guest had been boasting of New York's growing population, impressive skyline, bustling nightlife, and breathtaking architecture. After pointing out all of the positive aspects of big-city life, he asked the humble civic leader, "And what do you produce on the hilly, rocky landscapes of south Georgia?" Dobbs didn't hesitate. "Strong men and women" was his reply.[13]

True to form, Herman Cain has enjoyed a stellar career in the business world and an impressive presidential run. In 1977, he became the youngest vice president in the history of the Minnesota-based Pillsbury Company after just three years on the job. He left this position in 1982 to take a stab at the restaurant business at Burger King, a Pillsbury subsidiary. Four years later, his success with the fast-food chain prompted Pillsbury to select him to assume the presidency of one of its struggling units: Godfather's Pizza. Due in part to his relentless focus, pursuit of excellence, and constant quest to add value every step along the way, Cain turned to the pizza franchise. As a result, he became the first Black president of the National Restaurant Association, the food service industry's leading trade organization. Let those who would follow in his footsteps remember that when Cain began his career at Burger King, no task was too menial for him. He answered phones, scrubbed floors, and even flipped hamburgers. After completing the franchise's required management training program in only nine months, Cain was named vice president and general manager for Burger King's Philadelphia region—a particularly gratifying accomplishment, considering that nearly 40 years prior, he and his Morehouse classmates were refused service in a southern restaurant.

To understand the arc of Herman Cain's business career, start with his modest beginnings. Though his home was small and his surroundings poor, his family was big on values. His parents provided excellent examples of hard work and self-determination, and they ensured that the Almighty served as a reference point in their children's lives. Cain's mother and father came up the hard way and fought for every inch of ground they covered. Together, they personally witnessed Jim Crow, worked at the most demanding labor, and received the type of racial oppression and bias that would make a weak person question his or her faith. Each had to lug the weight of an inferior education as well as poverty and low self-esteem.[14] Cain's parents were well into their fifties before they could vote or eat in a White-owned restaurant. Through it all, they could proudly say that no matter the injustice or indignity, they refused to be touched by bitterness or defeat. They would not allow the insensitivity of others to turn their hearts cold. Cain's mother worked as a domestic, and his father held a handful of menial jobs, including mopping floors on the evening shift of a local bakery when not serving as a chauffeur for the most senior executives at the Atlanta-based Coca-Cola Company. This work ethic would inspire Cain not only to work hard but to stamp his personal brand of excellence on every task he was assigned.

MANAGING THE TURNAROUND

In 1988, Cain, then president of Godfather's Pizza and a member of the management group that sealed the deal to acquire the fast-food chain from Pillsbury, was trying to shape a course of action for the fast-food chain. He had achieved what more than one industry analyst had characterized as a miracle. When Cain arrived at the pizza franchise, he found weak and indecisive executive leadership, a blurred corporate image, low morale, and poor training and support. How did he manage to turn the firm around? Here's a snapshot of the value-laden strategy he implemented, which you, the reader, can use to place yourself one step closer to your seven-figure goals.

- *"Believe that you can make a difference."* As he interviewed middle managers who sought to become members of his executive staff, Cain asked each two questions: "What excites you about your work?" "What type of person are you?" According to Cain, financial success requires more than just an expressive imagination or positive thinking; it requires *possibility thinking*. The difference between wealth and poverty, success and failure, is not nearly as great as most people believe. Your current thinking ultimately will affect your future economic conditions. Develop self-confidence and always advance. Confront your fears and face them squarely. Cain shared with me over lunch that those who constantly postpone their dreams, delay the execution of their ideas, and bottle up their grand plans to be implemented at a more convenient time are always relegated to the rear.
- *Love excellence.* It's no longer just companies that must raise the bar regarding performance, it's each of us individually. Due in part to our hyper-competitive marketplace, each

employee and business owner is pressed to keep getting better. In short, "just okay" is no longer okay. Since the days of Adam Smith and his fellow Scottish philosopher and reformer Samuel Smiles, the scarcest resource in business has always been capital. If you had it, you possessed the means to create additional wealth. If you didn't, you lacked the one resource necessary to grow your business. Today that line of thinking is outdated. The scarcest resource is no longer money; it's *personal excellence*. If you fail to continually grow, learn, develop, and upgrade your skills, somewhere, someone else will. And the day you meet that person, you will lose.

- *Develop an obsession with customer service.* Kill 'em with service! I forget who uttered those words, but it's still the key to financial success. Not only is this the best way to add value and build a business, but it's the single most effective strategy in which to stay employed. My philosophy has always been to exceed the expectations of the job. I always knew that for me to do well, I couldn't be just as good as the next person. I had to exceed the next person.[15] Your rewards in life will be in direct proportion to the value of your service. Don't look for easy money. Search and identify genuine ways to offer value. Seek a product or service that provides an important contribution to the quality of life or work of your customer. Everyone earns a living by serving others. Each of us serves at least one customer—including your boss, those who report to you, as well as your spouse or family members. *Who is your number one customer?* Put fortune on your side. Look for opportunities to serve others. Regardless of who signs your paycheck, the principal function of your business or vocation is the winning and retention of customers. Countless people have been led to believe that the goal of a business is to earn a profit. Well, this statement is somewhat true, but the real purpose of a business is to create and retain a customer. You would do well to constantly ask yourself: What can I do to improve the quality of my service?

- *Pursue dirty jobs.* The wealthy do things that others don't like to do. Those who become financially successful never consider themselves above any task or chore. With regard to prosperity and abundance, they come to recognize that there is a price to be paid, and the sooner they pay that price, the sooner they can gain the financial independence they desire. In short, be willing to perform the dog work. Volunteer for assignments that others avoid. Put in the extra hours, and make the extra phone call. Search for unsolved problems as well as unmet needs. A willingness to work hard does not negate working smart—longer does not always equal better—but you will be known for going the extra mile as opposed to doing the bare minimum. In the words of the writer and poet Maya Angelou, do what you do so well that others cannot ignore you.

- *What Does it Take?* It takes your ability to embrace the calculated risk. There is no greater question that anyone can ask. These four simple words stand between you and your moment of prosperity. If you dare to accomplish your financial goals, if you aspire to the Creator's grand scheme, if your existence depends on it, and if you are willing to give up your time, money, and effort for it—then you must face the eternal question that confronts every would-be millionaire: *What does it take?* If you dare to walk through the gates of financial independence, you must answer this question. Doing so requires the courage not to bend to popular opinion. It calls for courage to refuse to follow customs and rights that run contrary to our own sense of morality.[16]

Many would-be millionaires are stymied by the prospects of forgoing a steady paycheck or facing the unknown. Most simply cannot withstand the risk. But, to be creative, to venture forward, to succeed, you must be willing to *lose* all that you possess—to embrace uncertainty, to replace security with insecurity. To find true happiness, to be fulfilled, to be at peace with yourself and others, you must learn to *embrace the calculated risk and accept complete responsibility for your actions.*

HOW TO GET RICH

Countless feet below the pyramid at Giza lies its foundation, unseen by those who visit the historic landmark. But make no mistake, the foundation—invisible and unrecognized by most—enables the timeless treasure to stand upright and true. So it is regarding the fifth law of wealth. A large part of every financially successful life must be spent in laying foundation stones of work, perseverance, faith, and service to others in order to endure the test of time. History is replete with examples of men and women who have freed themselves from poverty and misfortune by their optimism, faith, and values.

What power can poverty hold over a home where loving hearts recognize the untold riches of the head and heart? Those who can face poverty and misfortune with cheerfulness and courage are rich as well as brave. Brave and honest men and women do not work for gold; they work for love, for honor, for character. The object for which we strive tells the story of our lives. "Character before wealth" was the motto drilled into Colin Powell by his Jamaican working-class parents. Ordinarily, those words might not seem to provide the springboard to prosperity, but Luther, a shipping clerk in New York City's Garment District, and Maud Ariel, a seamstress, knew the force of their example. Today, as the retired four-star general and sought-after public speaker looks back over his life, he openly states, "It was the manner in which they lived their lives that spelled the difference. Their spirit took me past ambushes and land mines in Vietnam; isolation in Korea; surface-to-air missiles throughout the Middle East; roadside bombs in Baghdad; racism and humility in Columbus, Georgia; and finally to my American dream. The great aim of your life is to hold dear to your values."[17]

"*How to get rich?*" Pamela Thomas-Graham asked an audience of hypersuccessful Harvard law school alums during their annual year-end celebration. And who would know better than she? Thomas-Graham has always been a woman of bold ambition. Her DNA strand spells "superwoman." She is a Phi Beta Kappa graduate of Harvard College and graduated from both the School of Business and Harvard law. In 1995, she was named the first Black female partner at McKinsey & Company, the industry leader, followed eight years later by *Ms.* magazine's "Woman of the Year."[18] Recently, her rising-star status plunged her into the world of finance as the Chief Talent, Branding and Communications Officer for industry leader Credit Suisse. Thomas-Graham never sought public favor or applause. Yet she has received both in abundance. She credits her success to her parents—her mother, a social worker, and her father, who sold real estate in urban

Detroit. Their philosophy? "We tried to teach our children that it's fun to stretch your mind; to challenge yourself intellectually. We can give our children the right ideals, the best education, and open doors for them, but the rest is up to them."[19] Thomas-Graham is a change agent who was raised to place a premium on integrity and making a difference. "Do more than is required, and do what's right," she advises. "Your reputation is your greatest asset. Not product, not price, not service, not promotion. People will buy you before they will purchase your product. Everything flows from this single trait. You can earn it only by earning it. Once you do, don't ever let it slip away."[20] The main focus of wealth is not to *do* but to become. Integrity cuts its own channel and does its own talking.

What a lesson Sylvia Rhone's life is for the indolent, indecisive, aimless, and plodding who hang about neighborhoods and cities complaining of their tough circumstances, dreaming of financial success, and wondering why they are left behind in the great race of life. Wealth depends largely on personal values, and whatever weakens or impairs those qualities diminishes any chance of success. In 1983, the music industry's good ol' boys club was finally forced to open its doors—doors that never should have been closed—when Rhone, generally regarded as the most powerful woman in the recording industry and who served as president of Universal Motown Records until 2011, never doubted that she'd one day run her own company. Nothing could discourage her from believing that she would carve out a career in this competitive field. The Harlem, New York, native, who grew up listening to Aretha Franklin and Marvin Gaye, says repeated encounters with bias and sexism in the music industry fueled her commitment to push harder and leave her mark. Today's music industry demands imagination and grit, and Rhone possesses both in bulk. In 1988, she became the first Black woman to serve as vice president of a major record company, Atlantic Records. Three years later, she was named co-president and CEO of her own Atlantic label, EastWest Records America.

Although she began her career in banking and finance, Rhone has a knack for discovering and developing new music talent and for salvaging financially struggling record divisions. "For years," says the Wharton graduate, "colleagues have mentioned that when it comes to business, I'm more man than woman. I was never sure whether to take that statement as a compliment or an insult. I now know they didn't mean that I lack femininity. Far from it. I love my fitted designer clothes and high heels. They meant that I'm confident, assertive, persistent, tough, analytical, and strategic. To be fair, both men and women need these qualities if they are going to excel financially in the business world. Take my word for it. Women need not act like men to succeed, but to compete, we must combine male and female behaviors—assertive as well as confident, decisive as well as hardworking—if we are going to shatter the glass ceiling. This is a business, and I wouldn't be here if I failed to make an impact on the bottom line."[21]

As you gather your millions, the following questions are sure to be asked. The correct answers will seal your destiny forever. How did you acquire your fortune? Can the lives of others be found in it? Are the hopes and dreams of your fellow man and woman buried within it? Have others sacrificed their God-given rights and opportunities because of it? Has the growth of your neighbor been stunted by it? Was your character and honor stained by it? Was your pride and ego enlarged by it? Did envy and greed help in its accumulation? If so, you have *not* succeeded. As Daniel pointed out to the prophets, "Thou hast been weighed in the balance and found wanting."

TO WHOM MUCH IS GIVEN . . .

As profiled in the *Washington Post*, it was billed as the largest, most eye-popping of the inauguration hotel packages: the J.W. Marriott's $1 million build-your-own-ball offer. You got 300 rooms, four suites, $200,000 worth of food and drink, and a front-row seat overlooking the Pennsylvania Avenue parade route. And it was snapped up within hours of Barack Obama's presidential election by a customer the hotel declined to identify.[22] Just hours before the gala, Marriott hotel officials announced that the buyer was a Virginia businessman who simply wanted to bring to the inauguration the disadvantaged as well as the terminally ill, wounded veterans, and others down on their luck. In the midst of the worst economic recession in more than 70 years and a downturn in corporate giving, Earl W. Stafford bucked the trend. Instead of cutting back and trimming costs, Stafford gave abundantly to those hoping to see better days. By his own estimation, the high-tech entrepreneur wrote checks for nearly $2 million to fund his People's Inaugural Project—a sprawling three-day philanthropic effort to bring more than 400 disadvantaged citizens, including the homeless and elderly, to Washington, DC, to participate in this once-in-a-lifetime event. Stafford said the idea was inspired by his deep religious faith and the good fortune that has come his way. The inauguration was an opportunity to remember the less fortunate and remind the country of its traditions of benevolence. "We wanted to . . . bless those who otherwise would not have an opportunity to be a part of this grand celebration," he explained. "We've gotten away from those core values that made America great. We need to get back to the business of caring for each other. We must become our brothers' keepers."[23]

Earl W. Stafford, the ninth of 12 children, was born in Mount Holly, New Jersey. His father, a Baptist minister, worked as a laborer for 40 years while his mother cooked and cleaned in the homes of the well-to-do. Although money was scarce, Stafford and his siblings never considered themselves poor. At an early age, each child developed a strong work ethic. A can-do attitude was the rule, not the exception. After high school, Stafford entered the air force, where he became an air traffic controller. While off duty, he pursued college-level courses at the University of Massachusetts and later earned an MBA from Southern Illinois University before completing executive course work at the Harvard Business School.

Following his air force career, Stafford founded Universal Systems & Technology (UNITECH) in 1988. Under his leadership, UNITECH grew from a small professional services firm to a robust business with more than 400 employees. After leading UNITECH for 21 years, in 2009, Stafford sold it to Lockheed Martin. At that time, the company had surpassed the $150 million mark in annual sales.

. . . MUCH IS REQUIRED

The project was inspired by his deep religious faith—that Stafford should direct a portion of his fortune to help the underserved. A few months later, he cornered the presidential suite at Washington, DC's Hay-Adams Hotel, adjacent to Lafayette Park as well as the White House. His initial thoughts were to hire a caterer and then depart, but that changed weeks later when his brother-in-law shared a newspaper story regarding an inaugural package offered by the Marriott. The next day, Stafford bought the package.

Once news of his plans hit the streets, Stafford and his foundation were overwhelmed. More than 7,000 phone calls, emails, and messages poured into his nonprofit foundation requesting tickets, nominating deserving individuals, or offering to lend a helping hand by volunteering to aid such a worthy cause. Hundreds of well-wishers even sought him out at home, some just to say thank you. Like so many of the wealth creators interviewed in this study, Stafford loves his life. Due in part to the windfall the wealth creators received after dedicating a lifetime to building their business or pursuing their financial goals, most openly state that the money is great because it buys freedom while offering a greater degree of choice. But it doesn't end there. Each is quick to point out that wealth translates into happiness only when it is self-earned and, specifically, is the direct result of individual effort. The highest degree of happiness occurs only when you begin to affect the lives of others. Here lies the *real value* that you've added to the world.

Each of us would do well to admit that circumstance *does* play a role; that wealth often places unworthy sons and daughters into high positions of influence; that contacts may place ordinary clergymen into extraordinary pulpits; that status and pedigree do gain a lawyer clients, a physician patients, and the marginal student acceptance into the most prestigious programs. However, in the long run, position, clients, patients, and schools do not necessarily constitute financial success. We would be better served to realize that the best man or woman does capture the victor's cup and that character and persistent merit do win the race. You doubt me? Paul was never revered until he occupied a prison cell in Rome; and the carpenter from Galilee reached the height of his success when smitten, spat on, tormented, and crucified. He cried in agony and yet with triumphant satisfaction said, "It is finished." Here is the key that looks beyond all boundaries, transcends all limitations, and penetrates all obstacles. "There's a saying in the Bible," Stafford reminds us, "to whom much is given, much is required."[24]

NEW RULES OF MONEY

Two key concepts stand front and center in nearly every profile mentioned within this chapter. First, each person, whether it is Bob Johnson, Herman Cain, Pamela Thomas-Graham, or Earl Stafford, could best be labeled the ultimate renegade. That is, each broke the rules and thrived on the process of change. Starting from scratch, these millionaires established a clear plan for their financial future and set goals in motion regardless of the obstacles or roadblocks that stood in their path. Second, their financial dreams did not become a reality until they implemented the fifth law of wealth. The millionaires in this study clearly understand the difference between adding value and the sad cost of mediocrity.

During a King Day celebration hosted by Spelman College—the historic all-female institution—former U.S. ambassador Andrew Young spoke before an eager student body and tried desperately to bring closure to an all-too-familiar refrain. Throughout his remarks, he explained there is no better way to honor and continue the legacy of Martin Luther King Jr. than by pursuing his life's passion of freedom and equality. Leaning on the insightful thoughts of the social activist John Hope Bryant, the former congressman and King confidant crafted his words by clarifying that the next phase of the civil rights movement will focus on "silver rights"—the financial empowerment of those who fought so valiantly to win their basic human rights. "The dollar," Young admonished, "speaks with a universal voice and dialect, challenging the underserved to seek a hand up and not a hand out. It's time that each of us learns how to fish. Give a man or woman a fish and feed them for a day—but teach them how to fish and you feed them for a lifetime. In this competitive and information driven economy we must learn how to fish so we won't go to our neighbors asking for fish. We must learn how to fish so we won't go marching to the mayor's office begging for fish. We must learn how to fish so we don't go picketing Congress demanding fish, *because Congress is running out of fish*. God places into our hands the Book of Life, bright on every page with open secrets, and we will indeed suffer if it drops out of our hands unread. No matter how tired or how tried, serving others blesses and curses not. The most important work you will ever engage in is the opportunity to be of service to others."[25]

AND WHAT OF THOSE WHO
WILL NOT OR CANNOT SERVE?

While the great majority of Black Americans embrace mainstream wealth-creating values, a clearly identifiable contingent does not. In the 1970s, we referred to members of this class as the hard-core un-employed. Graphic media depictions of the plight of the urban under-class have helped to underscore the compelling argument that at the base of much inner-city poverty lies the values and behavior of ghetto residents—values that, with concerted effort, can be changed for the better. They were made the poster children in the fight for civil rights and later the War on Poverty. The goal was to enable them, in addi-tion to the rest of Black America, to be free and self-sufficient. But in spite of a successful civil rights campaign and trillions of dollars spent over decades to combat poverty, as of this writing, a group of low-income African Americans have yet to set a course to fight their way out of poverty. They have yet to accept and implement mainstream values. They have failed to place a value on education—precipitating their own demise—either for themselves or their children. This dis-regard for knowledge results in a lack of job skills, opportunities for advancement, low self-esteem, and the inability to achieve economic independence. Mistakenly, they believe they are victims of crippling racism and thus refuse to accept any personal responsibility for their fate. This misguided faction has been bred to know only the lifestyle embodied in an entitled welfare culture based on racism, victimiza-tion, and defeatism. It is a lifestyle completely lacking in the laws of wealth and the promise that the future holds. Without the belief that you can be all that you want to be, this defeatist attitude leaves those trapped under its spell with little drive, forcing millions to live at the same level of misery. Without a wish to rise, a desire to accomplish, and a passion to attain, no life will succeed. Instead of developing the millionaire mind-set, these lost souls are held captive by a welfare mentality.

For those of you who fall under the latter category, please, I beg of you, don't misunderstand me. This passage is written with the utmost care and compassion. No blame game here. At first glance, much of what I'm sharing may seem radical or inconsistent with the thoughts and philosophies of established Black leadership. So be it; this is how *I* see it. Here is what I've discovered. Don't lament and grieve over lost opportunity or wealth. The Creator may see something mighty in you that even He cannot bring about as long as *you* persist in your ways. God may see a rough diamond in you that only the hard hits of lack and limit can polish. Here lies a philosophy that you must adopt and apply if you hold any hope of joining the ranks of this growing body of wealth creators. As my survey data and focus groups have revealed, the overwhelming majority of millionaires profiled in this study began their trek to wealth under the direst circumstances. Many were beyond the term *poor*, but few, if any, could be labeled *low income*. So many of these wealth creators, if not all, learned their values in middle-class households regardless of whether their parents were classified middle class. Their childhoods were infused with the virtue of work, education, respect for authority, modesty, independence, and self-determination. When I asked for the reasons underlying their achievements, these values were abundantly clear. Topping the list were middle-class values and the mainstays of entrepreneurial success such as hard work, perseverance, treating others in the manner in which you would like to be treated, as well as a bit of luck. Furthermore, despite several million dollars in liquid assets, nearly 80 percent of the Black financial elite call themselves middle class, more than 70 percent describe themselves as people with simple needs, and nearly 50 percent don't feel wealthy. Likewise, today's Black wealthy tend to think of themselves less as rich and more as people who came from modest means, worked hard, pursued their dreams, and achieved a level of success.

Furthermore, society is cajoled into believing that the poor are poor simply because they lack money. A popular solution suggests that alleviating poverty is quite simple: Just get money into the hands of the impoverished. If that were true, we, as a nation, could easily rid ourselves of poverty by printing more money. At various points in their development, nearly every millionaire in this study was broke. By the simplistic definition just discussed, he or she would be considered poor—equally poor to the millions of Americans who fall below the poverty line. Yet each millionaire was motivated, eager, teachable, and bent on rising to the top by starting at the bottom. Now compare this man or woman to his or her impoverished counterpart who lives life at the margin. At one time, both lacked money, but only one was poor. So for those of you who have decided to use *The Wealth Choice* as the linchpin on your journey to financial success, do not be dismayed or deceived. Poverty is an all-too-familiar starting point. Whereas the term *poor* refers to the absence of wealth, *low income* means much more. A man or woman who has no or little money is indeed poor, but an individual who lacks values as well as hope and ideas is poorer still.

Be poor, if you must—but never be low income. Though a rich mind and a noble spirit will lift anyone from the most humble beginnings, to be low income is to lack all values that can and will eventually lead to wealth.

"YOU CAN'T GET POINTS TODAY
FOR YESTERDAY'S GAME"

While seated in the Potter's House in Dallas, Texas, Bishop T. D. Jakes shared his wisdom on economic empowerment in an interview: "So many times I advise young men who are experiencing difficulty finding a job to create one. I do so because I learned as a little boy that if success doesn't come after you, you must go after it. Tears will get you sympathy, *but sweat will get you change.*"[26] No truer words have ever been spoken. There is so much to do and so many to serve; all you need is one good idea. But the extent of your opportunity to be of service will invariably correlate with your imagination coupled with your education. And the best place to begin is where you are.

The men and women profiled in this book are by definition self-made. Most have delivered themselves from garages to greatness, from basements to owning professional sports teams, from bootstraps to big time. Throughout my research, none of my survey respondents ever blamed anyone for their own failures or struggles as they marched to wealth and success. Nor did they bemoan the fact that they may have been forced to deal with life's recesses while others pursued their financial goals in relative ease and comfort. They simply took responsibility for their lives. Perhaps David Steward—CEO and founder of World Wide Technologies—said it best. Here is a man who built from scratch the nation's largest Black-owned company, a $4 billion monolith. In 1981, while working as an account executive for Federal Express, he was recognized as salesman of the year and inducted into the company's hall of fame. Steward was presented with a trophy—an ice bucket on which his initials were engraved. When he peered inside the bucket, he noticed that it was empty. Steward saw this as his defining moment, and he asked himself if that was what he wanted out of life. At the time, he and his wife had two small children, a mortgage, and "all the trappings of success that could keep you locked into a job," but he was ready for so much more.[27]

"Years from now," he said, "when I would look back over my life, I don't want any regrets. I don't want to say the reason why I didn't chase my dream was because I lacked faith in God, or that I was comfortable with the status quo. I had so much more to give. Others are quick to point out what you *should* be, but you're the only person who can decide what you *will* be."

Feel free to disagree, but I don't see much merit in poverty. Frankly, I can't see poverty being eliminated in your lifetime or mine. Still, I believe each of us can do our part toward that goal by creating wealth for ourselves in a way that adds value—serves—and enhances the lives of others. If you are fortunate to join the 35,000 or so Black millionaires who currently live in the United States, your actions and efforts will undoubtedly impact countless consumers or businesses—across all economic strata—in a positive and fruitful way, one hopes. I can only offer the words that the singer and actor Tyrese Gibson shared with my students nearly a year ago: "You can't get points today for yesterday's game. So every day you've got to be focused on being bigger, better, and greater than you've ever been. Each day you must change the 'war on poverty' to a 'prosperity program for abundance.' And the process begins by serving others." Or, in other words, by implementing the fifth law of wealth: How may I serve thee?

MILLIONAIRE LESSON NO. 6

"Others are quick to point out what you should be, but you're the only person who can decide what you will be."
—*Dave Steward*

SIX

THE ROAD NOT TAKEN

The Sixth Law of Wealth

"Dare not" is one thing. "Cannot" is another. Not everyone can be rich. But anyone can dare to. Somebody has to.

—Felix Dennis, British publisher and philanthropist

It's okay to be a superstar—to be the man in L.A., but sooner or later you need to start owning things.

—Magic Johnson to Shaquille O'Neal

WHEN ROBERT FROST WROTE HIS AWARD-WINNING poem "The Road Not Taken" in 1916 while living on an idyllic farm in New England, his life bore little resemblance to what most of us enjoy today. Many of the amenities that we take for granted had yet to be invented. Our country hadn't developed commercial air travel, television, talking pictures, traffic lights, photocopiers, color film, calculators, frozen food, antibiotics, insulin, a cure for polio, or any form of nuclear energy. The uniform wage for unskilled labor was a paltry ten cents per hour. Yet, thanks in part to the thoughts and ideas behind Frost's inspiring words, we now enjoy prosperity greater than ever imagined. The slow progress of the early 1900s is over, and today great possibilities are rushing forth.

Frost's poem doesn't just describe his feelings regarding his own personal choices; it contains a secret that lies at the center of the sixth law of wealth. Concealed within these lines is a wealth-creating formula utilized by nearly every millionaire surveyed in this study. This life-altering secret is so powerful that it can spell the difference between you living an existence of "false security," engaged in the monotonous routine of performing the same task day in and day out, and living a life of power, possibilities, and control. This widely known principle could mark the difference between spending every waking moment of your life in neutral, content to place your destiny in the hands of others, and utilizing your God-given gifts and talents. This law separates those who live in a world bounded on the north by mediocrity, on the south by indecision, on the east by past thinking, and on the west by "if only." By the time you finish this chapter, you will realize that the door to the millionaires' club is open. Contrary to popular belief, it never was closed. You will grow tired of being characterized as someone who avoids risk and perpetually shrinks from the fight. Or as someone who depends on others for his or her daily bread; someone who is constantly forced to adjust, robbing Peter to pay Paul, living only for the fifteenth and thirtieth day of every month. Here is the single truth that will define the difference between you violating your sacred birthright or unleashing your hidden forces, standing your ground, and fulfilling your dreams.

But no one knows when or under what circumstances this law will appear in your life. When that moment arrives, its demands are few, but they are binding and nonnegotiable. Many a bright and talented individual died in poverty and relative obscurity because he or she failed to embrace this one simple rule.

RICHES WITHIN YOUR REACH

Isn't it ironic that every individual is a stranger to his or her greatest strength until some crisis summons it out? Some of the wealthiest men and women in the annals of commerce and industry—examples who can be found in these pages—never caught a glimpse of this slumbering giant until they lost everything, until misfortune overtook them, until every bridge was burned and all possible avenues of retreat were closed off. It was only then that they found a way out of their dilemma, a way to lean on their own initiative. Many of the financial elite were forged in the stern school of necessity by way of the sixth law of wealth.

No amount of discouragement could force Mark Wilson to scrap his plans. *Why?* Because he saw the handwriting on the wall. When Wilson, a 15-year Dun & Bradstreet veteran, realized that the industry powerhouse was on the verge of outsourcing its call center operations, he seized the opportunity. "I thought that would be a great chance to approach management about my alternative strategy," Wilson shared in an interview. "I knew it would be risky but I was prepared to take the gamble." It was a risk that paid off. Embracing the sixth law of wealth, in a seven-year period, Wilson has grown his company, Ryla Teleservices Inc., from a 20-seat operation in 2002 to more than 3,500 employees. And revenues have climbed accordingly—from $1.1 million at start-up to more than $100 million in sales from 2002 to 2009. The firm's rapid expansion has not gone unnoticed. As of this writing, according to *Inc.* magazine, Ryla is one of the 5,000 fastest-growing private companies in the United States and is ranked as one of the top 500 African American–owned businesses in the nation by Diversity-Business.com.

No amount of rejection could ever deter Sylvia Woods. She discovered the sixth law, applied the secret, and made a huge fortune in both money and opportunity. Born on a farm in South Carolina 85 years ago, Woods ventured to New York in 1945 in search of brighter tomorrows. She soon landed a job waiting tables at a local Harlem, New York, eatery. Surprisingly, she didn't even know how to prepare coffee and burned herself trying to serve her first customer. But she learned, and seven and a half years later, the owner offered to sell her the restaurant. "I thought the man was crazy," she recalls. "I had no idea how to run a business."[1] Pulling out all stops, her mother mortgaged the family farm and loaned Woods $20,000. "Scared to death," in August 1962 Woods took charge of the restaurant, changed the menu, and, under the name Sylvia's, began serving southern-style home cooking. Her husband and four children pitched in, clearing tables, seating guests, and launching a family tradition. Today, hordes of patrons descend on this landmark that draws an international clientele. All wait patiently to sample Sylvia's spicy barbecued ribs, fluffy corn bread, and sweet potato pie.

There's no limit to how far or wide the power of the sixth law can reach. Nearly a decade ago, Ken Brown discovered the secret, and not a moment too soon. Seated before an apologetic boss, Brown was informed that his position would be terminated. The cause? Corporate downsizing. Vowing never to be caught off guard again, with pink slip in hand, Brown fought back tears as he explained his dilemma to his wife and children. As discussed earlier, Brown went on to make a name for himself in a host of fields. Today, after the sale of his McDonald's restaurants, he spends most of his time promoting his company, Ken Brown International, as well as lending a hand and breathing life into the dreams of those who need to hear his message most: aspiring entrepreneurs.

The secret was passed on to Lonnie Johnson, and, once he received it, no obstacle or roadblock could ever quell his spirit. Johnson is a member of what seems to be a vanishing breed: the independent inventor. As the third of six children born in Mobile, Alabama, Johnson was inspired by the legend of George Washington Carver. Growing up, Johnson was quiet and curious, driven by a fascination with how things worked. As he grew older, he began constructing a variety of gadgets and contraptions, including rockets powered by fuel cooked up in his mother's saucepans. At 13, he bolted a discarded lawn-mower engine onto a homemade go-cart and took it to a local interstate highway, only to have a bemused policeman escort him home. It was then that Johnson realized "engineers were people who did the type of things that I wanted to do."

Historically, engineering was hardly an obvious career path: Then, as now, the profession was dominated by Whites. In high school, a standardized test from the Junior Engineering Technical Society informed Johnson that he had little aptitude for the field; but he persevered and, as a senior, became the first student from his all-Black high school to enter the organization's regional engineering fair. The event was held at the University of Alabama at Tuscaloosa in 1968, just five years after then-governor George Wallace unsuccessfully attempted to block two Black students from enrolling.

Johnson's entry in the competition was a creation he called "Linex": a compressed-air–powered robot assembled from electromagnetic switches he salvaged from an old juke box and solenoid valves he fashioned out of copper tubing and rubber stoppers. His imagination was shaped by what he had read in books and soaked in through the television series Lost in Space. For nearly a year, he scavenged junkyards searching for the parts he needed to build the robot's base. He constructed wheels and used his sisters' reel-to-reel tape recorder for its eyes. The guts from his brothers' walkie-talkies transmitted signals to the hunk of metal and controlled its movements. The finished product wowed the judges, who awarded Johnson first prize: $250 and a plaque. University officials didn't trumpet the news that a Black teen had captured top honors. "The only thing anybody from the university said to us during the entire competition," Johnson remembers, "was 'Good-bye, and y'all drive safe, now.'"[2] Johnson went on to win math and Air Force ROTC scholarships to Tuskegee University, where he received a bachelor's degree in mechanical engineering before receiving a master's in nuclear engineering. He joined the Air Force in 1975 and subsequently held jobs at the Air Force Weapons Laboratory, NASA's Jet Propulsion Laboratory, and the Strategic Air Command—solid, respectable positions that made him a part of the scientific community. But at each stop, he felt that his creativity was stifled. In 1987, at the age of 38, he could take it no longer. He would go into business for himself, he decided, focusing on his own projects, which included a thermodynamic heat pump, a centrifugal-force engine, and a pressure-action water gun. "All I needed was one to hit," he reasoned, "and I'd be fine."

IT ALL BEGAN BY ACCIDENT

In 1982, while debating the idea for an environmentally friendly heat pump that would use water instead of Freon, the concept for a water gun surfaced in his mind. Johnson had built a prototype pump, attached rubber tubing, and held the device over his bathroom sink. Aiming the nozzle at the tub, he turned it on and produced a blast of water so powerful that the mere wind from the spray ruffled the curtains. Wow, he thought, this would make a great water gun. He developed a prototype for his six-year-old daughter, and rave reviews from neighborhood children convinced him that the device held commercial appeal.[3]

For nine stressful and uncertain years, Johnson hawked his water gun to toy makers. After countless presentations, not to mention sinking close to $15,000 of his own money into the project, he finally reached a deal with the Larami Corporation. Larami's goal was to produce 100,000 units per year of what was originally dubbed "the

Drencher." In 1990, despite little advertising, the gun became an instant hit. Renamed the "Super Soaker" one year later, Johnson's invention became the number one toy in the country.[4] Today, the Super Soaker has been tweaked and repackaged, with more than 20 different variations, and remains a fan favorite. In the years since Johnson received his first U.S. patent, more than 200 million Super Soakers have been sold. Revenue estimates for the toy range as high as $400 million.[5]

Today, Johnson is finally in his element. He no longer operates in the basement of his home but in a meticulously refurbished three-story brick loft featuring soaring ceilings and antique wood floors. His laboratory, however, is a no-frills space, with galvanized electrical conduits descending from the ceiling through gaps where acoustic tiles are missing. On one wall of his office is a promotional poster created by the retail chain Target that features Johnson's face amid a pantheon of nineteenth- and twentieth-century African American inventors. Along another wall visitors will find a row of plaques commemorating a dozen of Johnson's 100-odd patents. And hanging crookedly above his desk is a cheap black frame that contains an inspirational quote that has been attributed to Calvin Coolidge. Under the heading "Press On," it reads: "Nothing in the world can take the place of persistence."[6]

IT WAS A CASE OF BEING SWEPT ASIDE

Oddly enough, those who acquire this secret and use it often find themselves literally swept up in financial success. This hidden key was passed on to Mannie Jackson, and he was more than receptive. "Like every young executive," he said during an interview with best-selling author Harvey Mackay, "I made a run for the CEO position at Honeywell. I didn't get it. As an executive vice president in charge of mergers and acquisitions I was well compensated. My office in the executive wing was elegant and contained all the trappings. Despite that, you know what stared me in the face every morning when I arrived at work? The fact that I knew I was being underutilized."[7]

To say that Mannie Jackson is ambitious would be a gross understatement. Born in a railway box car in southern Missouri, Jackson lived with 12 family members before moving into a two-bedroom house in Edwardsville, Illinois. There he would accompany his mother and grandmother as they cleaned homes throughout the mostly White wealthy neighborhoods. "For most children my age," Jackson admits, "watching your mother and grandmother scrub floors and clean toilets would've been demoralizing. But I viewed their line of work as a learning experience. When I walked into these palatial homes I'd go into the libraries and look at the books the wealthy read. I'd listen as they spoke and interacted with each other. And I'd watch my mother proudly discuss her duties and responsibilities. Believe it or not, I came out of it a better person."

Jackson took up basketball, grew to be six feet two inches, and worked to perfect the jump shot that would become his trademark. At Edwardsville High School, he led the 1956 team to the state final—the only time the school has made it that far. Jackson was named first team all-state and, two years later, became the first of two Black players to letter in basketball for the University of Illinois.

After graduating in 1960, Jackson took his jump shot to New York, intent on making it in the NBA. Ironically, he started in the National "Industrial" Basketball League instead—a collection of company-run semipro teams whose players were also being trained for the corporate world. When Jackson failed to make the New York Knicks, he decided to delay his business career a few years longer in order to suit up for the Harlem Globetrotters—a show-stopping, all-Black barnstorming basketball team. Founded in 1927 by Chicago entrepreneur Abe Saperstein, until 1950, the first year the NBA featured integrated teams, the Globetrotters were the only game in town willing to sign talented Black players. Like many others before him, Jackson fell under Saperstein's spell. Apart from the fact that both had attended the University of Illinois, the two made an unlikely pair. Saperstein, the son of Polish immigrants, was a small, elderly Jewish man who took Jackson under his wing. As the Globetrotters toured the United States and the world, Saperstein introduced his mentee to a slew of high-profile business men and women as well as heads of state. "Abe was a mentor," Jackson says. "Outside of my immediate family, he was only one of a few adults who I thought cared about me personally. I observed him carefully. He was a world-class salesman and the ultimate promoter."[8]

Saperstein also encouraged Jackson to continue his studies, which he did in his spare time and during the off season. Shortly after

Saperstein's death in 1966, Jackson left the Globetrotters to pursue a master's degree in economics at the University of Detroit. He left the program to pursue a position with Honeywell, the Minneapolis-based industrial controls company. By the early 1980s, Jackson was managing Honeywell's Venture Center, spearheading its new ventures division. He thrived in this business environment, acquiring and restructuring numerous deals for Honeywell and building several enterprises from scratch. In 1986, he played a pivotal role in the creation of the Executive Leadership Council, a networking organization comprised of African American Fortune 500 executives. The council gave senior-level Black executives a leadership forum. Two years later, he was promoted to senior vice president at Honeywell and recognized by *Black Enterprise* magazine as one of the 40 most powerful and influential Black corporate executives in the country.

The business and basketball cultures came together for Jackson in 1993 when he acquired the Globetrotters for $6 million. He had hoped to form an investment team to launch an NBA franchise in San Diego, but when he was unable to do so, he turned to his former team.

To save the brand, Jackson implemented three operating principles he had used while working in corporate America. First, the product had to be reinvented in order to become relevant; second, customers had to be shown that management really cared; and third, everyone within the organization—from the marketing department to the players on the court—had to be accountable.[9] Jackson acted quickly to revamp the team's outdated operations. On the basketball side, he kept former Trotter teammate Tex Harrison as coach but replaced much of the roster, updated the music and routines, introduced a mascot named "Globie," and scheduled games against quality opponents. On the business and marketing side, he signed a string of marquee consumer brands, such as Northwest Airlines, Wheaties, Sony, Apple, Reebok, Disney, and Burger King. To expand the brand profile, he convinced Columbia Pictures to produce a feature film profiling the Globetrotters' early days and increased the team's commitment to charity and youth work. The strategy worked. Jackson's rags-to-riches experience has convinced him that he can change people's thinking on the subject of race relations. "I think the most significant element about the Globetrotters being owned by a Black man is not just that I'm African American. It's that I'm committed, and I'm bright, hardworking, and I possess a vision of where we're going. I have the opportunity to impact nearly two million followers a year worldwide. I can tell people outside the U.S. about the greatness of this country. I can go into inner-city Philadelphia or St. Louis and give hope to Black children. People now understand that these tall Black athletes wearing those eye-catching red-white-and-blue uniforms are serious human beings."[10]

Is there life after leaving corporate America? Jackson explains the benefits of the sixth law of wealth: "Within the first 14 months after leaving Honeywell, I made more money than I earned during my entire 25-year corporate career. Both my net worth and—more important—my self-worth are at levels well beyond my wildest dreams."

YOUNGEST CEO

When Robert Frost wrote those insightful lines, "I took the one less traveled by, and that has made all the difference," it would be difficult to think that he didn't have Ephren Taylor in mind. When Taylor—a millionaire on paper by age 16, and less than a decade later the youngest African American CEO of a publicly traded company—confronted the secret of the sixth law of wealth, he jumped at the chance. He launched his first business, a video game development company, when he was 12 years old. "My parents refused to shell out 50 dollars for video games," he explained in an interview, "so I had to figure out how to program them on my own." While still in his mid-teens, he launched GoFerretGo.com, an online employment resource for teenage job seekers, after receiving extensive training at the Kauffman Center for Entrepreneurial Leadership. The company, now with an estimated value of more than $3 million, boasted a staff of 13 employees, including Taylor's former history teacher. Today, Taylor's interests have shifted to real estate, particularly in depressed inner-city areas.

But Taylor's story really revolves around the subject of choice. Henry David Thoreau, the nineteenth-century writer, stated, "If a man does not keep pace with his companions, perhaps it is because he hears the beat of a different drummer." While most of us are not as insightful as Thoreau, each of us is unique. I may not possess your talents or special gifts or be able to do what you do, but each of us has the ability to choose our own path and lifestyle. You may opt to stay with those who bemoan their fate as they constantly point out the lack of opportunities, or—like Taylor, who from an early age opted to march to his own cadence—you may follow the desires of your heart. Perhaps this young Black millionaire says it best:

> True success begins when we simply find that inner spark, that talent, that passion in our lives, and go after it to the exclusion of all the other things. You can work harder, or you can work smarter. I believe the most difficult task is the work you are forced to do for someone else. There's just something mentally draining about it. While we should all be grateful for the opportunity to earn a living and support our family, it's difficult to get into the mind-set that we're doing it for ourselves, when in reality we're working for someone else. Working smart really means thinking about the path that you've taken and analyzing if this chosen line of work suits your talents and gifts.
>
> As you consider this question, picture two roads before you. Call them "Option One" and "Option Two." Option One: Work forty to fifty years for someone else, and do as little as possible in order to keep the boss happy; after all, he or she is the person who pays you and who is buying your time. You're not giving it away, you're selling it. The individual buying your time is purchasing the hours of your life. That's why you are earning "slave-wages." You've sold out to the highest bidder. Along the way, you trade one owner for another. Sometimes they leave you hanging, struggling to find another owner to buy the hours of your life. Hours for dollars—that's all you know. Literally shortening your life, by selling off the hours and the days, the months and the years. Take a couple weeks vacation each year. Show up every day at eight, go home around six. Paint your house on weekends and try to grow a little savings account so you don't have to search for crumbs when you finally retire—if you retire, that is, and don't have a chest blowout by age 45 or 50. Keep your head down, don't create too many waves. Don't worry—be happy!
>
> Sometimes the whole deal fakes us out so much we actually feel as if we are in control!
>
> The only problem is, at this pace, it takes years and years to reach your goal, and your treasure is floating out to sea more and more with every wave, every minute, every day. How much of your goal, your prize, will be there when you finally make it? Who knows? It's more uncertain now than ever, because retirement programs are being

raided, social security is being gutted, medical costs are rising, and very few people even start thinking about retirement until it's too late. When you finally reach your goal decades later, you find just a few shekels stuck in the sand where your treasure was supposed to be, and another beach full of people ahead of you. Broken, worn-out, broke people mostly sitting and wondering what went wrong. For those who choose option one, life drags on, day after day, paycheck to paycheck, "blue Mondays" to TGIF, weekend to weekend, vacation to vacation, finally retirement–then it's gone. Game over.

Option Two: Make a decision to gain all the knowledge you can and keep growing. I think of this option as running on the beach and scooping up a few sea shells (new knowledge, new skills) without missing a beat. You get tired, you stumble, but you get back up and keep running. For how long? Sometimes it may seem like forever, but you know you're closing in on the goal a whole lot faster, and when you get there, there's a whole lot more of it to enjoy. Not only that, but you notice the beach isn't crowded . . . very few people are around, and they're all running in the same direction. No one is dragging his or her heels, wasting years in the sand. They know there's a prize up ahead. You get there after a few years, and there's this monstrous pile of gold, more than you can spend. Plenty to enjoy and create a lifestyle and a future for your family, and plenty to share with your church and charities.

Just past the pile of gold is another beach, and there aren't many people either. They're all full of life and enjoying every moment. That's the rest of your life, and you're still young so you'll be able to really enjoy it to the max, too! You've won your race, you've claimed your prize and you own your life. You own your minutes and hours, and you pay yourself royally. When it is all said and done, the only way to gain your freedom is to buy it. You can't lease it, nor can you wish for it. You buy it and then you own it. You enjoy your health, your family, and your financial security. Think about that goal, of owning your own life and doing what you love. From just barely getting by to living life on your own terms. Now, you can begin to take responsibility for your success and failure . . . and your own life. Which option will you choose?[11]

What makes these millionaires' stories and their achievements so compelling? Is it the daring that seems to lurk behind their decisions to apply the techniques and ideas contained within the secret of the sixth law? Is it the apparent willingness of these men and women to *leap* before they *look?* Is it their amazing ability to hang on—to struggle tooth and nail—long after others have given up? What of the never-say-die attitude that can turn seemingly certain defeat into victory? Is it the wealth and value these individuals create in the lives of others? What about their ability to move at the drop of a dime when opportunity presents itself? What of their ability to see the *unique* in the *familiar?* Is it their grit and white-hot desire to do the impossible or to be somebody? What about their relentless optimism? As one respondent mentioned early in my research, "If you hold any hope of joining this elite club, you must learn to meet hard times with a harder will." When I asked a young Detroit-based millionaire for his thoughts on the matter, he said, "I never think *probably,* only *possibly.*"

Dr. Shirley Bailey, one of the first Black women to graduate from Howard University's School of Dentistry, shared her thoughts regarding pursuing opportunity and overcoming obstacles. After a 30-year dental practice, filling teeth was no longer enough. During whatever spare time she could find, Bailey built a real estate brokerage firm that now boasts more than 85 agents. Today, through her highly celebrated Las Vegas–based agency, she is licensed to sell everything from casinos to cruise ship condominiums. But Bailey's journey has been anything but easy. Listen closely as she offered me advice on the sixth law of wealth: "When it comes to chasing your dreams, each of us must begin somewhere—and there's no better time than when you're starting off at zero. *Why?* Because when you're on the bottom anywhere you go will be an improvement." Her words may seem simple, but nothing is closer to the truth. In short, you learn, persist, and adapt.

Finally, what must you do to uncover and implement in your own life the secret that is contained within the sixth law of wealth? First, you must make a conscious decision that when your moment arrives, you are going to embrace and pursue this course of action. *You choose* to make the sixth law a part of your life; the sixth law does not choose you. The power is in your hands. And second, you must *act.* This law is as much about doing as it is about thinking and believing. It's about seizing opportunity, charting your own course, courage, executing ideas, refusing to take no for an answer, creating your own luck, and being true to the dream that beats in your heart. Believing and conceiving alone won't make it happen. All the wishful thinking you can muster will not manifest this simple principle. Taking action makes all the difference in the world. As you continue to read, I suggest you take note of Leah Brown. I doubt you can find a better example.

THE ROAD TAKEN: WHAT IF YOU WERE SOMEBODY AND NO ONE KNEW IT?

Launching her own business and filling a market niche wasn't enough for Leah Brown. She wanted something more meaningful. For years, Brown worked as an engineer and a lawyer before a personal family crisis caused her to rethink her career choice. She eventually turned her uncle's untimely death into a personal battle-cry for improved health-care. Now, her company, A10 Clinical Solutions, wants to provide minority and underserved communities better clinical trials and research.

Brown grew up in New Jersey with no real interest in healthcare or medicine. Like her parents, she originally thought she would become a teacher. Instead, she studied computer science in college. It wasn't until 1987 when she would discover her true calling. That's when her favorite uncle was diagnosed with AIDS. Though she desperately tried to help him, four months after his diagnosis, he was gone. Despondent, Brown reasoned that her uncle's doctors could not find the right combination or formulation of drugs to keep him going. This would prove to be the defining moment in her life. Angry and confused, she lamented that there wasn't much that could be done for him, nor was there even enough information available to seek proper treatment for those afflicted with the AIDS virus. That frustration, fueled by "divorce and—after 15 years with a large consulting firm—corporate downsizing," brought her to a special place. It was here, during a trying time in her life when pain and anger can either destroy or inspire you, that Brown discovered this sixth law, a place where only this principle resides—where there is no past, no regret, and only the anticipation of future success. With rare exceptions, luck or chance have no bearing on the sixth law. It is simply a matter of finding yourself and building on what you find. It is being able to place yourself in a state of mind that makes the creation of wealth possible. *What was her secret?* After losing her uncle, her husband, and her job, Brown knew the direction in which she would turn: *She would finally control her life and never work for someone else again.*

In the years following her uncle's death, Brown began to channel her negative energy into an unrelenting focus to form a company that could provide clinical testing of the biologics for diseases that were impacting the African American community. Seven years later, A10 Solutions, Inc., now A10 Clinical Solutions, was formed. A10 manages clinical trials for pharmaceutical giants such as GlaxoSmithKline and Merck. The firm also partners with the National Institutes of Health and other government agencies while specializing in research aimed at underserved populations. Today, the firm provides customizable clinical solutions and unprecedented service that eventually develops and provides lifesaving, innovative, and investigational drugs to market faster and safer through the quality management of critical clinical trials. The company's revenue has climbed steadily—from $6 million in 2008 to nearly $20 million in 2010, the same year Brown was named as one of *Fortune* magazine's Top 10 Most Powerful Women Entrepreneurs.

"WHY GET A JOB? I WANTED THE JOURNEY!"

Brown knew that if she was going to enter the healthcare field, it would have to relate to the law. That was the attorney in her. It was part of her comfort zone. But to enter the always-innovative, always-daunting world of clinical trials, money is vital. A fiscally conservative person by nature, Brown knew that her work would be cut out for her. "The entire idea of clinical trials is intriguing," she admits, "but if you lack the funding to keep things going, it could be a problem. So the big picture became: '*I had this great business idea, but how am I going to finance it?*'" Brown recognized that if she were going to enter this arena, she would need capable and talented people to help guide her through the process. That meant hiring high-quality clinicians right out of the gate. "The researchers who I initially brought on really cared and had a passion for the A10 mission. Some stayed. Others moved on. Those who remained did so through all the highs and lows—and, with any start-up, there were some really difficult times. There were defining moments when we had nothing, zero revenues for the first 18 months."[12]

But Brown kept plugging away. A10 eventually landed its first clinical study with Talecris Biotherapeutics, a global biotechnology company that produces critical care treatments for life-threatening disorders in the fields of immunology and neurology. After Talecris's much-needed push, A10 sought a major pharmaceutical company to add to its fold, something Brown calls a true sign that the company had arrived. Before long, the start-up landed Merck & Co. and Glaxo-SmithKline, two internationally recognized conglomerates that placed her enterprise on the clinical research A list. It was only a matter of time before other Fortune 500 pharmaceutical companies jumped on board. In the face of it all, Brown maintains that success means never having to say you're afraid. "Fear nothing. Fear can cripple you and stop you in your tracks.

"Seven years ago I knew where I was going to take this company and use all the knowledge and best practices that were at my disposal. Was it daunting? Yes. I constantly questioned myself. As soon as I solved one problem, I'd ask, 'Did I do the right thing?' There was always probing, always self-evaluations. But if you're not asking the tough questions, you are not doing the right thing.

"Through it all, I knew that we were going to make a difference. When you have an opportunity to do something special, to impact others and to touch pretty much everyone in the world, why wouldn't you sign up for that? *Why get a job? I wanted the journey.*"[13]

FINALLY, HERE'S THE SECRET: THE SIXTH LAW OF WEALTH

Why would anyone choose the life of an entrepreneur? Why would anyone agree to work 60- to 80-hour weeks with no letup in sight? Why would anyone tolerate the headaches and aggravation associated with this line of work? Why would anyone willingly agree to be constantly berated by the doubters, naysayers, and so-called experts who know what's best for *your* life? Why would anyone relinquish the security—either perceived or real—of employment in a Fortune 500 company or a cushy government job to toil at low wages? Why on earth would any man or woman openly commit to bet the farm and place it all on the line—home, savings, and financial future—to walk a daily tightrope of success or failure? In the midst of constant activity, amid a swirl of interactions with exhausted employees, disgruntled customers, and indifferent suppliers, why would anyone sign up to possibly experience the loneliest feeling in the world? Why would anyone in his or her right mind embrace ambiguity and openly wonder where the next investment will come from or how to make payroll? Come push or shove, hell or high water, why would anyone choose to walk this lonely road? It's simple. As stated eloquently by Robert Frost nearly a century ago, because it "has made all the difference."

What is the sixth law of wealth? Do you know? The overwhelming majority of people will never recognize the true difference between wealth and poverty, between living day to day and financial independence. They will never sense freedom and fulfillment, nor will they awaken to their highest potential. A seven-figure income is a mosaic composed of very small stones. *What is the sixth law of wealth?* In six unforgettable words: *Thou shalt own thy own business.*

TOUGHEST QUESTION IN THE WORLD

Which came first—the chicken or the egg? This question has baffled scientists, researchers, and academics throughout the ages. To many, the idea of business ownership—which has come to be viewed as the most traveled route to financial independence—poses an equally debated conundrum: *Are entrepreneurs born or made?* Or, specifically: *Can entrepreneurship be taught?* Some people, including a handful in this study, say no. They argue that entrepreneurs are "born." The hidden assumption in this argument is that there are only a small, select few who have what it takes to start, build, and grow a thriving enterprise. Yet evidence abounds that countless men and women from all walks of life are launching businesses at this very moment.

The same people also contend that management skills cannot be taught. An effective or a good manager is a "born manager." Today, however, the discipline of management is something that academia takes for granted. To further drive the point home, a similar debate surrounds the concept of leadership. And now, leadership training abounds and is second in demand to entrepreneurial development. Until researchers pinpoint the entrepreneurial gene, entrepreneurs will always be "developed." As pointed out by David Butcher in the article "Entrepreneurs: Born or Made," "Consider the long hours, lack of sleep, high risk, high stress and often slow financial return. More than four decades' of research has sought to answer why people become entrepreneurs. Until now, answers have been vague and uncertain, and much of the literature has assumed that the tendency to engage in entrepreneurial activity is explained by learned individual differences or situational factors."[14] Although several Black entrepreneurs can be found among the world's wealthiest, all but a few in this study began their trek to a seven-figure income at the bottom, broke or with little to no capital or savings. Entrepreneurship isn't about who or what you know; it's about what you do (see Table 6.1).

DEMOGRAPHIC PROFILE: BUSINESSES OWNED AND OPERATED BY BLACK MILLIONAIRES*

Q. 17: "If self-employed, state type of business"

% Sample	Type of Business	% Sample	Type of Business
1	Advertising	4	Food Service
1	Architect	16	Franchising
4	Auto/Dealer	1	Funeral Parlor
1	Beverage/Wine/Spirits	1	Grocery Store
1	Bonding Co.	2	Healthcare
2	Building Materials	2	Healthcare Management
1	Carpet/Flooring	3	Hotel/Motel
1	Cleaning Services	3	Insurance
1	Clergy	4	Manufacturing
3	Clothing/Retail	1	Music Distribution
2	Communications	2	Nursing Homes
3	Construction	1	Personnel/Staffing
2	Consulting	1	Photography
2	Convenient Stores	1	Psychologist
1	Cosmetics/Skin Care	1	Public Speaking/Training
2	Direct Sales/MLM**	8	Real Estate
1	Dry Cleaning	2	Real Estate Development
1	Education/Charter School	4	Restaurants
2	Electronics/Technology	2	Securities/Investment
1	Engineering Research	1	Sports Management
2	Entertainment Productions	2	Venture Capital/Private
1	Event Planning		Equity

* Business titles are categories taken from Census Bureau listings. Percentages were based on a sample pool of 500. Physicians, dentists, and surgeons are listed under "Healthcare." Stocks and personal investing are listed under "Securities/Investment." ** MLM = multilevel marketing

Table 6.1

What do highly successful Black millionaires do? They work *for profits, not wages.* Obsessed with perfection, they are a combination of passion, commitment, creativity, drive, and a global perspective. And that mix isn't easy to find. Bottom line: They know what it takes to draw a crowd. Their behaviors revolve around six core strategies:

1. *Desire for independence.* Although research suggests that entrepreneurs are made rather than born, my data pointed out that those business owners who built enterprises with seven-figure-plus revenues shared a combination of behaviors and attitudes that differed from those of their peers who presided over less successful start-ups. When asked for the top three most important entrepreneurial qualities, nearly 75 percent cited "vision," 73 percent cited "passion," and 64 percent cited "drive." As Jeffrey Gitomer, a well-known author and motivational speaker, says, "When you're in business for yourself, you create your own destiny, you write your own story, you design your own legacy, and, most important, you sign your own paycheck. I get to choose when I work, how I work, and who I work with. Being in business for yourself gives you the opportunity to work your heart out for something you love."

2. *Deep sense of purpose.* One of the successful transformative aspects about being an entrepreneur is that you define a moment, an age, or sometimes an epoch. Over the past 50 years, Black entrepreneurs have launched ideas and products that have changed the way society approaches everything from politics to business strategy. The vision and grassroots efforts of these men and women are adjusting the way we think and behave as a people—not only in the context of industry and commerce but, perhaps more important, in the art of wealth creation. How we define a generation is no longer in the hands of corporations and unions. Black business owners who have reached millionaire status are shaping this country, and those examined in this study have done their part to nudge our nation from a W2 economy to a 1099 economy—from employee to employer. What are the secrets of America's greatest Black entrepreneurs? The answer, in one sense, is simple: They are driven by a fire in the belly that makes the improbable possible.

When Charlotte, North Carolina, businessman Bob Johnson set a goal to purchase a professional basketball team or when Cathy Hughes sought to acquire a string of radio stations, they focused on worthwhile and attainable objectives. "I always keep my creative forces at work by keeping my eyes open," Johnson stated. Hughes, on the other hand, replied, "Everything that I achieved began with an idea. The secret of my success involves being able to distinguish good ideas from potential failures."

3. *Believing is seeing. Black millionaires have adapted a new business model—from "find a need and fill it" to "imagine a need and create it."* Refusing to bow to precedent, the most successful Black entrepreneurs are people who are driven by an overmastering purpose and are fueled by an unwavering aim. These innovators are no longer content to supply consumers with products that are simply better at filling existing needs; rather, they choose to create entirely new needs to fill. They know that the consumer appetite for new products is unlimited. Entrepreneurs like Daymond John, Lisa Price, Cathy Hughes, and David Steward have redrawn the lines of what it means to be in business. These serial entrepreneurs will stop at nothing to have their dreams and visions recognized.

For John, it is not enough to launch a ubiquitous urban clothing brand; he now wants to create a lifestyle and experience around it while deciding which batch of would-be entrepreneurs to fund. Steward's reshaping of telecommunications and cellular mobility has changed our world. Hughes has shaken a staid and established old-boy industry. For Price, it's not enough to develop a skin care line—she wants to create a lifestyle, an experience, for an overlooked and once-neglected market segment and create demand for a product nobody knew they wanted. These visionaries are included in the elite club of America's successful Black entrepreneurs. The men and women who have left their mark on the world seized ordinary moments and made them great.

Moreover, successful Black entrepreneurs do not believe that the success or failure of their venture will be governed by fate, luck, "the system," or other circumstances or external forces. They believe that their accomplishments as well as setbacks lie within their own control and influence. Case in point, one-time Tuskegee, Alabama, mayor Johnny Ford shared with me the following anecdote that epitomizes the concept of inner belief and self-worth. More than 50 years ago, he and Earl G. Graves, the eventual editor and publisher of *Black Enterprise* magazine, were riding down a busy Manhattan street when Graves, an entrepreneurial hopeful at the time, pointed to the city's skyscrapers. With a serious expression, he said, "See those buildings up there? That's where I'm going. I'm going to launch my business. It's going to be about Blacks and enterprise. *I'll be a millionaire by the time I hit 40. Johnny, are you coming with me?*" Ford had political ambitions while Graves set his sights elsewhere. He found true success as publisher of a magazine that is primarily a how-to-guide for Black entrepreneurs and professionals. And yes, Graves was a millionaire by age 40.

4. *Tolerance for uncertainty: The ability to take risks and engage in the unknown.* Survey data conclude that most high-profile Black entrepreneurs see opportunity where others see only risk and also tend to be optimists, who believe they can succeed despite the fact that so many suggest that they can't. There is a general consensus among survey respondents that each is committed to begin their day with thoughts of "Why not?" rather than "I can't." Or, as one interviewee stated in the starkest terms, "If you don't get what you want in life, it's a sign that you either didn't want it bad enough or you tried to haggle over the price." The majority of entrepreneurs in this study are convinced that the future will be better than the past, and they will go to great lengths to improve the present.

5. *Iron will/sheer determination and an overriding commitment to succeed.* When genius fails and talent says impossible, when tact and diplomacy flee, when power and influence have done their best yet retire from the field, when resources dry up, when logic and sound advice call it a day, and when belief turns its back—at these times, iron will and gritty persistence step in and, by the sheer force of holding on, convince customers, win the order, close the contract, and seal the deal.

With more persistence and determination than financial backing and a heartfelt goal of offering cardiac healthcare to many overlooked rural communities, Colleen Payne-Nabors, a former nuclear technologist, debuted her vision with a single employee, one mobile van, and a handful of freshly printed business cards. Her first attempt at launching a business of her own was met by mockery, ridicule, and doubt. But in 1998 and barely in her thirties, Payne-Nabors took the first step on her road to wealth—a seemingly endless journey that ran uphill. Consider how she was raised—nine family members in a three-bedroom house on a small central Oklahoma farm; empathize with her as a college admissions officer stamps "rejection" across her file; shake your head in disgust at those who dismissed her business plan as a pipe dream; and come to your feet when she is named "Oklahoma Small Business Person of the Year." Perhaps no one has ever battled longer, or tougher, or in the face of more opposition and roadblocks that would dishearten most would-be entrepreneurs.

From the outset, Payne-Nabors was committed to enduring long days and even longer nights. Battling for what she believed in, she survived her first 18 months, as she described, "by hanging on only by her fingernails." Eight years later, however, her company diversified and has been rebranded into Mobile Cardiac Imaging (MCI) Diagnostic Center, replete with nine mobile units, two diagnostic clinic locations, and a full-time staff of 24. In little more than a decade, Payne-Nabors's enterprise has evolved into the largest fully functional diagnostic center in Tulsa, Oklahoma, closing a gap in much-needed healthcare services. As a result, her earnings have soared from a $40,000-a-year paycheck to owning and operating a business with revenues in excess of $12 million. In terms of what it takes to build a multimillion-dollar enterprise, she got straight to the point in our interview: "In three words: Passion and perseverance. Though I don't believe or suggest that anyone burn bridges, my company forced me to grow up quick and keep my emotions in check. My once-orderly life has taken on a massive change. I try not to be overly disappointed, discouraged, or depressed by setbacks. When they do occur I view them as learning experiences. I try to see adversity and obstacles as opportunities and possibilities. I've been in business for nearly 14 years and I'm still a young woman, and thankfully, I don't have to answer to anyone. *But let's be clear—business is not for the weak.*" The story of Colleen Payne-Nabors proves again—as if proof were still necessary—that wealth and achievement are the predictable result of diligence, ingenuity, and perseverance. Millionaires behave in a way that is more consistent with their stated values and beliefs. They don't simply assert the importance of persistence. They *are* persistent.

6. *Multiple streams of income: The one money rule that all Black millionaires have mastered.* John D. Rockefeller Jr., son of the billionaire founder of Standard Oil, was not hoping to save money when he decided to offer his five sons a weekly allowance. To ensure that each child mastered the sixth law of wealth and the true value of money, his weekly gift came with numerous strings attached. According to Nelson, his second oldest, who eventually became a successful businessman, philanthropist, governor of New York, and owner of the most expensive piece of real estate in Manhattan—the Rockefeller Center—each child would receive 25 cents per week but was required to earn the rest by operating a series of family enterprises. "To earn extra money," the former vice president recalled, "my brothers and I diversified and managed an array of businesses—from growing vegetables to raising rabbits to marketing dry goods, to saving 10 percent of our earnings as well as supporting our favorite charity." Another brother, David, who would become chairman of Chase Manhattan Bank, said, "We all profited by the experience, especially when we understood the value of money and the most efficient way to earn it."[15]

Some would expect that Rockefeller's children, raised in the lap of luxury, would be spared such chores and trivial duties. Yet the oil baron wanted his sons to understand the value of money and believed this was the best way to convey the message. As a rule, success and wealth are the triumph of common, ordinary virtues. Rich beyond any measure, Rockefeller taught a specific pattern for creating wealth and the wisdom each quality contained.

1. Be prepared to work—whatever you work to acquire, you value.

2. Know where your money is going. Account for every penny; maintain accurate and itemized records of your daily expenditures. Whatever you can account for, you control.
3. Save 10 percent of your earnings—the root of wealth and prosperity can be found in saving.
4. You are not wealthy because you possess a lot of money; *you are wealthy when your money works for you.*

Be your own boss—the sooner the better. Black millionaires never depend on one income source; instead they create a number of revenue streams.

Arguably, here lies the quickest way to build a fortune. Though Steve and Pasha Carter never met the oil magnate, they certainly subscribe to his wealth-building formula. It would be too simplistic to say that this husband-and-wife team ditched promising careers to start their own home-based network marketing business just because they wanted to get rich. The Frisco, Texas–based couple felt stifled in their respective lines of work. For example, while growing up, Steve never recalled his dad being forced to punch a time clock. His father operated a court reporting agency, and it was generally assumed that once his son finished college, he would run the business. Pasha managed patient billing for one of the largest hospitals in the Atlanta, Georgia, area, but she clearly had loftier goals. The former Atlanta Falcon cheerleader wanted it all: a fulfilling career with all the financial trappings wrapped around a loving and supportive family. However, what her nine-to-five life provided left her wanting. Even after taking on a second job, she could not make ends meet. But, for both Steve and Pasha, their prospects for the future drastically improved. The potential upside of a multilevel marketing start-up tipped the balance. What drove Steve and Pasha, who were single at the time and did not know one another, to pursue the same opportunity from different parts of the country was a promise—a promise to be given the opportunity to finally master money rather than permitting money to master them. A promise to live life to the fullest and to bathe each day in the golden glow of enthusiasm. And, most important, a promise to share their knowledge, lifting countless men and women out of poverty and altering thousands of lives for the better.

Nearly 16 years ago, after reviewing the same multilevel marketing opportunity, Steve and Pasha each dove in. While he searched for the chance to carve out a business of his own—one that would offer flexibility and residual income and would not chain him to a desk— Pasha was driven by the bottom line. "I was asked to look at this business model during the middle of the day," she shared in our interview. "Leading the discussion was an unassuming young man in his early twenties. Once I pushed my ego aside, it didn't take me long to realize that he was making more money in a month than I was earning all year. At that point it was a no-brainer. I got started in 1995 and never looked back." Though their rise to millionaire status was anything but easy, each understood that whatever hurdles they had to clear or walls they had to knock down, reaching their goal would only be a matter of time. "In network marketing," Pasha claims, "you can either make money or you can make excuses—but you can't do both." Steve chimes in, "For those who are considering a network marketing business you should begin by asking yourself three key questions: Am I happy? Do I deserve more? Do I want more? If the answer is yes, I suggest that you begin to walk to the beat of your own drum and dismiss what others may think, say, or do."

After making huge strides on parallel paths for the better part of five years, the two joined forces and combined their businesses into one highly profitable organization under the 5LINX umbrella, a unique home-based business that offers a variety of computer and telecommunications products. Their seamless new team is focused on the same wealth-building core values—to broaden their audience and personally empower each individual who is exposed to their business. According to the Carters, successful networking is a skill that comes through experience and belief. From day 1, they believed in the networking profession and never wavered in their conviction that they were going to succeed. They just didn't know how soon. But they are equally committed to a deeper cause: "I want to show people how to *earn* more so they can *keep* more, *invest* more in order to *live* more," Pasha explains. "In this economy, if you are tied or confined to a single paycheck, you are really unemployed. We want to teach people not only how to make millions but how to keep it and pass it on through generations. Our goal is to leave a legacy." Collectively, their passion is to help others transform self-limiting beliefs into self-fulfilling breakthroughs. And the best way to do that is to utilize the proven ageless moneymaking formula at the heart of the sixth law of wealth: Create multiple streams of income.

NEW RULES OF MONEY: FIRE YOUR BOSS

Not so long ago, there was a basic recipe for wealth:

1. Start with four years of college.
2. Add one white-collar job. (For best results, find a Fortune 100 company with a huge pension fund.)
3. Slowly stir in equal measures of loyalty and initiative.
4. Wait 40 years before retiring.

Forging ahead isn't quite so easy these days. There aren't many companies that continue to search for lifetime relationships with employees; many aren't sure what industry they'll be in a few years from now or whether they'll have one at all. You could believe that your job seems safe today only to find yourself replaced by software or a cheaper overseas worker tomorrow. Even in a reasonably robust economy, an estimated 1.7 million employees will lose their jobs each year. Moreover, seasoned employees with peak salaries will inevitably be a chief target of layoffs, and once lost, such employees are the most difficult to place. Each of us is living with loads of uncertainty, adjusting and readjusting as our industry evolves, and putting in 50 hours per week or more in the meantime.[16] Here's a prediction: Sooner or later, you will reach a pivotal moment in your career—maybe close to your intended retirement date, maybe not—when you will want to look long and hard at the possibility of proceeding on your own terms, of living life without a paycheck.

Working solely for a paycheck is neither wrong nor bad, but it is a risky proposition. Risky because as your paycheck increases, so do your taxes; and, as your paycheck grows so does your dependence on others. Countless men and women struggle all the days of their lives with no stronger urge than to acquire the basic necessities: food, shelter, and clothing. Now and then someone will step out of the masses, flee from the ranks, and tip the scales to demand of him or herself, and of the world, more than a mere living. This individual is determined to leave a legacy—a solid faith in his or her mission—the rooted belief that this is the sole purpose to which this person has been called. "The greater danger," wrote Michelangelo, the sixteenth-century Renaissance sculptor and painter, "is not that our hopes are too high and we fail to reach them, it's that they are too low and we do." The world's wealthiest and most fulfilled are those who rose up and refused to be victimized by anything less than their individual destiny.

Job security is a phrase that our parents or grandparents frequently used. But in today's economy, the concept of any type of security—*job or social*—has gone the way of analog phones and eight-track tapes. Those who have retained their jobs must do more for less—shoulder more of the workload, work longer hours, and often forgo any form of additional compensation. As of this writing, seniority offers no safety net and fewer incentives. So why not take the road less traveled? Why do some people go through life imprisoned in a jail of their making—the jail of *ignorance,* the jail of *poverty,* and the jail of *fear*—when the sixth law of wealth—the key that would free them—is within their reach? Ironically, human nature seems to have an ancient predisposition to say no. It is, of course, a conservative response—a status quo protector, a reactionary response that says, "I'm trying to cope with things as they are. Don't rock the boat." Change of any type always carries with it the possibility of change for the worse.

The social writer and philosopher Eric Hoffer, in his groundbreaking book *The True Believer,* stated that there is a conservatism of the poor as rigid as that of the rich and wealthy. The poor are constantly engaged in managing their survival. Regardless of how bleak or limited their circumstances, they feel that change of any kind may be for the worse. As a result, they approach life on that level. The wealthy, in contrast, are quite content with circumstances as they are; they hope to maintain the status quo and keep their lives in order. Unfortunately, we really can't keep saying no if we hold any prospect of succeeding. Survival should not be your only option. It's fine for those creatures on the left side of the evolutionary chart, but for the man or woman front and center in the twenty-first century—ripe with opportunities—simply surviving is out of the question and the beginning of a long slide toward oblivion. Humanity requires much more. It is important that we enjoy our time in this free and open society and make some sort of contribution to the welfare of others. Personal fulfillment (a subject that is discussed in detail in chapter 7) is the result of producing, creating, and serving others.

Security? There's no such thing. There's only opportunity. For the business owners highlighted in this study, entrepreneurship is an endless adventure. For these creative souls, it offers them the opportunity to test their ideas, creativity, abilities, moral stamina, and, most of all, faith. Like some, you may lack the ambition, desire, or inclination to assume full responsibility for the outcome of your life. You may prefer steady employment. You may choose to allow others to fret over payroll and sweat over inventories, expenses, slow sales, and impending debts. But recognize that, by doing so, you will never enjoy the freedom, ownership, or chance to enjoy the fruits of your labor. If you expect to call on your greatest qualities in your finest hour, you cannot be risk averse—which, for too many people, is the unheralded side effect of working too long.

And when that entrepreneurial bug begins to bite, I urge you to place the new start-up failure rate in proper prospective (as if budding entrepreneurs must be crazy to take the risk). For example, a 2010 Kauffman Foundation study revealed that nearly 50 percent—one half—of new business start-ups survive the first five years.[17] So whether the figurative glass is half full or half empty rests entirely on your perspective. If controlling your own schedule and income, as well as possibly joining the ranks of Black America's financial elite, is important to you, who wants to play it safe? "The only way to create wealth," advised Michael Roberts in an interview, one-half of a highly successful sibling partnership, "is to vow early in life never to allow opportunity to slip by." Two decades ago, Roberts and his brother Steven couldn't find two quarters to rub together. Today, these African American business leaders estimate their holdings—from hotels, to real estate, to telecommunication outlets—to be worth more than $1 billion.[18] Amazingly, one St. Louis, Missouri, hotel in their portfolio once refused to serve Blacks. "Never shrink from anything that will give you more discipline, enhanced training, or broaden your experience," Mike Roberts continued. Sooner or later each of us must address the question: 'If not, why not? If not now, then when? *If not me, then who?*'" The answers will jump to life *if* you are ready to receive them. Again, Thoreau wrote, "If one advances confidently in the direction of his dreams, and endeavors to live the life which he has imagined, he will meet with a success unexpected in common hours." Closer to home, Leah Brown may have said it best during a recent interview: "We need more faith-filled men and women who are energetic enough, bold enough, determined enough, and gritty enough to sign their name on the front of a paycheck as well as the back." It is *you* who must develop a deep desire for independence as well as a proclivity to act if you are to pave a new road to your financial future. Remember, the *teaching* is in the words, but the *learning* is in the silence. I now urge you to move boldly and take the first step on the road to the sixth law of wealth: Thou shalt own thy own business.

MILLIONAIRE LESSON NO. 7

"We need faith-filled men and women who are energetic enough, bold enough, determined enough, and gritty enough to sign their name on the front of a paycheck as well as the back."

—*Leah Brown*

SEVEN

MAKE THY MONEY GROW

The Seventh Law of Wealth

Success in life comes not from holding a good hand, but by playing a poor hand well.

—Robert Louis Stevenson

NOW THAT YOU HAVE REACHED THE FINAL CHAPTER OF *The Wealth Choice,* you know that those men and women who have achieved both financial comfort and wealth are distinctly different from those who struggle paycheck to paycheck or who sink deeper into debt. Thanks in part to the research on which this book is based, I can tell you precisely what comprises the difference between the roughly 112,000 African American households or the 35,000 Black men and women who possess a net worth of $1 million or more—.01 percent—and the scores of Americans, Black and White, who struggle to pay their bills.

First, they differ in their attitudes, behaviors, personalities, and goals. In short, the .01 percent are driven; they are deeply passionate about what they do. It's as if their chosen field of work or endeavor is a calling, not a career.

Second, they have a certain quiet inner peace regarding their ability to meet any challenge, to rise above any situation or circumstance. They are overcomers. Though the overwhelming majority did not experience an easy path, Black millionaires are nonetheless more optimistic and infinitely more resilient than the average man or woman. They know the deepest truths of giving and sacrifice and the miraculous power of commitment and faith. They give of themselves, their time, their resources, and their sleep, reinvesting every dollar and mortgaging every property. They are more likely to find inspiration in a pink slip than in a promotion.

Third, Black millionaires are innovative and creative; they not only think outside of the box, they create their own box.

Fourth, the Black financial elite are grateful—incredibly grateful—for the blessings and good fortune that life has thrown their way. They tend to be goal setters committed to doing more than expected and giving more than required.

Fifth, the Black financial elite are always on a personal quest to learn something new, to absorb new information. Rather than focus on the next best thing, they are more apt to focus on what's now. However, most important, they approach life with a different mind-set and a unique set of skills, especially regarding the seventh law of wealth. The story of S. B. Fuller provides an excellent example.

FROM HAVE NOT TO HAVE

Wealth and self-development were S. B. Fuller's two most conspicuous qualities. They soon became a lifelong obsession. No one shared or believed in this concept and the spirit of enterprise more than Fuller. Born in Monroe, Louisiana, Fuller was always a picture of energy and full of plans, someone who was ahead of his time. Brought up in poverty and receiving only a sixth-grade education, he began to teach himself and bolster his professional development by reading such books as *The Art of Selling* and *How to Win Friends and Influence People*. In the early 1930s, Fuller sold insurance for the Commonwealth Burial Association, a Black-owned firm, and soon he was supervising company employees. Through daily morning lectures to his sales staff, he honed a philosophy of self-help and financial independence.

By the 1950s and 1960s, Fuller had built a multimillion-dollar conglomerate of businesses that boasted sales of more than $15 million a year and employed 5,000 sales representatives in 38 states. Fuller Products controlled eight other corporations, including a Chicago-based department store, Fuller-Philco Home appliances, the Regal Theater, a real estate trust in New York, farming and cattle interests, and the Courier chain of newspapers serving Black subscribers throughout the Midwest, New York, and Pittsburgh. Fuller's mother, who died when he was 17, had convinced her son that the best way out of poverty was through sales and entrepreneurship. As a result, Fuller hitchhiked to Chicago and tried his hand in sales but felt confined; he knew he would no longer be trapped working for someone else. Acting on his own philosophy and in the teeth of the Depression, he launched his first enterprise with $25—the Fuller Products Company—buying soap wholesale and then selling it door to door. He later used these sales techniques to offer a briefcase full of items under a little-known line of cosmetics.

In 1951, Fuller purchased a seven-story building in the heart of downtown Chicago, where he held incentive-laden sales conventions rewarding top producers for their efforts. In one case, the top earner received a Cadillac.[1] In a September 1956 "Businessmen in the News" profile, *Fortune* magazine noted that Fuller Products Company's gross sales reached $18 million.[2] During this period, Fuller reportedly became the wealthiest Black man in America. His business flourished, prompting him to further expand his own brand and auxiliary products, which were marketed across the country. He was the first African American to employ cross-country marketing. Speaking before the Baptist convention in Chicago in the early 1960s, Fuller shared a snippet of the seventh law of wealth and urged Blacks to collectively assume the responsibility for their own growth and development. "The ultimate weapon in the fight against discrimination is self-help," he urged, "and a refusal to remain dependent on others for your own sustenance. Dependence on others is no better than updated slavery."[3]

This rags-to-riches story should have made him a hero within the Black community, and to some he was. That was until 1963, when, at the request of the National Association of Manufacturers, Fuller—the organization's first Black member—gave a keynote address in which he stated in part:

> Whenever there are people, there is progress, and whenever there is progress, there are problems. The number one domestic problem in America today is the race problem. It is contrary to the laws of nature

for man to stand still; he must move forward, or the eternal march of progress will force him backward. This the Negro has failed to understand; he believes that the lack of civil rights legislation, and the lack of integration have kept him back. But this is not true; the lack of initiative, courage, integrity, loyalty, and wisdom are responsible for his not making the rate of progress that he should make. . . . If the Negro had the amount of initiative, courage, and imagination required, he could control the retail selling in his own community. A lack of understanding of the capitalistic system and not racial barriers keeps the Negro from making progress.[4]

DEATH OF A SALESMAN

Fuller's message to the manufacturers was not particularly new for him, but the level of coverage of his remarks was. Moreover, several days later, in an interview with *U.S. News & World Report,* Fuller elaborated: "The minute that Negroes can develop themselves so they excel in whatever they do, then they are going to find that they don't have many problems."[5] Black leaders were incensed. His remarks touched off a firestorm of rage that—driven by the NAACP—would lead much of Black America to boycott his products, thus destroying most of his fortune. But others pointed out that Fuller was not the first Black leader to address these issues; Frederick Douglass, Booker T. Washington, and Marcus Garvey openly shared similar views at different times in history. The problem was that this topic was and, to this day, remains taboo. Some African Americans not only questioned the strategy but wondered how bankrupting the Fuller Products Company would move the civil rights agenda forward. Here was a man who was confined by race as well as all aspects of building a business. Civil rights leaders had to be reminded that many of Fuller's problems were related to bias in the banking community. The normal channels of credit and investment open to his competitors were closed to Fuller. If it wasn't for Fuller and fellow Black millionaires Arthur G. Gaston and T. M. Alexander, who provided much-needed financial support for a host of Black causes, icons such as Martin Luther King Jr. and Medgar Evers would have spent more time in jail instead of leading their troops. It was Fuller—the budding entrepreneur who at one time could barely read or write—who rescued the influential Black newspaper the *New York Courier* from bankruptcy—the same newspaper that played a key role in placing Jackie Robinson between the White lines in organized baseball. Unfortunately, the boycott had a profound effect. When the dust settled, Fuller's multimillion-dollar nest egg had shrunk to $300,000.

I share this story not to force you to choose sides, take issue with a generations-old argument, or even cast blame, if blame is due. If I did, all those who picked up this book would surely miss my point. No, the purpose of this brief profile is to highlight the internal mission of one individual whose goal in life was to ensure that all of God's children were given full access to the tools and principles that are beyond necessary for those who hold any hope of rising financially. Once each month, more than a half century ago, like clockwork, Fuller would share his wisdom and business prowess—labeled his gospel of success—with would-be entrepreneurs, power brokers, and corporate climbers alike. Those in attendance included Joe Dudley, chief executive, Dudley Products; George Johnson, who would make his mark in the hair care field; Mary Ellen Schadd Strong, the future publisher of *Black Family* magazine; Rick McGuire of Seaway Furniture Store, Inc., who as part of his marketing campaign featured a sign in his store window stating "A S.B. Fuller-inspired business"; Daryl Grisham, president of Parker House Sausage; John Lawson of the Dallas, Texas–based Lawson Cosmetics Co.; Dr. T. R. M. Howard, president of the National Business League; as well as a young and impressionable John H. Johnson, who would listen to his mentor with rapt attention before returning home to hock his mother's furniture in order to build his publishing empire. Each proudly professed to their mentor, "If there had been no you, there would have been no us." And Fuller's sales and promotion insight did not stop at the outer edges of the Black community. Far from it. His marketing, placement, and advertising principles, specifically among female consumers, are still used to this day in Fortune 500 powerhouses such as Avon and Mary Kay.

During these monthly meetings and pep talks, each of these people, and many others, would listen intently and constantly, probing their teacher for additional strategies and solutions. These millionaires-in-the-making wanted to know what they had to do to live a seven-figure life. While thousands, if not millions, of African Americans judged Fuller—a man they had never met or encountered—on his remarks, he was a visionary, a difference maker who was committed to changing his life as well as his community all because he took this statement to heart: "Poverty is not the enemy. The enemy is the man or woman who not only believes in his or her own helplessness but actually worships it." And then he gave his charges a hint as to the seventh and final law of wealth: "If we could save money as well as we save souls, many of our problems would be solved."[6] Fuller's main message centered on individual freedom and personal responsibility, so why was there so much hostility toward this man who made such a difference in the lives of others? Perhaps that answer lay in his favorite quote written by his favorite philosopher—Plato: "Better be unborn than untaught, for ignorance is the root of misfortune."

SEVENTH LAW OF WEALTH

S. B. Fuller's advice regarding the discipline of saving cannot be over-stated. As a citizen in this land of opportunity, nearly anyone who reads this book has and will earn enough money during his or her working life to be classified as wealthy. That's right, you read it correctly. Each of us will eventually earn *enough money to live our days in endless comfort.* Over our lifetimes, regardless of our education, you and I will more than likely earn more than $1 million in wages. *So, why aren't more men and women within our community wealthy?* Simple. The problem doesn't lie with how much we earn—our problem rests squarely with the issue of what we do with our money once we earn it. My interview with one of Black America's entrepreneurial icons is indicative of how Black millionaires handle and view their money.

T. M. Alexander's story is the American dream made manifest, a plot straight out of Horatio Alger. In 1931—during the bleakest days of the Great Depression—Alexander graduated from Morehouse College, finishing with honors. John Wesley Dobbs, grandfather of Atlanta's first Black mayor, Maynard Jackson, would tease, "I remember when he came out of Morehouse. Here was a Black man with a head full of dreams and a brief case full of ambition. Getting started for T. M. was not easy, but success rarely is," he continued. "Instruments do not become sharp on soap rock; *it's difficulties that make men invincible.*"

To help celebrate his accomplishment, an uncle surprised Alexander with $100, which he used to start the same business that he ran until the day he died: Alexander & Associates, one of our nation's oldest and most successful Black-owned insurance companies. In those days, a Black man in business was not only an entrepreneur but also an unwitting crusader. Often isolated and misunderstood, Alexander was a success by any definition, as he fought to preserve both space and dignity in a society that wielded racism and discrimination like a sledgehammer. "When I started out I peddled insurance like produce from door to door, often with little success. However, over time, I was able to gradually build up a loyal clientele, quietly and without fanfare." For nearly 70 years, Alexander, a millionaire several times over, could be found at the helm, still climbing and expanding by utilizing the same principle—the seventh law of wealth—which he shared throughout his life.

One spring afternoon, Alexander and an associate took a leisurely stroll down Peachtree Street, the heart of Atlanta's bustling marketplace. The entrepreneurial stalwart and pillar of the Black community made it his business to enter every shop along the way, stopping long enough to handle a piece of merchandise and commend the owner on his or her wares before moving on. After nearly two hours of witnessing this routine, his friend asked Alexander why he loved to frequent the market but never purchase a thing. "I am always amazed," the frugal chief executive replied, "to see just how much stuff I don't need. Every man is needy who spends more than he has; no man is needy who spends less. So what is the best way to build a fortune? *Don't waste it.*"

So many times we manage our monthly income in a manner that prevents us from appreciating the true level of wealth that we possess. We pay the butcher, the baker, and the candlestick maker as well as anyone else who finds us in the mood. So many people commit their total income and then some without retaining any portion for themselves. The problem is that we forget to make ourselves just as important as those who are competing for our hard-earned dollars. So few realize that regardless of what we do for a living, each of us can be financially independent by the time we reach age 65 if we only give a dime out of every dollar to the most overlooked person—*ourselves*—as well as that forgotten family—*our own.* As the noted author and intellectual W .E. B. Du Bois says, we've given all of our economic power away. "When you owe another, your freedom is impaired," Du Bois counseled. "Your ability to decide your destiny is tainted by the amount you owe."[7]

Why is saving so important? Several reasons come to mind.

1. Without a basic savings account—an emergency cushion—you might be continually stuck in a cycle of debt.
2. Saving is synonymous with peace of mind, greater options, and power: the power to leave a dead-end job or a bad relationship, or to avoid difficult circumstances altogether.
3. If you can't save, you cannot invest. And investing—whether in stocks, bonds, mutual funds, real estate, or commodities—or preferably some combination thereof—is the cornerstone of the seventh law of wealth. Saving and investing is the only way in which your income will not only keep pace with inflation and taxes but multiply.

MAKE THY MONEY GROW

The task of building wealth may be daunting, but it is not insurmountable. Once you understand how to hold on to your economic power, in the form of spending, saving, and investing, your focus shifts. You no longer concern yourself with every nickel and dime but rather with the financial strategies that have and will create substantial wealth. On the surface, this may not sound like hard financial advice, but it is true. If you desire to join the Black financial elite, I suggest that you begin to shift your thinking: Rather than focusing on your lack of money, concentrate instead on your abundance of financial resources. As discussed earlier, whatever we envision expands. I urge you to take hold of the seventh law. By mastering this principle of wealth conservation, you are satisfying a crucial prerequisite to all that you desire.

I have traveled extensively and observed a variety of diverse cultures. I have watched those who resent the affluent and wealthy as well as others who consider wealth's magical charms the be-all, end-all final destination of life. T. D. Jakes tells us in *The Great Investment:*

I have experienced success and struggle, power and poverty. I have thrived and been thwarted by a fluctuating economy. I have lived on both sides of the track, and my shoes have walked down shantytown streets and sidewalks paved with gold. I know that hard work and determination can overcome humble beginnings, and that circumstances beyond our control can tumble fortunes like a house of cards. For some, success was handed to them as they were born into wealthy families and were given choices and opportunities denied to most. I have seen people go from wealth to gross poverty through one bad business decision, one prolonged illness, a lawsuit, a problem child. Success is fragile.[8]

Due, in part, to the 2009 recession, the following data highlight far too many disturbing trends with regard to the current state of Black wealth.

- According to the Economic Policy Institute, as many as 40 percent of Black households had a zero or negative net worth in 2009. Compared to their White counterparts, this economic gap has quadrupled in recent years. During this period, the median wealth of White households stood at $113,149 compared with less than $6,000 for African Americans.
- In 2010, the Insight Center for Community Economic Development released their report, "Lifting as We Climb: Women of Color, Wealth, and America's Future," which found that nearly one-half of single Black women have zero or negative wealth, meaning their debts exceed their assets; one-fourth of single Black women have no checking or savings account; and only 33 percent of single African American women are homeowners.
- In 2009, the National Foundation for Credit Counseling stated that 51 percent of African Americans admit they do not pay their bills on time, and 84 percent carry a monthly credit card balance.
- After peaking at 50 percent in 2006, African American home ownership dropped to nearly 44 percent. As of this writing, many Blacks are at least two months behind on their mortgages, placing them at risk for foreclosure; others are dealing with subprime loans they can no longer afford. It has been estimated that 1.1 million African Americans will lose their homes—the number one generator of net worth and equity—by 2012.
- Not only are African Americans more likely to be unemployed and experience longer periods of joblessness, but as of March 2012, our country's Black jobless rate remained at 13.6 percent, well above the 9 percent national average.

- According to a recent Federal Deposit Insurance Corporation report, more than half of Black households use alternative financial services, including payday lenders, check cashing companies, or pawnbrokers.
- One out of five Black households lack either a checking or savings account; only one in four African Americans owns stocks, bonds, or mutual funds.
- Of the 1.4 million individuals who filed for bankruptcy in 2011, nearly 55 percent were African American.

PART OF ALL YOU EARN IS YOURS TO KEEP

So what is the answer? How can you apply the life-changing seventh principle of wealth in your life? In your finances? Here is the single key that not only made these Black millionaires wealthy beyond their wildest desires but permitted them to hold onto the vast majority of their earnings. After all, the overwhelming majority did not create their millions overnight. Nor did they find themselves on the threshold of a seven-figure income because someone died or bequeathed a check. In fact, nearly nine out of ten explained that their wealth developed over time. How can you use and practice this final law of wealth that continually allows the well-to-do to stand on solid financial ground?

The power of this principle cannot be overstated. Remarkably, this final law of wealth can be traced back 6,000 years to ancient Babylonia. It was in this setting that Babylon—a city that was bordered by the Euphrates and Tigris rivers and was the capital of the Persian Gulf—became the wealthiest city of the ancient world because its citizens were the richest people of their time. They appreciated the value of money. They practiced sound financial principles in acquiring money, growing their income, and building their net worth. The financial accomplishments of those who lived in this region and time period would have been forgotten had it not been for the writings of a twentieth-century map maker.

George S. Clason was the creator of a series of short stories, which he called the Babylonia Parables. In the stories, he described the success secrets of the ancients and how they handled their financial affairs. Read by millions, this timeless book—*The Richest Man in Babylon*—has been hailed as the greatest of all inspirational works on the subject of thrift and financial planning. In 1926, Clason, a successful Colorado businessman, began to explain the lost virtue of thriftiness and the process of saving money to build wealth. He compiled his thoughts in pamphlets and distributed them through banks as well as the financial community. After the stock market crash in 1929 and the onset of the Great Depression, Clason's message had particular relevance as he sought to bring his financial advice to an expanded readership. By 1930, he compiled his favorite stories in what would be the best-selling book *The Richest Man in Babylon,* publishing the 144-page tome through a company bearing his name.

The short, allegorical self-help reader struck a chord with Depression-era consumers, who clamored for its easy-to-read financial advice and wisdom on wealth creation. Rather than writing in a dry business tone, Clason delivered his lessons through parables set in ancient Babylon. His premise was that today money is governed by the same laws that controlled it when prosperous individuals thronged the streets of Babylon, 4,000 years before Christ. To this day, the book remains popular, gaining exposure as new generations of readers pick it up, learn from it, and apply the principles contained within. "The secret to prosperity," the author pointed out, "is to believe and practice this axiom: Part of all you earn is yours to keep. Learn to live on less than you make and save the balance for yourself."

So what would you do to become a millionaire? Most people would reply with a variety of answers, some difficult and challenging. What if I mentioned that keeping track of your weekly or monthly expenses could and would add to your earnings? *Would you do it?* I would hope so, but the sad truth is that most people would not make this simple effort. With the addition of one important element—saving and investing—this is a fundamental strategy that the Black financial elite practice on a daily basis (see Table 7.1). It is not enough to earn a decent living—or even a living that is beyond decent. Black millionaires take their earnings and put them to work. It is no wonder their nest eggs continue to increase. *Why? Because money goes where it is treated best.*

PATIENT INVESTOR

Searching for silver linings inside the derailed U.S. economy? They are out there for the brave and resilient. Just ask John Rogers Jr., as seasoned investors have for more than 35 years. The stockbroker pioneer

INVESTMENT BEHAVIOR CALCULATED
IN PERCENTAGES (N = 500)*

How much money will you need (in total) for a secure retirement?

Less than $200,000	1%
$200,000–$249,999	1%
$250,000–$499,999	4%
$500,000–$749,999	5%
$750,000–$1,000,000	21%
More than $1 million	67%

What percent of your monthly income (gross) do you save or invest?

Less than 5	11%
6–10	27%
11–15	23%
16–20	18%
21–25	7%
More than 25	14%

How much money do you invest per month into your retirement account?

$50–$100	3%
$101–$200	8%
$201–$299	5%
$300–$399	6%
$400–$499	7%
More than $500	63%
Nothing at this time	8%

Are you investing in the stock market right now?

Yes	72%
No	28%

If "yes," how long (in years) have you been investing?

Less than 5	8%
6–10	17%
11–15	24%
16–20	20%
21–25	20%
26–30	4%
More than 30	6%

Total amount invested in specific retirement account?

Less than $5,000	3%
$5,000–$24,999	4%
$25,000–$49,999	9%
$50,000–$99,999	9%

| $100,000–$200,000 | 21% |
| More than $200,000 | 52% |

How confident are you that you will have saved enough money for a comfortable retirement?

Very confident	44%
Somewhat confident	46%
Not confident at all	10%

Do you or your spouse participate in any of the following retirement programs?

401(k)	46%
IRA**	38%
403(b)	13%
Other	2%

* Survey responses to questions 1, 3 to 10. Questionnaire administered May 2005 to February 2011.
** IRA = individual retirement account

Table 7.1

maintains that amid the ashes of the financial crisis of 2009 exists one of the greatest entrepreneurial environments in years for those determined to make their money grow.

Once his father gave him shares of stock as a twelfth-birthday gift—IBM, Greyhound, General Motors, and American Can—John Rogers was hooked. By his senior year in high school, he hired his own broker, whose office he visited to read the ticker and pore over stock quotes in the *Wall Street Journal*. Four years later, he became one of only a handful of his race gutsy and resilient enough to try his hand within this unsure and sometimes volatile industry.

John Rogers Jr. was born in 1958. His well-to-do family regularly discussed politics, money, and philosophy at the dinner table.[9] Always an inquisitive student, Rogers graduated from the University of Chicago Laboratory School in 1976, the same year he was selected "All-State" by the class A Illinois basketball committee. After graduation, he headed to Princeton, where he thrived in the classroom as well as on the basketball court. Rogers starred as guard for the legendary basketball coach Pete Carill and the Princeton Tigers. His appetite already whetted with the endless possibilities of markets, earnings yields, and profit margins, Rogers spent the next four years effectively dividing his time among economics, investments, and zone defenses. Even as his teammates discussed upcoming games and tournament hopes, Rogers could be found in the library soaking up the latest market figures or visiting a local brokerage office. During this time, he also latched onto value investing after reading Burton Malkiel's classic *A Random Walk Down Wall Street*. With an Ivy League degree in hand, Rogers landed a job as a stockbroker with William Blair & Company in Chicago. Besides being the first recruit hired straight out of college in more than four years, he was the first Black professional to work at the 400-employee firm. For Rogers, Blair & Company was the ideal place to learn the business; it was a one-stop shop encompassing corporate and public finance, trading, money management, mutual funds, and research, and specializing in small-cap stocks.[10] For the next three years, Rogers successfully guided clients in their investment transactions while continuing to refine his own growth strategies.

Though his reputation soared, Rogers was determined to follow his own star. In 1983, he traded the comfort of working with a reputable firm and steady income for the nonstop, high-stakes roller coaster world of running his own shop. He ventured out on his own and immediately turned to those who had initially piqued his interest—his parents. Based on the confidence of personal contacts and seed money from family and friends, Rogers launched his company, Ariel Capital Management, named after the African and Asian mountain gazelle. In his tiny downtown Chicago digs, John Rogers equipped himself with the basics: a phone line, a calculator that slammed out numbers with strings of zeros, a stack of business cards, and the morning edition of the *Chicago Tribune*. From this starting point, he single-mindedly viewed his world.

SLOW AND STEADY WINS THE RACE

Rogers took on an associate and experienced two grueling years. Though business was promising, his parents' connections with would-be investors became increasingly more valuable. But eventually even this revenue stream dried up. By the close of his second year, Rogers was riding a dead horse. His total investment fund barely reached $400,000, which was hardly enough to pay the bills. And things got worse before getting better. Although the work was satisfying, Rogers's faith was put to the test. He toiled from sunup to sundown—Saturdays and Sundays included—grinding out dozens of scenarios and market calculations. The weekends included more paperwork, mass mailings of his investment newsletter, and non-stop phone calls searching for new portfolio entries as he sifted for new leads. With his client list dwindling, his dream of operating a successful management fund seemed to diminish with every passing day. Rogers was running out of cash fast and had no alternate plans. At the end of its first year, Ariel had $22,000 in revenue, barely enough to keep the lights on. Rogers desperately tried to hold his ground.

"Not only did I lack revenues, but I had no hope of accruing any revenues in the near future. It was tough keeping your composure when everything you worked so hard for begins to unravel."[11] Rogers's breakthrough came in 1985 when he received a phone call from Howard University's endowment office. The predominantly Black institution was searching for safe havens for its investment dollars and had discovered Rogers's outfit through a mutual friend. Understandably, the school was willing to invest only $100,000, a tiny slice of its pension fund, in his firm, making Rogers's reprieve bittersweet. He had hoped for more, but he was confident that his strategies would turn the collective heads of the school's development office. Toward this end, he deployed his game plan and invested Howard's portfolio in stocks with price to earnings ratios lower than that of the overall market. This strategy became a recurring theme. He also socked away a portion into small-company stocks that were dramatically undervalued. The result: Howard's nest egg grew appreciably, catching the eye of hungry investors. Within six months, Rogers had raised an additional $190,000 in investment capital, and, at that point, 1986, Ariel Capital moved as swiftly as its namesake, growing to $45 million in managed assets. Rogers quickly perfected a creative but conservative investment style best summed up by Ariel's motto borrowed from an Aesop's fable: "Slow and steady wins the race." Rogers's overriding philosophy is one of patience, timing, and making the most out of a down market.

"Warren Buffett has captured my attention for close to thirty years. I have read nearly every book and article about him as well as his investment strategy. Buffett's main principle—his circle of competence—never deviates. In other words, you only invest in products and companies that you understand. *Period.*" By 2004, Ariel employed more than 70 analysts, researchers, and traders while managing nearly $17.5 billion in assets for an array of clients. Moreover, Rogers reached a personal goal. He created the first two U.S. mutual funds managed by African Americans; the Ariel and Ariel Appreciation Funds each received four-star ratings. By his mid-forties, *Black Enterprise* magazine recognized him as a "master wealth builder."

Believe it or not, at 54, this trailblazing, ahead-of-his-time financial investor has seen it all—the booms and busts, the money rushing hungrily into stocks and then fleeing in fear. From the time his investment firm broke ground to the endless days when Rogers was forced to travel with hopes of convincing the endowed to divvy up parcels of their funds to smaller but no less capable Black investors, skeptical Whites and overly cautious Blacks nearly ran him out of business. *What turned Rogers's fortunes around?* Obviously, the general easing of opportunities within the finance arena for minorities, not to mention a burning gumption to succeed. However, his textbook approach, which pruned the recklessly speculative aspects of investing, was what won investors over. His ability to produce under fire, to employ cautiously aggressive growth strategies, and his immensely popular message: *Slow and steady wins the race* won the race for Rogers. And throughout that time, Rogers has never regretted that it was his name on the letterhead.

However, what does concern Rogers is that more African Americans have yet to tap into the power of the market. Since 1998, Ariel has cosponsored an annual study in conjunction with Charles Schwab that examines African American investing behavior. The latest research highlights the fact that African Americans are 35 percent less likely to invest than Whites.[12] Rogers is searching for ways to expose middle-class Black Americans to the stock market, and no investor is too small or too young. His starting point is inner-city school children. Inspired by a symposium he attended on financial literacy, Rogers had Ariel team members, with fellow Chicago investment firm John Nuveen & Company, fund the innovative school program. Unlike similar academic programs, the Ariel Community Academy, with more than 300 students, offers a curriculum with a decidedly financial spin: The basics of investing, from selecting stocks to tracking leading economic indicators, are woven into the daily lesson plans in math and history classes. The academy has been recognized for its above-average student retention rate and its 69 percent student participation in after-school programs. What's Rogers's motivation? "I feel guilty that I was not there in the 1960s to march with Dr. King. A big part of his dream was economic empowerment. I haven't been forced to render that type of sacrifice in my life. But this is a start."[13]

FIVE WEALTH-BUILDING STRATEGIES OF THE BLACK FINANCIAL ELITE

Most Black millionaires subscribe to personal investment strategies that are customized for individual needs. As a part of this study, when respondents were asked, "Who or what is your single most reliable source for investment strategies?" more than 40 percent replied "my broker." Nearly 25 percent said that "diversifying their portfolio was the smartest money move they made" (see Table 7.2). But, over the course of his career, John Rogers removed much of the guesswork from investing by casting a sharp eye out for small stocks and adhering to his proven maxim. He has no use for market forecasts or economists' predictions, nor does he pay much attention to volatility. Instead, like his peer group, the proven pro focuses solely on five wealth-building strategies that will help you crack the millionaire code. Like a compass, these five rules will direct you to security and prosperity. Each rule points out what you *want* to know and what you *need* to know regarding your money. I suggest that you put these strategies into action and watch as they manifest in your life.

Rule 1. The Best Investment Will Always Be Yourself

Master networker George Fraser shared a timely story about the life and spending habits of his cousin Bobby who had recently died. Fraser wrote in part:

> *My cousin Bobby was buried in a designer suit, but he died broke. He made plenty of money using his boomer generation MBA to get good jobs at Ford Motor Company and later at Honda in Marysville, Ohio. He loved automobiles. His gas-guzzling Jeep Cherokee was spotless, but hardly paid for. He had maxed out most of his seven credit cards on designer clothes.*

INVESTMENT BEHAVIOR CALCULATED
IN PERCENTAGES (N = 500)*

Outside of a 401(k) or other retirement plan, which of the following investment or insurance plans do you own?

Savings account (bank)	71%
Certificates of deposit	45%
Insurance (whole life)	63%
Stocks	63%
Mutual funds	73%
Fixed/Variable Annuity	36%
Money market	53%
U.S. Savings Bond	27%
Rental property	51%
Other	13%

Compared to 12 months ago, how would you rate investing in the stock market today? (select one)

A lot less risky	3%
A little less risky	15%
No more or less risky	41%
A little riskier	24%
Much riskier	13%

What annual return do you expect from the market over the long term? (10 years or more)

0%–5%	7%
6%–10%	56%
11%–15%	30%
16% or higher	4%

What or who is your single most reliable source for investment strategies?

Your broker	43%
Newspapers and magazines	18%
Internet	26%
Friends and family	13%

Of the following, which is your prime motivation for saving or investing?

Retirement	40%
Financial independence	31%
Send children to college	8%
Prepare for emergency fund	4%
Leave money for children	15%

What is the smartest money move you've made?

Buying your home	31%
Investing in the stock market	3%
Diversifying portfolio	23%
Reducing debt	24%
Paying cash for all purchases	5%
Reducing taxable income	6%
Real estate	2%

Not including your mortgage, how much do you owe?

Less than $10,000	50%
$10,000–$19,999	13%
$20,000–$29,999	15%
$30,000–$39,999	6%
$40,000–$49,999	4%
$50,000–$59,999	6%

* Survey responses to questions 1, 3 to 10. Questionnaire administered May 2005 to February 2011.

Table 7.2

Bobby was always as clean as his Mama's chitlins.

He was divorced and faithfully paying child support for his two beautiful children. His definition of community service was when the community was helping to serve his monthly sales quotas.

Bobby had some good, honest side hustles, but he was always running on empty. His well-appointed two-bedroom condo north of Columbus, Ohio, ate up nearly half his take-home pay. So his lifestyle meant he was good at robbing Peter to pay Paul.

Bobby reminded me of the joke about the optimist who jumped from a 12-story building. As he passes the third floor, he says, "So far, so good," not realizing that he's about to crash.

He died of a heart attack at 54. At the reading of his one-page will, there was little to distribute to his children. The creditors and IRS got most of it. He was house poor, car poor and stuff poor; his children would have to start from scratch, just as he had. I thought if he only had treated his wealth with the same pride and support with which he treated his family and friends, he would have died rich.

This forced me to reflect on two things. Were we living Dr. King's dream of economic development? Was I, too, suffering from economic illiteracy and a compulsive spending disorder driven by what many believe to be the United States' reckless marketing of easy credit and a mass media focus on materialism and instant gratification? Or, was I driven by low self-esteem, the remnants of hundreds of years of oppression and denial producing a personal philosophy that dictates high social status as more important than financial freedom? Perhaps there is a little of both lurking below the surface of still too many "successful" African-Americans, who end up in debt and support every institution but their own.[14]

I imagine most families have at least one cousin Bobby. No family is immune.

Unfortunately, we live in a consumer-driven society where, for some, shopping is a sport. We feel good, we buy. We feel bad, we buy. We rent when we should buy and buy when we should rent. We think in terms of jobs when we should think of careers. We are forever stuck on how much money we earn rather than how much money we are retaining, saving, and investing. We think credit when we should think cash. We think minimum payment instead of ending balance. We think tomorrow when we should think today; we think later when we should think now. And, most important, we look without when we should look within. Such is the ongoing dilemma of the have nots.

At last count, Tyra Banks's net worth was estimated at $90 million. But her personal finances were not always this rosy. While Banks doesn't feel the need to own the latest designer this or that, her wardrobe, which features form-fitting, low-cut dresses on the air and jeans in the office, generally fits the budget and tastes of her audience. As she has stated on numerous occasions, "I grew up wearing a uniform to school, and if my stylist did not create my outfits to wear on camera, I would never get dressed."[15]

"I'm frugal," Banks continued. "I have always been this way. When I was young, my mother would give me my allowance, and I would peel off a little each week with the aim of saving a little for that rainy day. A penny saved is a penny earned is more than a proverb; it is a value I look for in others. When interviewing potential candidates to handle the financials for my company, I make it my business to ask a question or two regarding their personal spending habits. *Why?* Because how you spend money reveals a lot about you."[16]

Richard Parson's road to a $100 million fortune began nearly 60 years ago in his Brooklyn, New York, home. It was there that the Citigroup chair and former Time Warner chief executive learned the power of the seventh law of wealth. He watched in earnest as his mother, a homemaker, and his father, an electrical worker, sat twice a month at the kitchen table to allocate and prioritize his father's paycheck. "With pad and pencil," Parsons recalled in an interview, "he would pay his mortgage before buying food and necessities. Next, he would place aside a modest sum specifically for savings. Our family would then live on whatever was left." Whatever money was left went toward educating Parsons and his four siblings, sending the former to Washington, DC, to be a direct report to the vice president, Nelson Rockefeller, before Parson took the helm of Time Warner, the largest media and entertainment conglomerate in the world. "As a society, we must learn to rely less and less on credit and borrowing," he advises. "The ability to borrow is like dynamite—it must be handled with care. That is a lesson each of us should learn. Just because we can qualify for credit does not mean we should."[17]

"On every hand," says Kirbyjon Caldwell, pastor of the Houston, Texas–based Windsor Village, "we see signs advertising 'No Money Down' or 'No Credit Check Required,' or 'Unemployed? No Problem.' With each catchy scheme comes offers of cars, clothing, furniture, and appliances all promising 'easy payments.' As I preach to my congregation every Sunday when it comes to staying afloat financially and living within your means, there is nothing *easy* about *easy payments*."[18] And who would know better than this one-time Wharton-trained fast-track bond broker? Though Caldwell grew up in a middle-class home, his neighborhood was adjacent to Kashmere Gardens, one of Houston's tougher areas. After graduating from high school, Caldwell left the Lone Star state to attend Carleton College in Northfield, Minnesota, where he earned an undergraduate degree in economics before measuring himself against the best and brightest finance students at the University of Pennsylvania. With an MBA in hand, he was gobbled up by First Boston, a Wall Street investment bank, and eventually returned to Texas to join a Houston-based bond firm. Never one to regret any decision, at age 25, Caldwell listened to his heart and opted out of investment banking to enter the ministry. The result? What his congregation has come to know as the gospel of good success, a 16,000-member, 120 ministry, $14.5 million mega-church. Though many still seek his insight regarding investments and the stock market, Caldwell is crystal clear as to where people should invest first: "On themselves," he replied.

Rule 2. Managing Your Finances Is Your Responsibility

In the discipline of sound money management, the unit measure of prosperity always begins with the smallest coin. As a result, millionaireship is measured not by the pound but by the penny, not by the dollar but by the cent. To hear the reserved and shy Dr. Roosevelt Peebles describe his most routine procedures would literally cause anyone to pause. This Nashville, Tennessee–based board-certified plastic facial and reconstructive surgeon boasts a wealth of knowledge not only about beauty and form but about function as well. Changing the lives of his patients for the better has become his magnificent obsession. Like Dr. Maxwell Maltz, the famed plastic surgeon who stated years ago, "The incisions I make run more than skin deep. They frequently cut into the psyche as well," by correcting a perceived flaw here or removing an aggravating blemish there, Dr. Peebles's skilled hands have been known to enhance the appearance of his clientele, giving all who walk through his doors a sense of well-being as well as improved self-confidence and self-esteem.[19] But regardless of how much he loves his work, at 54 years of age and working in a field that demands precision, Dr. Peebles is the first to admit that retirement looms just around the corner. "No rational physician could ever believe that he or she could last forever within this highly specialized field. Personally, saving and investing for the future is not only a worthwhile endeavor but a necessity. I've never been one to live an ostentatious life. Though it would be easy to do so, conspicuous consumption does not hold my interest. Living beneath my means and saving at a minimum 30 percent of my earnings is my path to building lasting wealth."

It is impossible to map out a route to your new financial destination—in this case, to join the ranks of the affluent men and women profiled within this text—if you don't know your point of origin. With that in mind, it would be wise to open every single financial statement—bank, credit card, mortgage, 401(k), brokerage account—and gauge where you are. Only when these documents lie before you can you set priorities and calculate what to do next, and it's always a good idea to secure the services of a qualified professional to take an independent look at your overall financial picture. Living in the past will not create your future.

Trish Millines-Dziko was a gifted, geeky 13-year-old who excelled at math and enjoyed operating the school film projector when she suddenly informed her mother that she saw no use for college. Her mother was 50 years older than her only child and had spent much of her life working as a maid in hotels and for wealthy families in the small New Jersey beach town of Belmar. As a single parent, she bought her own home, a small bungalow, by working 51 weeks a year and saving the cab fare and lunch money her employers provided. Though she never said a word about her daughter's decision, she moved decisively. That summer, Trish accompanied her mother five days a week scrubbing floors and cleaning toilets as she made her rounds. The point was made. A few months after her mother died of cancer, Trish enrolled in New Jersey's Monmouth College.

Originally an electrical engineering major, she switched to computer science. It was love at first sight. Here was a Black woman who excelled at circuitry and deductive and inductive logic. It wasn't long before a handful of high-tech giants came calling—specifically Microsoft Corp. In 1988, Millines-Dziko began working at Microsoft in its technical systems division. Although she was the only team member of her race and gender, she felt at home. From a pool of 200 majority White computer wizards, she was selected as the company's first Black female program manager.

I share this story with you not to highlight the technical exploits, career advancement, or one corporate climber's rise through the ranks. It is obvious that the circumstances surrounding Millines-Dziko's childhood might have discouraged a lesser man or woman from pursuing his or her goals. Nor does her example expand the ever-growing need for people of color and corporate America to work together to bridge the digital divide. Clearly, what is on display is the one quality greater than wealth, the one trait that will confer prosperity on all those who seek it. To the average person, there is, was, and always will be another—more pressing—need for your money than putting it away to grow for the future. There will be the car you want to buy, the house you want to renovate, and the vacation you want to enjoy. And because each option will arrive far sooner than retirement, they all will appear much more enticing than a routine deposit into a 401(k) or an IRA. Many who know Millines-Dziko's story have called her lucky, and because of her "instant success," some say she is a financial genius. But whatever the reasons for her accomplishments, the seventh law of wealth—the ability to save and max out a 401(k)—certainly played a major part in her success. Nine years after working for the highly touted, blue-chip software firm, Millines-Dziko earned so much money from company stock that, at age 39, she walked away and retired a Microsoft millionaire. Regarding retirement and investing, what is her course of action? "Never take advice from someone who is not where you want to be in life," she counsels. "Remember, if you buy someone else's opinion, you buy their financial statement."

Rule 3. Get Your Spending Under Control

"Ladies and gentlemen, we've got a problem." The voice barking out this admonition belongs to one of America's five Black billionaires. But his story does not begin or end here. The purpose of sharing this brief passage is not to discuss the challenges of wealth creation with regard to the Black community, nor is it to point blame or single out those who constantly struggle to attain wealth. No, this anecdote runs far deeper than a few paragraphs. As Bob Johnson walked from his table to position himself behind a microphone, a throng of reporters and attendees detailed his every move. Despite the lighthearted atmosphere eased by cocktails and finger food, the billionaire businessman could not hide his emotions. And then he not only made his point but clarified the finite effects of this ubiquitous seventh law.

"I want to deal with an issue that should be on everybody's mind," he said to a packed room of chief executives, entrepreneurs, and wealth creators at a Washington, DC, focus group.

Most of you know me as the proud owner of the Charlotte Bobcats— one of 30 NBA teams. What you probably don't know is that each team fills a roster of 13 to 15 players who earn, on average, $5 million over a three-year period. Furthermore, in terms of race and ethnicity, each team—mine included—is nearly 80 percent Black. So you do the math. Economically speaking, and to the surprise of no one, the NBA boasts the wealthiest and most powerful group of Black males in the world. That's the *good news*. The *bad news* revolves around the disturbing fact that *no one knows how these players save or invest their money.*

This game is not about *bling-bling* or diamond-studded earrings— it's about using your influence; it's about making a difference, and saving and investing your resources wisely.

I admonish you to get your spending under control. Does the dreaded "b" word—budget—make you cringe? It really shouldn't. Not when you realize that developing a budget and sticking to it offers a host of wealth-bearing benefits. A budget aids your monthly cash flow, prevents overspending, and helps you avoid living paycheck to paycheck. The economy is within you, and here lies your first step. The difference between wealth and poverty or between have versus have not is not nearly as great as most people believe. Your current thinking ultimately affects your future economic condition. Again, I suggest that you take the road less traveled. Quick question: How many credit cards do you own? Count the number of credit cards—excluding debit cards—in your wallet. If you carry more than one, then you are, in all likelihood, overspending and incurring debt. Make this the year that you finally retire credit card debt. Whatever occurs in the stock market or the housing market is completely *beyond* your control. Credit card debt, however, is completely under *your* control. Each time you pay off a credit card with a 15 percent interest rate, you earn a 15 percent return on your money. And yes, it is important that you carry some cash. Studies reveal that when consumers use credit versus cash, they spend 12 to 18 percent more.

Arguably, the most influential Black entrepreneur of the twentieth century was Arthur G. Gaston, the Birmingham, Alabama, native who took his life savings—$500—and transformed it to a net worth of more than $40 million. Vision and a legendary work ethic played a part in Gaston's amassing such a huge financial portfolio, but these qualities paled in comparison to the root cause of all that he was to achieve. Nearly 30 years ago, I sat at his feet seeking his wisdom and keys to success. "Pay as you go and keep a handle on unnecessary expenses," he said to me during an interview without blinking an eye. "Even the Almighty, it has been written, cannot afford to be extravagant. When He increased the loaves and fishes, He commanded the disciples to gather up the fragments that nothing be lost."

By any measurement, Sheila C. Johnson, the chief executive of Salamander Hotels and Resorts, a sprawling 165-acre luxury compound nestled in the horse country of northern Virginia, is rich. The ex-wife of Black Entertainment Television founder Robert Johnson, she now presides over her own expansive empire. Johnson is the first African American woman to own a stake in three professional sports teams: She is president and managing partner of the WNBA's Washington Mystics, the National Hockey League's Washington Capitals, and the NBA's Washington Wizards, and her net worth has been estimated at $400 million. But don't let that fool you. As you stroll the grounds of her home, what is obviously missing amid the guest cottages and horse stables is opulence and bling. Her lifestyle is understated. An excellent example, she has been known to urge her players to be smart about their financial future, too. As she and a reporter toured her grounds, Johnson summed up her thrifty mind-set: "There are a lot of Black folks with money. I just handle mine differently; I'm not in-your-face money."[20] Johnson's fiscal approach is so simple and yet so difficult for many people to comprehend. As of this writing, U.S. credit card debt rests at an all-time high—more than $60 billion. The average family owes more than $8,000. While Black millionaires are apt to take a credit risk on their business for strategic reasons, they are highly unlikely to take a risk in their personal spending.

In closing, remember the point about a fool and his money. Like Cousin Bobby, most people spend their surplus assets on the appearance of wealth: fine clothes, fancy cars, jewelry, and lavish vacations. Ironically, the wealthy can spot a dead give-away in an instant. Again, as previously stated, one member of this study told me that "if someone looks wealthy, the odds are he or she isn't." This outlook was underscored by A10 Clinical Solutions' Leah Brown, who stated, "I choose not to spend $500 on a Gucci bag. Why should I brand some else's company when I can brand my own? As a community, we will not build lasting wealth utilizing these kinds of business practices. Being poor does not help those behind you; poverty only perpetuates poverty."

Rule 4. Pay Yourself First. Saving Is Permissible

For the first decade of Victor MacFarlane's life, his mother's living room couch also served as his bed. The product of a single-parent home, MacFarlane sought neither sympathy nor pity; that was not his nature. Nearly 50 years later, when asked for his proudest accomplishment, he didn't cite the 80-story Time Warner Center in New York that his real estate company helped to build. Nor did he mention the countless urban revitalization areas that he transformed along the West Coast as well as the Eastern Seaboard. Oddly, he didn't even acknowledge the $4 billion in real estate and private equity funds that MacFarlane Partners currently manages. History clearly states that Victor MacFarlane created the first urban investment fund in 1990. What he did bring to my attention was that it was in that one-bedroom Middletown, Ohio, home where he ultimately decided that poverty would not be given a place in his life.[21] This resolve has helped him amass a varied and valuable real estate portfolio, including inner-city housing and commercial space, high-end condo developments, and planned communities. His company's diversification helps it to thrive even in the slow markets of the past few years, consistently generating returns of 20 percent or more.

MacFarlane is quick to point out that in this game, capital is king. But he is equally as quick to admit that all fortunes have their foundation in the first great principle of wealth building: saving. He then began to share his four rules for prosperity. "First, establish a budget and live within it," he explained during an interview. "Live within your means. If you are not careful, any amount of money can be spent— whether you earn $70,000 a year or $70 million. Second, create and adhere to a savings plan. Each of us needs some amount of liquidity. To capitalize on opportunity, I always keep some amount of cash on hand. Third, separate your needs from wants. The vice of our age is the desire to keep up with the Joneses, to outshine our neighbor. It's time to let your neighbor go. Trust me, this negative habit is the bedrock of poverty. And, four, diversify your funds. It is wise to participate in a variety of assets."

When it comes to saving and investing for your future, the historic rule of thumb is 10 percent. By saving 10 percent of your income each month, you will grow wealthier than you dreamed possible. In some cases, it is necessary to save more, particularly if you have ambitious retirement goals. But now is the time to adopt the rule that so many of the financial elite apply. Begin by acting on the wisdom that 10 percent of all that you earn is yours to keep.

After a celebrated career with the Milwaukee Bucks and Los Angeles Clippers, Junior Bridgeman, a former NBA standout, shared the following story with a fresh group of retired professional athletes. One day while Bridgeman was working the line at a Wendy's fast-food restaurant in Milwaukee, a woman approached the counter to place an order acting as if she might have recognized the one-time six-foot-five point guard. Once she left the store, Bridgeman didn't give the matter a second thought until the following morning, when he heard the comments of a caller on a local radio talk show. "I think it is a shame," the caller explained. "I was eating at a Wendy's yesterday and I saw *Junior Bridgeman* working behind the counter. Oh, my God! *Is that the best these ex-athletes can do?*"[22]

As Bridgeman concluded his remarks, a few of the athletes in attendance shifted uncomfortably in their seats. *And why not?* In an age of in-your-face ballers, high-priced pleasure seekers armed with an inflated self-worth and egos, and extravagant spending habits to match, it is pretty easy to visualize the reaction of today's pampered NBA stars, but not Bridgeman. He is a throwback; he just smiled. Perhaps it is because the last laugh was his. Unlike so many of his ex-teammates, he refused to squander his earnings. Instead, he saved every dime and purchased a string of fast-food franchises in 1987, the year he retired. Ironically, he owned that particular Wendy's plus 160 others, not to mention 121 Chili's restaurants. Today, Bridgeman Foods is number 3 on the *Restaurant Finance Monitor*'s top 200 franchisee-owned companies, surpassing the $530 million mark in revenue.[23] When asked how he got his start, the former swing man replied, "It all began with my first paycheck, really the first dime I earned. I knew that saving something was better than saving nothing. If you are careless with your nickels and dimes, fortune will never come by your hand. However easy it may be to make money, it is far more difficult to keep it."

Rule 5. Make Your Money Work as Hard as You Do

Across every aspect of the data, among Black America's wealthy, I found these statistics: Forty percent save 10 to 20 percent of their gross incomes, and nearly 75 percent have invested $100,000 or more in specific retirement accounts. Furthermore, the well-to-do don't like being in debt. When asked "Not including your mortgage, how much do you owe?" one-half of respondents replied "less than $10,000." Millionaireship begins with savings, with forgone consumption, which appears, from a sufficient distance, the same as poverty. The chief desire of the millionaires in this study is not money to waste on depreciating extravagances but the freedom and power to expand their entrepreneurial ideas. And forget about keeping up with the Joneses—the Black financial elite would rather identify the Joneses' strengths and work with them to uncover how they can leverage their own talents and skills in order to make smarter financial decisions. For the wealthy, earning, spending, and saving money is serious business—*very* serious business.

It is by the mysterious power of saving and investing that the loaf is multiplied, that little becomes much, and that out of nothing comes the miracle of something. In chapter 6, you read the daring mission of Colleen Payne-Nabors to launch her enterprise. It is true that those who will pay the price of victory never need to fear final defeat. But truer still is the fact that the real secret to her success rests squarely on the seventh law. *Why?* Because investing is second nature to this savvy entrepreneur. As a freshly minted college graduate, she joined her employer's 401(k) plan without hesitation. To further augment her earnings, at age 25, Payne-Nabors began purchasing Treasury EE savings bonds. Every two weeks, her bank automatically deducted $50 from her paycheck to purchase the bonds. Seven years later, when she was ready to buy her first house, she cashed in those bonds to make a $12,000 down payment. And you guessed it. Roughly five years later, when her rural Oklahoma town grew too small for her dreams, it was the equity in her home that served as leverage to her shaky start-up when area bankers were noncommittal.

As I wrote this chapter, the stock market stood at its most volatile point in decades. Stocks were up hundreds of points—if not thousands—one week and down thousands the next. The world is still sorting out this financial mess, both in the United States and abroad. In the near term, unemployment barely remains stable, business activity is moderate at best, and, in some sectors, the economic headlines continue to be scary. "Clearly, the novice investor needs the most basic information regarding investing and who can afford to do so," John Rogers points out. "Before you figure out how to invest, you must decide if you should be investing at all. If you are going to invest on your own, invest in those companies you know and understand." I include these words here because they echo an important finding in *The Wealth Choice* data: *The wealthy buy stocks.* In order to generate multiple streams of income and diversify your portfolio, saving by itself is not enough. Unfortunately, the slim returns you might generate through a money market account or certificate of deposit will barely keep pace with inflation and taxes, let alone exceed them.

NEW RULES OF MONEY: SAVING MONEY TRANSLATES INTO SAVING THE INDIVIDUAL

Ask the majority of men and women who have built seven-figure bank accounts to what they owe their wealth or fortune. They will tell you that their financial success is not only the fruit of struggle but the fruit of habit; that they acquired their best quality when only a child; that they exercised the only discipline that would lead them out of bondage never to see the likes of poverty again. I do not believe that anyone can truly be happy until he or she expresses that which the Creator has made to dominate in his or her life; until the person has given vent to the grand passion that speaks loudest in his or her life; until he or she has made best use of that gift which was intended to take precedence over all other powers. No person can live a full life while bound in any part of his or her nature.

Saving and investing enables men and women to lift their heads above the crowd; to be independent, self-reliant, and shielded from debt and anxiety—that frightful obligation and emotion that destroys homes, ruins marriages, wrinkles the smoothest face, and stifles peace of mind. Thrift and saving place hope into the heart and raise self-esteem. There is an impressive fact in the gospel story of the Prodigal Son. The statement "he wasted his substance in riotous living" means more than that he wasted his funds; rather, it implies that he wasted *himself.* And the most serious offense of all waste is not the waste of substance but the waste of *self,* of your energy, capital, the lowering of morals, the gradual loss of character and self-respect that thrift encourages and promotes. The best form of insurance against poverty and failure, saving and investing, means a warm home and healthy children; a restful vacation and a college education; a secure retirement and help for the needy. In short, the saving of money translates into the saving of the individual. I suggest that you begin now to adhere to the seventh law of wealth and make your money grow.

MILLIONAIRE LESSON NO. 8

As I preach to my congregation every Sunday when it comes to staying afloat financially and living within your means, there is nothing easy about easy payments. Learn to say the words "I can't afford it."

—Kirbyjon Caldwell

EPILOGUE

ONE FINAL LESSON

"Mr. Secretary," I asked Ron Brown, then Secretary of Commerce in the Clinton administration, "what is the formula for wealth?"

"Simple," Secretary Brown replied. "Creative men and women with access to capital."

"So what is the formula for poverty?" I continued.

"Unfortunately, that's simple too," he explained. "If you associate with nine broke people, sooner or later you will be number ten."

IT HAS BEEN NEARLY SEVEN YEARS SINCE THE DEATH OF *Ebony* magazine founder John H. Johnson and nearly three decades since I sat in his thick-carpeted, exquisitely paneled office as he quizzed me on the inner secrets of wealth creation. At his peak, Johnson's financial portfolio included publishing, cosmetics, television, and radio. In 1982, he was the first African American to be cited on *Forbes* magazine's list of the 400 wealthiest Americans. Before Jackie Robinson integrated major league baseball, before Dr. Martin Luther King Jr. marched on Washington, before Motown changed music, in 1945, America had *Ebony*. During my interview, Johnson shared with me that he was in the business of inspiring people, heralding achievements of other African Americans that White mainstream magazines would never publish or simply would overlook.

Thirty years ago, I sat in the office of the one individual who would put my abilities to the test. Although Johnson did not create the American media, he drew awareness to the Black consumer market and eventually altered the industry's color and content. Born in poverty in Arkansas City, Arkansas, he was the greatest salesman, entrepreneur, and chief executive of his time. As my interview drew to a close and I began to gather my notes, my mind reverted back to his parting question: "*Young man, why aren't you rich?*"

After nearly an hour, it seemed as if Johnson had waited until the time was ripe, preparing to hear my vague, sheepish answer and subsequently dismiss any excuse that I might offer. To put it bluntly, he would have none of it. Yet he also was quick to point out my inherent advantages and gifts that I had overlooked or failed to consider. "Young man," he began, "with your youth and education, the opportunities that stand before you are beyond computation. There are no secrets to amassing a fortune. As this process was taught to me, I enjoy sharing these keys with you. And it doesn't take volumes to explain these principles. Never before was there such a demand for the energetic, resourceful man or woman; the individual who knows no limits; who will master his or her circumstances; who will never be satisfied with anything short of perfection; and who will manage his or her own business. Your hour of opportunity is at hand."

Mr. Johnson had made his point. He was obviously probing me in search of the keys to wealth creation; the same keys that his mentor, S. B. Fuller, sought to find in him. Short of demanding an answer, he waited for my response, and it was only fair. After all, Johnson had given me a portion of his day—nearly one hour of his most precious resource—time. Though each of us is blessed with the same twenty-four hours, it is not the hours of the day that concern the Black financial elite, but how we account for our time that matters most. And within that timeframe, Johnson's thoughts never shifted. As he shook my hand and bade me farewell, this giant of a man found the time to teach me one final lesson. He told me to imagine the life I wanted and decide to live it. He urged me to discover my calling and make it my vocation, and then devote my energy and lifeblood to its attainment. He admonished me to set clear goals and a timetable for their completion. He warned me to never quit in the pursuit of my goals. Be persistent, he implored. See possibilities where others see problems; and, remember, rules are made for those who will follow them. And finally, to live by the infallible rule—to whom much is given, much is required. Give back and give thanks.

As he walked me to his door, he closed by saying, "Never forget, until you are free economically, true independence will always be an afterthought. Today, we, as Black Americans, can *live* where we want, *eat* what we want, *sleep* where we want, and send our children to the finest schools we so desire. But for far too many of us this form of freedom is difficult to express. Why? Because in most cases we cannot afford to. Unless you are free economically and financially, you will never be free personally."

I'm honored that you took the time to read *The Wealth Choice*. It was my intention that this book would not only place you on the road to true independence but would be the most substantive analysis of Black America's most successful self-made millionaires to date. With regard to money and your finances, by reading this book, you have embarked on a journey that instructs how to earn more, save more, serve more, dream more, and spend less. So many people will purchase a book with great intentions. Many readers generally skim a few pages, consider an idea or two, and then place the book down. You, however, have actually read this volume and are poised to act on what you've read and focus your time and energy on what matters most. I wrote *The Wealth Choice* to provide a road map to a life of more wealth, more freedom, and infinite joy and well-being. By now you've come to realize that wealth follows seven divine principles that are as definite as the laws of gravity and finite as the concepts surrounding the discipline of mathematics. As hundreds of Black millionaires indicated—through interviews, focus groups, or surveys—true prosperity is an inward transformation of knowledge, belief, effort, discipline, and faith. We can neither feel nor experience poverty if we are conscious of our all-encompassing supply, that the Almighty is our partner, our shepherd, and that "we cannot want," for there is no lack in "Him in whom all fullness lies." The following story provides a good example.

A dear woman who had lived her entire life in the outer reaches of the back country moved to a progressive little village. There, to her great surprise, she found that her new home was equipped with electricity. Though she heard of the wonders that electricity provided, she had never seen or used an electric light before. As one could imagine, the dim low-watt electric bulbs with which her house was fitted seemed like an improbable marvel.

One day, a traveling salesman came through her town selling electric bulbs. When he peered into her home, he couldn't believe this gentle soul was still using such outdated lighting to illuminate her house.

He asked whether he could replace one of her small bulbs with a newer version. She consented. As he screwed the bulb into the socket, she stood transfixed. It seemed to her nothing short of a miracle that such a tiny bulb could radiate so much light. She never dreamed that such a powerful source of illumination had been there all the time and that the enormously increased light came from the same current that had been feeding her outdated low-watt bulb.

We smile at this woman's naiveté, but far too many of us are equally as naive and shortsighted in regard to our own innate power, which likewise can be multiplied and increased beyond measure. When it comes to the subject of wealth, abundance, and prosperity, so many approach life using a dim bulb, falsely believing that somehow, some way, our Creator would either want to limit our power or force us to live within the confining shadows of poverty and want when so much more is available. Unfortunately, multitudes of my race unknowingly go through life blind to the fact that there is unlimited light and limitless power flowing right past their doors ready for their use, primed for their drive, their ideas, their vision, and free to use all the resources and blessings their individual heart desires. They are receiving no more and no less from this vast unlimited resource that waits their command. All that is required is for them to flip the switch, step into the light, and tap into that limitless wealth-providing current.

No one need tell you how tough it has been for ordinary men and women to inch ahead financially during the past few years. In fact, you probably have your own story to tell. As *Ebony* magazine pointed out, "Although economists say the Great Recession technically ended in 2009, it is painfully obvious that, especially in the African American community, the economic slowdown still lingers. Jobs are scarce, wages are down, and prices are up. But consumer advocates say the housing crisis—combined with chronic unemployment—has dealt the single biggest blow to the state of Black wealth this past decade, undoing years of economic progress."[1] And to compound matters, unlike the example just given, so many of us deepen the hole in which we find ourselves by our undisciplined spending habits and failure to delay gratification. We are so bombarded with the new, the flashy, and the up to date, which soon will be the out of date, that we unconsciously buy into the message that we must own the latest fad, fashion, or style *now*. We have ignored the common virtue of saving and living within our means. And why should we wait when our line of credit allows us to make any purchase and have it delivered to our door? In the blink of an eye, we inadvertently run up unnecessary credit card debt, buying things we don't need and can't afford, all with the hope of impressing someone we don't know. Today, bankruptcy has become an acceptable way to eliminate once-avoidable financial obligations.

Now is your chance to embrace these seven laws of wealth and flip the switch. Now is your opportunity to increase the power, to walk out of the darkness; to be done with poverty; to refuse to dwell on it, speak it, dread it, expect it, fear it, worry about it *any longer.* You need not concern yourself with your current state of affairs. Circumstances have rarely favored great men or women. A lowly beginning is no bar to a wealthy life. The determined soul cannot be stopped from reaching his or her financial objectives by indifferent or poor parents; by inadequate schooling or shoddy teaching; by lack of books or contacts; by questionable backgrounds or vocations; by poverty or ill health or affliction; by hunger, abandonment, or weariness.

Yes, the rich *are* different. Generally speaking, Black millionaires think and act differently. They believe in the greatness of this country, and they want to help write the next chapter of American history in ways that benefit them as well as their fellow man. The Black financial elite want a seat at the table, not because they feel entitled but because they know they have something unique and valuable to offer. Dissatisfied with just getting ahead, these wealth creators not only want to corner the market but to change the game. So if millionaireship is what you desire, how will you achieve your goals? Own a business? Remember David Steward, Cathy Hughes, and Leah Brown—they did what you propose to do on a shoestring. Is writing your passion? Lean on the words of Terry McMillan when editors and publishers trashed her first submission. Oppressed by debt and struggling to make ends meet, she produced her greatest work—*Waiting to Exhale.* What about fashion? Reread the profile of Daymond John who, for six long years, slept on the floor of his Queens, New York, home until the world took notice of his youthful urban designs. Is it public speaking that drives you? I urge you to examine the life of Les Brown. Perhaps no one else has ever battled longer or more diligently to overcome obstacles that would dishearten most individuals. Brown had a weak voice and even weaker self-esteem. His initial attempts at public speaking were drowned out by hisses, jeers, and scoffs. Brown was so discouraged that he nearly relinquished his dream of pursuing a speaking career until he stumbled onto the following words of Berton Braley, the twentieth-century American poet. And he would've been content to remain on the sidelines of life had he not found the *will to win*.

> If you want a thing bad enough
> To go out and fight for it,
> Work day and night for it,
> Give up your time and your peace and
> your sleep for it
> If only desire of it
> Makes you quite mad enough
> Never to tire of it,
> Makes you hold all other things tawdry
> and cheap for it
> If life seems all empty and useless without it
> And all that you scheme and you dream is about it,
> If gladly you'll sweat for it,
> Fret for it,
> Plan for it,
> Lose all your terror of God or man for it,
> If you'll simply go after that thing that you want,
> With all your capacity,
> Strength and sagacity,
> Faith, hope and confidence, stern pertinacity,
> If neither cold poverty, famished and gaunt,
> Nor sickness nor pain
> Of body or brain
> Can turn you away from the thing that you want,
> If dogged and grim you besiege and beset it,
> You'll get it!

Don't settle for less than you can be financially. You would do well to remember: Millionaires make money while others make excuses. When you come into the realization of that great, silent, vital energy that lies within that is able to satisfy all the soul's desires, all its yearnings, you shall no longer hunger or thirst, "for all the good things of the universe will be yours." No life can be poor when enfolded in the Infinite Arms and living in the midst of abundance, the source of all supply. So until we meet again, if you are ever given the choice, *Choose wealth!* Enjoy your life as well as the journey.

> *There's nothing to fear—you're as good as the best,*
> *As strong as the mightiest, too.*
> *You can win in every battle or test;*
> *For there's no one just like you.*
> *There's only one you in the world today;*
> *So nobody else, you see,*
> *Can do your work in as fine a way:*
> *You're the only you there'll be!*
>
> . . .
>
> *There is nothing to fear—you can and you will.*
> *For you are the invincible you.*
> *Set your foot on the highest hill—*
> *There's nothing you cannot do.*

—*Anonymous*

SEVEN LAWS OF WEALTH

First Law of Wealth	**Wealth begins in the mind but ends in the purse.**
Second Law of Wealth	**Decide that you will not be poor.**
Third Law of Wealth	**Believe in thyself when no one else will.**
Fourth Law of Wealth	**To thine own self be true; find your unique gifts.**
Fifth Law of Wealth	**How may I serve thee?**
Sixth Law of Wealth	**Thou shalt own thy own business.**
Seventh Law of Wealth	**Make thy money grow.**

NOTES

INTRODUCTION

1. W. E. B. Du Bois, *The Negro in Business* (Atlanta, GA: Atlanta University Press, 1899), 13.
2. Derek Dingle, "Why Reginald Lewis is Important to the Future of Black Capitalism," *Black Enterprise,* June 25, 2009, http://blackenterprise.com /small-business/why-reginald-f-lewis-is-important-to-the-future-of-black -capitalism (accessed October 24, 2012).
3. Sean D. Hamill, "For Casino Owner, Winning a License Was Not a Matter of Luck," *New York Times,* December 12, 2007, http://nytimes. com/2007/12/12/12/us/12pittsburgh.html.
4. Maggie Walker National Historic Site, http://www.nps.gov/mawa/the-st-luke-penny-savings-bank.htm.
5. Don Wallace, "100 Anniversary Issue: A Century of Success," *Success Magazine,* November 1991, 36.
6. Jim Emmert, "Rich Man, Poor Man: The Story of Napoleon Hill," *Success magazine,* http://www.success.com/articles/515/-rich-man-poor-man (accessed October 24, 2012).
7. Dennis Kimbro, *Think & Grow Rich: A Black Choice* (New York: Fawcett Columbine, 1991), xiv.
8. Ibid., 15.
9. Paul Taylor, Rakesh Kochhar, Richard Frey, Gabriel Velasco, and Seth Motel, "Twenty-to-One: Wealth Gaps Rise to Record Highs Between Whites, Blacks and Hispanics," *Pew Research Center,* July 26, 2011, 1–5.
10. Ibid.
11. Ryan Mack, "Establishing a Legacy of Wealth: We Must Take Stock of How We Spend," Part 3, *Black Enterprise,* July 29, 2009, http://www. blackenterprise.com/money (accessed August 17, 2012).
12. Thomas M. Shapiro, Tatiana Meschede, and Laura Sullivan, "The Racial Wealth Gap Increases Fourfold," *Institute on Assets and Social Policy,* May 2010.
13. "A Special Report on Global Leaders: More Millionaires than Australians," *The Economist,* January 20, 2011, 1–2.
14. Robert Denk, "Home Ownership: The Engine of Wealth Accumulation," *National Association of Home Builders,* July 17, 2006, http://www.hahb. org (accessed August 17, 2012).
15. U.S. Department of Commerce, *Survey of Business Owners: Black-Owned Businesses: 2007,* http://www.census.gov/econ/sbo.html (accessed August 17, 2012).

16. Kristin Anderson Moore, Zakia Redd, et al., "Children Poverty: Trends, Consequences, and Policy Options," April 2009, http://www.childtrends.org/files/child_trends-2009_04_07_rb_childreninpoverty.pdf.

17. Saul McLeod, "Maslow's Hierarchy of Needs," *Simply Psychology,* 2007, http://www.simplypsychology.org/maslow.html (accessed October 24, 2012).

18. Roger Brooks, "Least Likely to Succeed," *Success,* October 2011, 51-55.

19. Darren Hardy, "Innovate or Die?" *Success,* May 11, 2010, http://darren hardy.success.com/2010/05/innovate-or-die/ (accessed December 15, 2012).

20. Leslie Kaufman, "Trying to Stay True to the Street," *New York Times,* March 14, 1999, http://www.nytimes.com/2011/11/19 (accessed November 11, 2011) ; Roger Brooks, "FUBU's Stealth Marketing," *Success,* May 4, 2010, http://www.success.com/articles/1063-fubu-s-stealth-marketing (accessed December 15, 2012).

21. Alisa Gumbs, "Models Inc., One-on-One With B. Smith," *Black Enterprise,* September 1, 2006.

22. Brett Pulley, "Diamonds, Cars, and Confessions," *Forbes Magazine,* May 9, 2005, http://www.forbes.com/2005/0509 (accessed August 17, 2012).

23. Brian Tracy, *Getting Rich Your Own Way* (New York: John Wiley & Sons, 2004), 2.

CHAPTER 1

1.   As of 2009, according to an analysis of Federal Reserve data conducted by the Economic Policy Institute, 112,000 Black households (.01 percent) had a net worth of $1 million or more.

2.   Derek T. Dingle, "Madame C. J. Walker: Breaking New Ground," *Black Enterprise,* February 1, 2005, http://www.blackenterprise.com/mag/madame -c-j-walker-breaking-new-ground (accessed August 17, 2012).

3.   Paulette Thomas, "Number Crunching: What Does It Take to Deem a Business 'Minority-Owned?'" *Wall Street Journal,* July 26, 1999, 2.

4.   Michael D. Walker, "The 7 Success Secrets: Motown," April 15, 2010, http://www.the successsecrets.net (accessed August 17, 2012).

5.   Nadira A. Hira, "Diary of a Mad Businessman," CNNMoney.com, February 14, 2007, http://cnnmoney.com/magazine/fortune (accessed April 14, 2012).

6.   The Oprah Interview, "Oprah Talks to Tyler Perry," *Oprah magazine,* December 2010, 231.

7.   *New York Times,* "Times Topics," February 18, 2010, http://www.topics .nytimes.com/top/reference/timestopics/people/m/toni_morrison (accessed August 17, 2012).

8.   Adam Bryant, "Corner Office: Ensemble Acting, in Business," *New York Times,* June 7, 2009, http://www.nytimes.com/2009/06/07/business /07corner.html (accessed July 29, 2009); Chuck Salter, "Why America Is Addicted to Olive Garden," *Fast Company,* July 1, 2009, http://www.fast company.com/1297932/why-america-is-addicted-olive-garden (accessed December 8, 2012).

9.   Raymond W. Smilor, "Buying In and Cashing Out: Entrepreneurial Leadership in Growth Companies," remarks at the Annual Conference of the Ewing Marion Kauffman Foundation, San Diego, September 26, 1995,

http://apps.business.ualberta.ca/rfield/Speeches/Raymond%20Smilor%20
2%201996.htm (accessed December 9, 2012).

10. Richard Paul Evans, *The 5 Lessons a Millionaire Taught Me: About Life and Wealth* (New York: Simon & Schuster, 2004), Introduction.

11. Napoleon Hill, *Think and Grow Rich* (New York: Penguin Books, 1990), 82.

12. Diddy Biography, http://www.sing365.com/music/lyric.nsf/Diddy-Biography /7DD049DC35BC80CD48256A37002CED42 (accessed August 17, 2012).

13. Joe L. Dudley, Sr., *Walking By Faith* (Kernersville, NC: Executive Press, 1998), 75.

14. Carmine Gallo, "From Homeless to Multimillionaire," *Business Week,* July 23, 2007, http://www.businessweek.com/smallbiz/content/jul2007/sb2007 0723 (accessed November 11, 2009).

15. Libby Copeland, "With Gifts From God: T. D. Jakes Has Made Millions Reaching Millions," *Washington Post,* March 25, 2001, http://www.trinity fi.org/presstdjakes01.html (accessed July 26, 2011).

16. Ibid.

17. George S. Clason, *The Richest Man in Babylon* (New York: Penguin Books, 1988), 10.

18. Scott Ellsworth, "The Tulsa Race Riot," http://www.tulsareparations.org /TulsaRiot.htm (accessed December 15, 2012).

19. Ken Brown, *From Welfare to Faring Well* (Southfield, MI: Ken Brown Ministries), 107–108.

20. Ibid., 290–291.

CHAPTER 2

1. Daniel Indiviglio, "Chart of the Day: 9% of American Millionaires in 2011," *Atlantic Monthly,* May 5, 2011, http://www.theatlanticmonthly .com/business/2011.

2. Earl Graves biography, *Black Enterprise,* http://www.blackenterprise.com /management/earl-graves/.

3. Arlyn Tobias Gajian, "I Built a Magazine to Teach the Black Entrepreneur How to Tap Into the Billions of Dollars we Generate," *CNNMoney,* September 1, 2003, http://money.cnn.com/magazines/fsb/fsb_archive/2003 /09/01/350792/index.htm (accessed August 18, 2012).

4. Earl G. Graves, *How to Succeed in Business Without Being White* (New York: Harper Collins, 1997), 7.

5. Ibid.

6. Ibid., 23.

7. Linton Weeks, "The Sweet Sell of Success; Entrepreneur Earl G. Graves Has It Made. He Wants Black Americans to Share the Secret," *Washington Post,* June 17, 1997, http://washingtonpost.com/graves_success/6/17 /1997.

8. Graves, *How to Succeed in Business Without Being White,* 25–26.

9. George Gilder, *Recapturing the Spirit of Enterprise* (San Francisco, CA: ICS Press, 1992), 7.

10. Jim Rohn, *Leading an Inspired Life* (Niles, IL: Nightingale-Conant Publishers, 1997), 216.

11. Daniel P. Moynihan, "The Negro Family: The Case for National Action," U.S. Department of Labor Office of Policy Planning and Research, March

1965, http://www.dol.gov/oasam/programs/history/webid-meynihan.htm (accessed August 19, 2012).

12. Kathleen Cotton, "Educating Urban Minority Youth: Research on Effective Practices," The Carnegie Foundation: Office of Educational Research, March 1991, http://www.educationnorthwest.org/webfm_send/529 (accessed August 19, 2012).

13. National Commission on Excellence in Education, *A Nation at Risk* (Washington, DC: U.S. Department of Education, 1983), http://www2.ed.gov/rschstat/research/research/pubs/accountable/accountable.pdf (accessed August 19, 2012).

14. Julianne Malveaux, "Banking on Us: The State of Black Wealth," *Essence,* October 1998, 101.

15. Richard Paul Evans, *The 5 Lessons A Millionaire Taught Me* (New York: Simon & Schuster, 2004), 17-18.

16. Leah Samuel, "Poor Players Gamble on Illinois Lottery," *Chicago Reporter,* September 24, 2007, http://www.chicagoreporter.com/news/2007/09/Illinois-lottery-poor-play-more (accessed August 19, 2012).

17. Wendell Hutson, "Blacks Contribute Heavily to Lottery Sales," *Chicago Defender,* December 24, 2008.

18. Edward Banfield, *The Unheavenly City* (Boston: Little, Brown & Company, 1974).

19. Brian Tracy, *Getting Rich Your Own Way* (Hoboken, NJ: John Wiley & Sons, 2004), 4.

20. Lillian Lincoln Lambert and Rosemary Brutico, *The Road to Someplace Better* (Hoboken, NJ: John Wiley & Sons, 2010), 93.

21. Ibid., 217.

22. Malcolm Gladwell, *Outliers: The Story of Success* (New York: Little, Brown & Co., 2008), 37.

23. Debra Lee, "Defining Success," *Northern Trust* (Fall 2005): 11, http://www.northerntrust.com/wealth/05-fall/defininglee.html.

24. Tannette Johnson-Elie, "A Businessman and Lawyer, Daniel's One of the City's Brightest Stars," *Milwaukee, Wisconsin Journal Sentinel,* May 9, 2007, http://www.jsonline.com/business/29302569.html (accessed January 18, 2011).

25. Charles Darwin, http://en.wikiquote.org/wiki/charles_Darwin (accessed October 24, 2012).

CHAPTER 3

1. Karen M. Thomas, "Passion, Continuous Self-Improvement and Laser Like Focus on the Goal," *Positively,* Fall 2008, 31.

2. Charisse Jones, "Owning the Airwaves: Cathy Hughes Buys Radio Stations for African American Programming," *Essence* magazine, October 1998, http://findarticles.com/p/articles/mi1264/is_n6_v29/ai (accessed July 12, 2007).

3. Thomas, "Passion, Continuous Self-Improvement," 32.

4. Ibid.

5. Charisse Jones, "Owning the Airwaves: Cathy Hughes Buys Radio Stations for African American Programming," *Essence,* October 1998.

6. Cathy Hughes: Biography and Much More from Answers.com, http://www.answers.com/cathy%20hughes, 2 (accessed August 4, 2007).

7. "Cathy Hughes," BlackEntrepreneurship.com, http://www.blackentrepre neurship.com/cathy_hughes.cfm (accessed December 15, 2012).

8. Jones, "Owning the Airwaves."

9. Cochran's Closing Arguments, O.J. Simpson Civil Trial, *USA Today*, October 18, 1996, http://usatoday.com/news/index/nns17.htm (accessed December 28, 2008).

10. John Skow, "Some Groove," *Time*, May 6, 1996, http://www.time.com /time/magazine/article/0,9171,984507,00.htm (accessed August 8, 2010).

11. Laura Randolph, "Black America's Hottest Novelists: Terry McMillan Exhales and Inhales in a Revealing Interview," *Ebony*, May 1993, 28.

12. Anthony Evans, "Eternity: A Tale of Two Men," http://www.tonyevans .org/site/c.feIKLOOpGlF/b.2065683/k.75C2/Eternity_a_Tale_of_Two _Men.htm (accessed October 24, 2012).

13. Elwin L. House, *The World's Greatest Things* (New York: Fleming H. Revell Co., 1929), 101.

14. Martin S. Fridson, *How to Be a Billionaire: Proven Strategies from the Titans of Wealth* (New York: John Wiley & Sons, 1999).

15. Ting Yu, "Topping O' the Mornin'," *People*, July 29, 2002, http://www .people.com/people/archive/article/0,201376627,00.html (accessed November 12, 2009).

16. Ibid.

17. Barrington Salmon, "Success Story Started with Secret Recipe," *USA Today*, October 11, 2004, http://www.usatoday.com/money/books/reviews /2004-10-11-success_x.htm (accessed November 11, 2009).

18. Faye Rice, "Denny's Changes Its Spots," *Fortune*, May 13, 1996, 134.

19. Salmon, "Success Story Started with Secret Recipe."

20. http://en.wikiquote.org/wiki/williamjames.

21. http://en.wikiquote.org/wiki/maslow'shierachy_of_needs.

22. Maxwell Maltz, *Psycho-Cybernetics* (New York: Pocket Books, 1960), 17.

23. William James, *Psychology Briefer Course, Selected Papers on Philosophy* (England: J. M. Dent & Sons, 1917), 58-66.

24. Shelly Green and Paul L. Pryde, *Black Entrepreneurship in America* (New Brunswick, NJ: Transaction Publishers, 1990), p. 22.

25. Carter G. Woodson, *The Mis-Education of the Negro* (Radford, VA: Wilder Publications, 2008), 71.

26. Walter E. Williams, *America: A Minority Viewpoint* (Stanford, CA: Hoover Institution Press, 1982), 5.

27. T. Harv Eker, *Secrets of the Millionaire Mind* (New York: HarperCollins Publisher, 2005), 9.

28. Ibid.

CHAPTER 4

1. Julia L. Rogers, "Amos Winbush III Turns Catastrophic Data Loss into a Technology Win with CyberSynchs," *Small Business,* May 5, 2010, http://www.smallbusiness.aol.com/2010/05/05/amos-winbush-iii-turns -catastrophic-data-loss (accessed May 1, 2012).

2. R. Donahue Peebles with John Fried, "How I Did It: R. Donahue Peebles," *Inc.*, March 1, 2005, http://www.inc.com/magazine/20050301/howididit .html (accessed December 15, 2012).

3. Madison Gray, profile of John Hope Bryant, "The L.A. Riots: 15 Years After Rodney King," *Time,* April 27, 2007, http://www.time.com/time

/specials/2007/la_riot/article/0,28804,1614117_1614084_1614513,00
.html (accessed December 15, 2012).

4. John Bryant, *The Silver Rights Movement* (Los Angeles, CA: Operation Hope, 2003), 20.

5. Dennis Kimbro, *What Makes the Great Great* (New York: Doubleday, 1997), 201.

6. Caroline Clarke, "Winning on Wall Street: Carla Harris Uses Her Prowess to Make Billion Dollar Deals and Uplift Youth," *Black Enterprise,* February 2003, www.blackenterprise.com/mag/winning-on-wall-street/ (accessed November 6, 2010).

7. Julia Hanna, "Street Singer," Harvard Business School Alumni Bulletin, September 2006, http://www.alumni.hbs.edu/bulletin/2006/september/profile.html (accessed November 6, 2010).

8. Mary Speed, "Lending Her Voice," *Success,* April 2010, 78-81.

9. Cora Daniels, "Pioneers: Meet Six Unsung Civil Rights Heroes," *Fortune,* August 22, 2005, 74.

10. Good Morning America, "Women Entrepreneurs: Lisa Price," December 19, 2005, http://www.abcnews.go.com./GMA/story?id=1405821 (accessed June, 15, 2009).

11. R. Todd Eliason, "Shoot for the Moon," *Success,* August 2009, 69.

12. Les Brown, *Live Your Dreams* (New York: William Morrow, 1992), 27.

13. Wiki.answers.com, http://www.answers.com/topic/les-brown (accessed May 14, 2010).

14. Ibid.

15. Carla A. Harris, *Expect to Win* (New York: Hudson Street Press, 2009), 211.

16. Malcolm Gladwell, *Outliers: The Story of Success* (New York: Little Brown & Company, 2008), 19.

17. Patricia R. Olsen, "The Boss: Hard Work and Charity," *New York Times,* August 25, 2012, http://www.nytimes.com/2012/08/26/jobs/valerie-daniels-carter-of-vj-holding (accessed August 30, 2012).

18. Nancy Weingartner, "Faithful Franchising," *Franchising Times,* March 2008, http://www.franchinsingtimes.com/content/story/.php?article=00745 (accessed January 1, 2011).

19. Alex Markels, "How to Make Money: The Buffett Way," *U.S. News & World Report,* August 6, 2007, 46.

20. Bill Atkinson, "Stock-Picking Whiz Renown: Eddie Brown, President of Baltimore-Based Brown Capital Management Inc., Has a National Reputation as a Money Manager Who Picks Winning Stocks," *Baltimore Sun,* May 4, 1997, http://articles.baltimoresun.com/1997-05-04/business/1997124196_1_brown-capital-management-money-managers-texaco (accessed January 1, 2011).

21. Ibid.

22. Ibid.

23. Bio. The True Story, http://www.biography.com/people/steve-harvey-2063 1517 (accessed August 25, 2012).

CHAPTER 5

1. Cindy George, MLK Monument a Dream Come True: The Man behind the MLK Monument," *Houston Chronicle,* August 15, 2011, http://www

.chron.com/news/houston-texas/article/MLK-monument (accessed January 28, 2012).

2. Ibid.

3. Rebecca S. Rivas, "From the CBC to MLK," *The St. Louis American,* October 6, 2011, http://stlamerican.com/business/local_business/article _5c789608-ef9c (accessed October 10, 2011).

4. Robert Johnson and Brian Dumaine, "The Market Nobody Wanted," *Fortune Small Business,* October 1, 2002,

5. Susan Hamner and Tom McNichol, "Ripping Up the Rules of Management," *CNN Money,* May 21, 2007, http://money.cnn.com/galleries/2007 /biz2/0705/biz2/7.htm (accessed March 1, 2011).

6. Brett Pulley, *The Billion Dollar BET* (Hoboken, NJ: John Wiley & Sons, 2004), 44–45.

7. Ron Stodghill, "A Media Mogul Tries Remote Control," *New York Times,* February 18, 2007, http://www.nytimes.com/2007/02/18/business /yourmoney/18johnson.html (accessed December 24, 2008).

8. Ibid.

9. William Rhoden, "Sports of the Times; Finally, A Member of the Club," *New York Times,* December 19, 2002, http://www.nytimes.com /2002/12/19/sports/sports-of-the-times-finally-a-member-of-the-club.html (accessed February 22, 2011).

10. John Bryant, "Financial Literacy for All is This Generation's New Civil Rights Issue," *Huffington Post,* April 20, 2011, http://www.huffington post.com/john-hope-bryant/financial-literacy-civil-rights_b_848974.html.

11. Orison Swett Marden, *The Consolidated Library* Vol. 14 (New York: Bureau of National Literature, 1907), 135.

12. James 2:2–4, King James Version.

13. wikipedia.org/wiki/John_Wesley_Dobbs.

14. Wallace Terry, "Herman Cain: I Am the American Dream," *Parade,* October 13, 1996, http://www.parade.com/news/2011/10/herman-cain-i-am -the-american-dream.html (accessed April 2, 2011).

15. Ibid.

16. Herman Cain, *CEO of Self* (Irving, TX: Tapestry Press, 2001), 66–67.

17. Colin Powell and Joseph E. Persico, *My American Journey* (New York: Random House, 1995), 37.

18. Adam Shell, "CNBC Leader Gives New Meaning to Multi-Tasking," *USA Today,* March 22, 2004, http://www.usatoday.com/money/companies /management/2004-03-33-cnbc_x.htm (accessed June 4, 2011).

19. Ibid.

20. Pamela Thomas-Graham, "Celebration 50: What I Learned at Harvard Law," speech presented at Celebration 50 at Harvard Law School, May 3, 2003, www.law.harvard.edu/students/orgs/jlg/vol27/thomas-graham.pdf, 32.

21. Chuck Phillips, "She Advanced the Old-Fashion Way—She Earned the Promotion," *L.A. Times,* April 18, 1993, http://articles.latimes.com/1993 -04-18/entertainment/ca-24127_1_executive-vice-president (accessed August 26, 2012).

22. Michael E. Ruane, "The Benefactor of the Ball," *The Washington Post,* December 4, 2008, http://www.washingtonpost.com/wp-dyn/content/article /2008/12/03/AR2008120304095.html (accessed June 6, 2010).

23. Geri Coleman Tucker, "Businessman Throws Inaugural Party with a Heart," *USA Today,* January 19, 2009, http://www.usatoday.com/money /2009-01-15-executive-inaugural-events-disadvantaged_N.htm (accessed June 10, 2011).

24. Michael E. Ruane, "The Benefactor of the Ball," *The Washington Post,* December 4, 2008, http://www.washingtonpost.com/wp-dyn/content/article /2008/12/03/AR2008120304095.html (accessed June 6, 2010).

25. Elwin L. House, *The World's Greatest Things* (New York: Fleming H. Revell, 1929), 186.

26. T. D. Jakes, *The Great Investment* (New York: G. P. Putnam's Sons, 2000), 38.

27. Eve Tahmincioglu, "David Steward, the Boss: Stepping Out on My Own," *New York Times,* October 31, 2001, http://www.nytimes.com/2001/10/31 /business/31BOSS.html (accessed September 1, 2012).

CHAPTER 6

1. Lisa M. Hamm, "1 Restaurant to Go: Sylvia's Soul Food Expands," *Los Angeles Times,* October 11, 1996, http://articles.latimes.com/1996-10-11 /business/fi-52651_1_soul-food (accessed June 22, 2011).

2. Logan Ward, "Shooting for the Sun," *The Atlantic,* November 2010, http://www.theatlantic.com/magazine/archive/2010/11/shooting-for-the -sun/308268/ (accessed June 23, 2011).

3. Ibid.

4. Timothy Roche, "Soaking in Success," *Time,* December 4, 2000, http://www .time.com/time/magazine/article/0,9171,90514,00.html (accessed July 3, 2011).

5. Ibid.

6. Ward, "Shooting for the Sun."

7. Harvey Mackay, *We Got Fired!* (New York: Ballantine Books, 2004), 171.

8. Brad Snyder, "The Globetrotters Score Hoop Success," *Baltimore Sun,* January 5, 1996, http://articles.baltimoresun.com/1996-01-05/business /1996005001_1_harlem-globetrotters-mannie-jackson-corporate-executives (accessed July 1, 2011).

9. Mannie Jackson, "Bringing a Dying Brand Back to Life," *Harvard Business Review,* May 2001, http://hbr.org/2001/05/bringing-a-dying-brand -back-to-life/ar/1 (accessed July 1, 2011).

10. David Davis, "A New Spin on the Globetrotters," *Sports Illustrated,* November 13, 1995, http://sportsillustrated.cnn.com/vault/article/magazine /MAG1007379/2/index.htm (accessed June 28, 2011).

11. Ephren Taylor, *Creating Success From the Inside Out* (Hoboken, NJ: John Wiley & Sons, 2007), 16–19.

12. Michael J. Pallerino, "Healing the World," *Triangle Business Leader,* March–April 2011, 10.

13. Ibid., 11.

14. David R. Butcher, "Entrepreneurs: Born or Made?" *Industry Market Trends (IMT),* ThomasNet.com, May 25, 2010, http://news.thomasnet .com/IMT/2010/05/25/entrepreneurs-born-or-made-entrepreneurship -traits-are-they-genetic/ (accessed December 15, 2012).

15. Robert Allen, *Multiple Streams of Income* (Hoboken, NJ: John Wiley & Sons, 2000), 15.

16. Pat Regnier, "Getting Rich in America," *Money,* June 18, 2007, http://money.cnn.com/magazines/moneymag/moneymag_archive/2007/07/01/100116664/index.htm (accessed December 15, 2012).

17. Kauffman Fast Facts: Entrepreneurship and the Economy, "After Inception How Enduring Is Job Creation by Start-ups?" *Kauffman Foundation,* August 2010, http://www.kauffman.org/uploadedfiles/factsheet/entrep_and _economy_fast_facts.pdf.

18. Ed Lavandera and Wayne Drash, "Two Brothers, No Fears and $1 Billion Empire," CNN.com, August 24, 2009, http://articles.cnn.com/2009 -08-24/living/black.donald.trumps_1_steven-roberts-michael-roberts-busy-street?_s=PM:LIVING (accessed November 12, 2009).

CHAPTER 7

1. S. B. Fuller, "The African American Experience," http://testaae.greenwood .com/doc_print.aspx?fileID=GR3109&chapterID=GR3109-2480&path =encyclopedias/greenwood (accessed August 31, 2012).

2. "Aiming for $100 Million in Sales," *Fortune* 56 (September 1957): 76.

3. Elizabeth Wright, "S. B. Fuller: Master of Enterprise," *Issues & Views Winter 1989,* http://www.knowsouthernhistory.net/Articles/Minorities/sb _fuller.html (accessed August 27, 2012).

4. S. B. Fuller, "People, Problems, and Progress: Remarks before the 68th Annual Congress of American Industry, National Association of Manufacturers, December 6, 1963, http://www.knowsouthernhistory.net/Articles /Minorities/sb_fuller.html (accessed August 27, 2012).

5. Alphonso A. Narvaez, "S. B. Fuller, Door-to-Door Entrepreneur, Dies at 83," *New York Times,* October 28, 1988, http://www.nytimes.com/1988 /10/28/obituaries/sb-fuller-door-to-door-entrepreneur-dies-at-83.html (accessed July 18, 2011).

6. Ibid.

7. W. E. B. Du Bois, *The Negro in Business* (Atlanta, GA: Atlanta University Press, 1899), 13.

8. T. D. Jakes, *The Great Investment: Faith, Family, and Finance* (New York: G. P. Putnam's Sons: 2000), 9.

9. Lauren Young, "Mr. Rogers' Neighborhood," *SmartMoney,* February 21, 2002, http://www.smartmoney.com/invest/funds/mr-rogers-neighborhood -12405/ (accessed March 30, 2008).

10. John W. Rogers Jr. Biography, http://biography.jrank.org/pages/2767 /Rogers-John-W-Jr.html (accessed December 15, 2012).

11. Carolyn M. Brown, "Slow and Steady Wins the Profits," *Black Enterprise,* April 1992, reprint, http://www.questia.com/read/1G1-12039905/slow -and-steady-wins-the-profits (accessed August 30, 2012).

12. The Ariel Mutual Funds/Charles Schwab & Co., Inc., Black Investor Survey, 2005, 7, http://www.iamsaam.org/userimages/ArielSchwabBlack InvestorSurvey2005.pdf.

13. Jason Zweig, "Minds Over Money," *CNN Money,* July 6, 2007, http:// money.cnn.com/2007/06/19/pf/rogers_interview.moneymag/index.htm, (accessed March 30, 2008.)

14. George C. Fraser, "Riches Within Our Rich," *Financial,* May 19, 2011, http://frasernet.com/index.php?option=com_k2&view=item&id=86 :riches-within-our-reach&Itemid=16 (accessed July 4, 2011).

15. Lynn Hirschberg, "Banksable," *New York Times,* June 1, 2008, http://www.nytimes.com/2008/06/01/magazine/01tyra-html (accessed January 25, 2009).
16. Ibid.
17. Brett Pulley, "The View from the Top," *Ebony*, August 2011, 99–100.
18. Kirbyjohn H. Caldwell, *The Gospel of Good Success* (New York: Simon and Schuster, 1999), 193.
19. Maxwell Maltz, *Psycho-Cybernetics* (Englewood Cliffs, NJ: Prentice-Hall, Inc., 1960), vi.
20. Lonnae O'Neal Parker, "The State of Black Wealth: A Welcome Respite," *Ebony*, August 2011, 109.
21. Alan Hughes, "The King of Commercial Real Estate: Victor MacFarlane Reigns Supreme in America's Gateway Cities," *Black Enterprise,* January 2009, http://www.blackenterprise.com/mag/the-king-of-commercial-real-estate/ (accessed February 5, 2012).
22. Nancy Weingartner, "Junior Bridgeman Works the Same Way He Played Basketball Back in the Day—Teamwork," *Franchise Times,* November–December 2010, http://www.franchisetimes.com/content/story.php?article=01939 (accessed June 23, 2011).
23. Ellen Florian, "Where Are They Now? Ulysses 'Junior' Bridgeman," *CNN Money,* October 28, 2010, http://money.com/galleries/2010/news/companies/1010/gallery.where_are_they_now (accessed June 23, 2010).

EPILOGUE

1. Lynette Khalfani-Cox, "The State of Black Wealth in America," *Ebony*, August 2011, http://stage.ebonyjet.com/CurrentIssue/Aug2011_The_State_of_Black_Wealth_in_America.aspx (accessed December 15, 2012).

INDEX